FOR MAO

FOR MAO

Essays in Historical Materialism

Philip Corrigan, Harvie Ramsay
and Derek Sayer

© Philip Corrigan, Harvie Ramsay and
Derek Sayer 1979

All rights reserved. No part of this publication may be
reproduced or transmitted, in any form or by any means,
without permission

First published 1979 by
THE MACMILLAN PRESS LTD
London and Basingstoke
Associated companies in Delhi
Dublin Hong Kong Johannesburg Lagos
Melbourne New York Singapore Tokyo

Printed in Great Britain by
REDWOOD BURN LIMITED
Trowbridge & Esher

British Library Cataloguing in Publication Data

Corrigan, Philip
  For Mao
  1. Communism – 1945–
  I. Title II. Ramsay, Harvie
  III. Sayer, Derek
  335.43'4   HX44

  ISBN 0–333–22097–8

This book is sold subject
to the standard conditions
of the Net Book Agreement

By the same authors

SOCIALIST CONSTRUCTION AND MARXIST
THEORY: BOLSHEVISM AND ITS CRITIQUE

Also by Derek Sayer

MARX'S METHOD

Also edited by Philip Corrigan

STATE FORMATION AND CAPITALISM IN ENGLAND
(*with Michèle Barrett, Annette Kuhn and Janet Wolff*)
IDEOLOGY AND CULTURAL PRODUCTION

. . . he who never does anything never makes mistakes.

V. I. Lenin, 'On the significance of
militant materialism', 12 March 1922

Our European philistines never even dream that the subsequent revolutions in Oriental countries, which possess much vaster populations and a much vaster diversity of social conditions, will undoubtedly display even greater distinctions than the Russian revolution.

It need hardly be said that a textbook written on Kautskyan lines was a very useful thing in its day. But it is time, for all that, to abandon the idea that it foresaw all the forms of development of subsequent world history. It would be timely to say that those who think so are simply fools.

V. I. Lenin, 'Our revolution',
Pravda (117), 30 May 1923

Contents

Preface	ix
Introduction	xi
Chronology	xvii
Abbreviations	xix

Part One: MAO AS A MARXIST 1

1 Introductory remarks	2
2 Epistemology: where do correct ideas come from?	6
3 Practice	15
4 Political and cultural relations	24
5 Production	34
6 Conclusion	41

Part Two: ON PRACTICE: FOUR STUDIES 45

1 The Border Region years	45
2 The mass-line at work: the High Tide of socialism in the Chinese countryside	61
3 Bombarding the headquarters: the Great Proletarian Cultural Revolution	75
4 Gramsci and Mao	93

Part Three: ON CONTRADICTION 114

1 Introductory remarks	115
2 Socialist construction in China	116
3 The international Communist movement	123
4 Implications for socialist construction	129
5 Postscript, 1977	134

Notes	141
Bibliography	163
Index	203

vii

Preface

We have discussed the origins of these essays in collective work in the preface to the book which they complement: *Socialist Construction and Marxist Theory: Bolshevism and its Critique* (Macmillan; Monthly Review Press, 1978, hereafter *SCMT*). Although what follows stands independently of our other work, there is much to be gained by seeing *For Mao* as an extension of it. Some of the ideas expressed here originally formed part of the large typescript from which *SCMT* was eventually distilled and our thanks must be recorded to those who read that original formulation of our ideas.

We have indicated in our notes and bibliographies the texts which we have used. Apart from the classics of marxism, we acknowledge a special debt to the work of Charles Bettelheim and Jack Gray. We would also like to thank Tse Ka-kui for his valuable insights and Val Corrigan for preparing the detailed bibliography of Mao's writings and for providing significant critical comments.

We have signified the overall purpose of our essays in the title of this book.

PHILIP CORRIGAN
HARVIE RAMSAY
DEREK SAYER

January 1978

Introduction

This work is explained by its title. *For Mao*: on behalf of Mao; an intervention – given the circumstances, in fact, a *presentation* – of Mao against alternative positions. What alternatives? Alternatives within marxism, within 'Maoism' (a term as slippery and gauche as 'Stalinism') and, of course, within the vast apparatus of expertise: China-watchers, sinologists, Friends of China, visitors . . .

Moreover, these should be seen as 'Essays in historical materialism'. *Essays*: not a continuous narration providing a comprehensive story, but attempts, angles, representations, and glimpses. *Historical materialism*: the continually expanding core of theory and practice drawn from the explorations of Marx, Engels, Lenin, Stalin, and Mao, amongst many others, *in the light of* the combined historical experience of the international working class movement, above all, within socialist social formations.

This intervention, these essays, are part of our work over the last few years, especially *SCMT*, to which we refer those readers who seek further elucidation of our fundamental positions on marxist theory and socialist construction.

This is a work of theory. It is not a history. Nor is it a substitute for the closest possible reading of Mao's own work. Mao Tse-tung lived from 1893 to 1976 and, from the mid-1930s on, he wrote a series of texts which demand comparison with the classical texts of historical materialism. Indeed, his work, in quality and quantity, surpasses that of several marxists who have been the subject of the closest critical attention since the mid-1960s. It is against that background of plain ignorance that we write this book. It is for that reason that we have chosen to provide a presentational account of Mao's marxism.

It is worth drawing attention to this general lack of study of Mao's work, and, indeed, to the dearth of serious historical work of revolutionary China. There is, for example, nothing to compare with E. H. Carr's excellent history of the USSR. The immediate

xi

xii   *Introduction*

and obvious answer directs attention to problems of 'access' – to the 'language barrier'. But are there that many more fluent Russian speakers, reading, for instance, Lenin in Russian? Of course not. But that 'obvious' answer points us toward a possible solution to the riddle of why so many *marxists* can remain happily ignorant of Mao whilst consuming every word of Lukács, Gramsci, Sartre, Colletti and their epigones. If this seems a harsh judgement, scan a representative sample of English-language (although the point could be generalised) marxist journals over the last twenty years.

The obvious answer is one *theory* of Mao's marxism: that is, Mao's alleged sinification of marxism – leninism. This is true, but partial and trivial. As we have argued in *SCMT*, if marxism is not a *dogma* but a *guide to action* which *we learn in order to apply*, we cannot conceive of that learning without analyses of what Lenin described as 'concrete situations'. Indeed we would go further and ask that *all* major bodies of marxist writing be related to the circumstances of their original composition; we have attempted this with three essays in Part Two of this book.

But in arguing against the 'sinification' thesis, we are not agreeing with perhaps the largest group of commentators on Mao who consider him non-theoretical, a pragmatic nationalist and a true follower of former emperors. Our investigations show there to be a number of enduring, persistent and above all theoretical strategies which connect Mao's work to the mainstream of historical materialism. That unity, moreover, is founded upon a *political epistemology* which we sketch in Part One.

Both the above distortions of Mao's marxism can be summarised within a more general view which sees (and implicitly dismisses) China as *Oriental* or *Asiatic*. This view is particularly rampant amongst those whose self-identifying label is 'Western marxism'. Apparently there is but One Truth (which wears a European suit of clothes) which must be transported from here ('the West') to the rest of the world so that pure marxism may inhabit the globe. It is a view which is widely shared. Recently the national security adviser to the President of the United States, Zbigniew Brzezinski argued that 'a Communist society is really a derivative western society because Marxism is a western concept applied in semi-eastern societies' (*Times*, 10 October 1977, p. 6). In short, we have been through this tragedy before, it was called (capitalism's) imperialism. We welcome the thousand gaps that have been made in its network of exploitation and oppression.

Introduction

This general framework means that *geographical location* (distance from London or Paris, in particular) determines the 'worth' of any marxism. The interpenetration here revealed, of the culturally imperialist attitudes of formerly world imperialist classes and the marxist theory employed by intellectuals who seek to further socialism, is a fitting testimony to Máo's constant emphasis upon the ubiquity of class struggle under socialism. It also reminds us of the accuracy of his insistence that it will take one or two centuries before socialism is secured on a world scale.

Relatedly, many interpretations see the Great Proletarian Cultural Revolution as 'mob' activity incompatible with the deep rational traditions of 'Western marxism'. This is evident in the otherwise feeble 'analysis' by Isaac Deutscher: *The Chinese 'Cultural Revolution'* (1967), (quite congruent with his sneering assessment of Stalin as lacking 'refinement of thought' (1949:26)). The GPCR is now thought, by Perry Anderson, to be *both* 'an archivised chapter in the history' of the CPC (1977: 36) *and* part of some 'events in the Far East' (ibid., 39) with theoretical implications of only the most 'arcane' 'levity' for some territory called 'the West'. This framework is also revealingly present in such sympathetic accounts as *The Politics of Revolutionary China* by the British and Irish Communist Organisation (1977) which applauds Mao as 'certainly the most European spirit in the leadership of the CPC' (p. 45).

One of the major authors of the 'sinification' thesis, Stuart Schram, declared Mao Tse-tung 'obsolete' in 1963. Wisely reviewing this judgement in 1968, Schram wrote

> I still believe that to a large extent Mao's ideas and methods *are* ill adapted to the problems of building a new society in the last third of the twentieth century, but despite the excesses [N.B.] of the Cultural Revolution there is a sense in which this is less clearly the case than five years ago. (1969: 138)

Wisdom continues in later comments from this author (1973a) until, in assessing Mao as a marxist (1977), Schram has almost completely revised his earlier opinion. He thereby discovers, contrary to his view in 1968, that Mao *is* capable of 'imagining a viable alternative' to 'the seemingly implacable logic of advanced industrial society' (1969: 144).

It is worth stressing, for those who are only familiar with Mao's work

xiv   *Introduction*

through the filter of extensive interpretation, that Mao writes very well indeed. He wrote simply and directly on purpose (and he has been translated in this way) because theory should be available to a wide audience. This has reinforced much of the superciliousness from 'Western' intellectuals we have already alluded to and has led some to affect being affronted by Mao's 'pithy' and 'scatological' language. Mao's directness is to be contrasted with much writing of marxist theory in the last twenty years.

Mao's work has been available in English since the 1940s, and the four Volumes of his *Selected Works* have circulated since the early 1960s. In 1977 a fifth volume was published and more are promised; we could not fail to note the comparative silence which greeted this fifth volume, when the English translation appeared, in marxist journals and newspapers. Our bibliography contains an extended listing of Mao's work in English and, as with our listing of the writings of Marx, Lenin, Trotsky and Stalin in *SCMT*, we regard this as an integral part of this book.

We ought also to make clear at the outset that we are not providing another uncritical adjunct to that 'Maoism' which has shown itself, in the last year especially, to be monstrously adaptable to every inflection and substitution taking place in China. On the contrary, it is the very possibility of the dramatic reversals of 1977 taking place *in the name of Mao* (and employing his own texts) which means we must adopt a critical reading. In terms of our own analysis – presented most fully in *SCMT* – it seems to us that Mao's transformation of Bolshevism, as the self-proclaimed necessary route to socialism, is both partial and implicit. This moreover has led to certain theoretical problems in the accounts of those, notably Charles Bettelheim, who have followed a similar path to our own. Mao has elucidated a number of crucial relations, which Bolshevism frequently dichotomised and established causal relations between – such as forces/relations of production or base/superstructure. These are complex relations (contradictions, in fact) which are not to be understood in causal terms at all. Rather, he implies, these relations are internal to production.

But, and it is a far from simple matter of linguistics, Mao frequently remains within the conceptual field of Bolshevism, on the one hand, and – where he does not – he often erects what amount to metaphysical absolutes. Furnishing an example of the latter are certain formulations concerning *contradiction* (especially when used with notions of 'identifying the principal contradiction' and policies

Introduction

that flow from this, e.g. the 'three worlds' analysis). In the case of the former, Mao often provides a formulation which can be read as simple inversion (reversing the flow of Bolshevik formulations, while leaving the whole 'algebra' intact), as negation, or even equivalence. This is not a matter of 'theory', having theoretical effects alone. It is precisely these two areas – that of absolutes and that of untransformed Bolshevism – which have provided Teng Hsiao-ping and others with the maximum ammunition to argue for forces (as well as relations) being central to socialist productive advance; that expertise (as well as redness) is essential to socialist methods of work; that the struggle for scientific experiment (and those for production and amongst classes) is paramount . . .. In each case, the parenthetical addition has been downgraded to make the attempted reversal of the victories of the Great Proletarian Cultural Revolution that much more easily begun.

There is, finally, another 'linguistic matter' central to marxist theory and socialist construction. We have left the words of the classical writers as they employed them. This frequently means that they seem content to ignore one half of the human race. This is particularly true in some important passages by Marx in both *The German Idology* and his *Remarks on Adolph Wagner* (in the latter for example, pp. 190f in the TM edition, quoted by us pp. 18f below). As we pointed out in an early note to *SCMT*, our employment of these quotations without specific amendment does not mean we are ignorant of their *lacunae*. As Elisabeth Croll and Delia Davin have shown, in China the struggle for the fullest possible liberation has gone further (but not sufficently far) than anywhere else. The point is important since 'historical experience both negative and positive has shown that without specific organisations "armed" for struggle against them, socialist construction will be deformed by the reproduction of capitalist definitions of some people as less than fully human' (*SCMT*, p. 163, n. 2).

We hope that these essays will be taken as the start of a more open confrontation of contradictory currents within marxism and of more serious attention to those questions of socialist revolution and socialist construction which will always be associated with Mao's name.

The book is structured to facilitate three different kinds of intervention. Part One argues the case for Mao's overall marxist strategy. Part Two presents a series of three outline contextual xvi *Introduction*

studies relating to the Border Region years, the High Tide era, and to the years after 1963. The part concludes with an essay comparing Gramsci and Mao. Part Three synthesises the previous two and draws directly on our work in *SCMT* to explicate the relevance of Mao's marxism to various world-historical questions of the International Communist Movement.

Apart from our general Bibliography (pp. 163f below), we provide a list of 'Some Empirical Resources' (pp. 187f) for readers who wish to investigate the historical experience of socialist construction in China.

Chronology

(A fuller chronology will be found in other sources, e.g. the volumes of *China Readings*.)

1840–1949: *Era of semi-feudal and semi-colonial domination*
  1911–1912: Nationalist Revolution against Manchu (Ching) Dynasty
  1916–1926: Warlordism
      1919: May 4th Movement
      1921: Communist Party of China founded
  1927: Mao's investigations of the Peasant Movement in Hunan; April: Massacre in Shanghai
  1930–1934: Kiangsi Soviet
  1934–1936: Long March
      Japanese invasion extended
  1937–1947: Border Region years, Yenan Period
      1937: Mao's *On Practice* and *On Contradiction*
      1941: Mao's *Rural Surveys*

1949– : *Era of socialist construction*
  1949: Entry of Red Army into Peking
      1 October: People's Republic of China formed
  1949–1953: Recovery and consolidation
  1953: First Five-Year Plan
      Death of Joseph Stalin
  1955: High Tide years of agricultural co-operation
  1956: Mao's *Ten Great* [or *Major*] *Relationships* written. Mao authors, wholly or in part, two long editorials in the *People's Daily*: 'On the historical experience of the dictatorship of the proletariat'.
  1957: *On the correct handling of contradictions* written
  1958–1959: Great Leap Forward
  1959–1961: Three bad years
      1960: All Soviet assistance, experts, blueprints, etc., withdrawn from China

xviii   *Chronology*

1962:   10th Plenum of the 8th CC/CPC
              'Never forget class struggle'
1963–1965:   Socialist Education Movement
              1963:   Open dispute between the CPC/CPSU.
                        Where do correct ideas come from? written
              1964:   First edition of *Quotations* issued
1965–1966:   (and beyond) Great Proletarian Cultural
              Revolution
              1966:   11th Plenum of the 8th CC/CPC adopts
                        16-point directive
              1968:   12th Plenum of 8th CC/CPC condemns
                        Liu Shao-Ch'i, Teng Hsiao-ping and
                        others
              1969:   9th Congress of CPC
              1970–71: Lin Piao affair
              1973:   10th Congress of CPC
              1976:   Death of Mao Tse-tung, Chou En-lai,
                        Kang Sheng, Chu Teh
1977:   July: 3rd Plenum of 10th CC/CPC confirms Hua
              Kuo-Feng as Chairman SC/PB/CC/CPC; restores
              Teng Hsiao-Ping to Party and State posts; dismisses
              the 'Gang of Four' from all posts and from the CPC
              August: 11th Congress of CPC

Abbreviations

APC	Agricultural Producers' Co-operative
CC	Central Committee (of the CP . . .)
CP	Communist Party
CPC	Communist Pary of China
CPGB	Communist Party of Great Britain
CPSU	Communist Party of the Soviet Union
FLP	Foreign Languages Press
GLF	Great Leap Forward
GPCR	Great Proletarian Cultural Revolution
HSINHUA	New China News Agency
KMT	KuoMinTang
NEP	New Economic Policy
PB	Politburo (of the CC)
PC	Communist Party
PCF	Communist Party of France
PCI	Communist Party of Italy
PLA	People's Liberation Army
SC	Standing Committee
SCMT	*Socialist Construction and Marxist Theory*
SEM	Socialist Education Movement
Wansui	*Long Live* (a collection of documents by Mao, see Bibliography, under unauthorised collections of Mao Tse-tung's works)

Part One
Mao as a Marxist

I

Mistakes will inevitably be committed. It is impossible not to commit them. The commission of mistakes is a necessary condition for the formation of a correct line . . . The correct line is formed in the struggle with the incorrect line. To say that mistakes can all be avoided, [so that] there are only correct things, and no mistakes, is an anti-Marxist proposition . . . That there should be only correct things, and nothing erroneous, as [sic] without precedent in history, it amounts to denying the law of the unity of opposites. It is metaphysical. (Mao, 1958H: 113)

Marx's *Capital* started with the analysis of the dual nature of commodities . . . Things which are not commodities have a dual nature too. Our comrades likewise have a dual nature, correct and incorrect. Don't you have a dual nature? I know I have. Young people easily make the mistake of being metaphysical: they cannot bear to talk about their shortcomings. People improve with experience. In recent years, however, it is the young who have made progress; the hopeless cases are some of the old professors. (Mao, 1965H: 239)

Professors – we have been afraid of them ever since we came into the towns . . . When confronted by people with piles of learning we felt we were good for nothing. For Marxists to fear bourgeois intellectuals, to fear professors while not fearing imperialism, is strange indeed. I believe this attitude is another example of the slave mentality . . . (Mao, 1958H: 116)

For Mao

II

In 1816, he [Saint Simon] declares that politics is the science of production, and foretells the complete absorption of politics by economics. The knowledge that economic conditions are the basis of political institutions appears here only in embryo. Yet what is here already very plainly expressed is the idea of the future conversion of political rule over men into an administration of things – that is to say, the 'abolition of the state,' about which recently there has been so much noise. (Engels, 1894a: 307)

Politics must take precedence over economics. To argue otherwise is to forget the ABC of Marxism.
    . . . without a correct political approach to the matter the given class will be unable to stay on top, *and, consequently*, will be incapable of solving *its production problem* either. (Lenin, 1921a: 34)

Political work is the life-blood of all economic work. This is particularly true at a time when the economic system of a society is undergoing fundamental change . . . Before a brand-new social system can be built on the site of the old, the site must first be swept clean. Old ideas reflecting the old system invariably remain in people's minds for a long time. They do not easily give way. (Mao, 1955J: 302, italicization removed)

There is no doubt that politics and economy, and politics and technology should be united . . . This is what red and expert mean. In future, the term 'politics' will continue to exist but in a different sense . . . Ideological and political work is the guarantee for the accomplishment of our economic and technological work . . . (Mao, Instruction of 31 January 1958, quoted in Ch'en, 1970: 82).

1 INTRODUCTORY REMARKS[1]

In a famous passage, redolent with themes which we hope our own work will extend and clarify, Marx argued

Mao as a Marxist

Men make their own history, but they do not make it just as they please; they do not make it under circumstances chosen by themselves, but under circumstances directly encountered, given and transmitted from the past. The tradition of all dead generations weighs like a nightmare on the brain of the living. And just when they seem engaged in revolutionising themselves and things, in creating something that has never yet existed, precisely in such periods of revolutionary crisis they anxiously conjure up the spirits of the past to their service and borrow from them names, battle cries and costumes in order to present the new scene of world history in this time-honoured disguise and this borrowed language. (Marx, 1852b: 398)[2]

It is our central argument that Mao recognised that the central problem of socialist construction was to sustain the activity of 'revolutionising selves and things'. In this, to begin with a common misapprehension, Mao is not being 'idealist', 'utopian' or wagering on 'Man's better nature'; he is being fundamentally materialist. The only 'materials' for transformation are the people, the things (and knowledge of people and things), that now exist, albeit in a constant flux.

Mao is also – to stress another theme of our book – demonstrating that he has (and how he has) learned from history; he is being historical as well as materialist. If people are to transform themselves and their circumstances it must be recognised (literally, again, re-thought) that they *are* capable of doing this; they have – despite appearances to the contrary – the resources to accomplish this great task. Such a recognition only comes from a political inspection of history which reveals the myriad suppressions of alternative social forms and social development 'buried' within historical experience. People, in sum, can be more than they seem. This is what 'wagering on the people' (rather than on technology, cadres, economics, or gods) means.

If, therefore, people can be more than they seem, and, moreover, can only so become by transforming their circumstances as much as themselves, what prevents this taking place? Is it ownership of property (and rights) by a minority? Is it the 'logic of technology'? Is it the dominance of 'tradition'? It is, historical materialism argues, the social relations (and corresponding language and imagery) that make possible a particular way of 'pumping' surplus value out of labour-power to facilitate commodity production.

4   *For Mao*

But much follows from this. How to 'change' the social relations and social forms without 'reproducing' them? How, in short, to create something that has never yet existed? How to throw away 'time-honoured disguise and . . . borrowed language'? The manner in which the wager upon the people is conducted is as crucial as the fact of that wager. Time and again Mao returns to 'methods of work' and 'problems of organization' – to experience and its social modes. Unless, he is arguing, people experience this socialist construction as being more and having more, they will be disabled in their attempts at transformation. If they are crippled in this way it will be because we (the Party, cadres, intellectuals) will have continued the 'names, battle cries and costumes', retreated from that wager, and made 'wagering on the people' a rhetorical device to facilitate new Buddhas, new imperial envoys, and the cessation of the emancipation of labour.

We shall return to these themes throughout our book. We want first to briefly examine three representative texts which do, however partially, confront Mao's *marxism*: the work of Rossana Rossanda, Sam Mauger and Paul Sweezy.

Rossanda's text has circulated in Italy, France and England[3] and remains, in many ways, the best short statement of what is distinctive about Mao's marxism. Rossanda's significance, as a leading militant with *Il Manifesto* and as a theoretician, is exposed in the central recognition that the Great Proletarian Cultural Revolution is a world-historical action (similar to the Great October Socialist Revolution) which

> compels us to ask ourselves why we go on enduring, in a state of equivocation and helplessness, the crisis in the European socialist camp and the constant putting-off of the revolution in the West. Worse still, it compels us to do this not, as some would prefer, in moral terms, by summoning ourselves to self-mortification, to a regenerative bath of revolutionary purity, but by applying ourselves to thought about fundamentals, that is, to a search, right down to the very roots, for the reasons why, even when we pursue a worthy policy, we fall back upon a tradition that we would prefer not to reexamine.
>
> The Great Proletarian Cultural Revolution summons us to re-thinking and to practical activity which cannot but destroy something which is deeply rooted in the past and present of the working-class movement. (Rossanda, 1970: 54)

Mao as a Marxist

Fundamentally, Rossanda recognises, to use the words of Althusser in 1972:

> If we look back over our whole history of the last forty years or more, it seems to me that, in reckoning up the account (which is not an easy thing to do), the only *historically existing* (left) 'critique' of the fundamentals of the 'Stalinian deviation' to be found – and which, moreover, is *contemporary* with this very deviation, and thus for the most part precedes the Twentieth Congress – is a concrete critique, one which exists in the facts, in the struggle, in the line, in the practices, their principles and their forms, of the Chinese Revolution. (Althusser, 1972b: 92)[4]

Mauger's text is, for these purposes, emblematic: it may be taken to represent a fairly common form of analysis, that of the 'Friends of China'. Here there are, as it were, two sorts of 'borrowed language': largely Bolshevik readings of marxism–leninism as the dominant vocabulary, with a gloss provided from pronouncements of the CPC on this or that tactical decision. Not a few of such analyses are, in fact, quite congruent with bourgeois and other commentators on Mao who celebrate his profound 'flexibility' and his 'pragmatism', his freedom from (*sotto voce*: marxist) dogma. On the contrary, as we hope to show, it is his precise and enduring marxism which frees him from dogma; just as it is his withering attention to 'reality' and 'experience' that frees him from slavish cringing before the 'facts'.

But Mauger's analysis (1973) does provide a useful illustration of the central problem with which we began this section: much of the profundity of Mao's critique is hidden within a vocabulary which appears to indicate continuities from Bolshevism, rather than any break with it. This is partly because, in our view, the break is only partial – indeed its partialness is displayed in many a Friends of China account (or rather 'accounts') read over the last five years – but there does remain an adherence to certain formulations which are a barrier to coherent articulation of just what it is that Mao, and the CPC, have accomplished. In Mauger's first article (1973: 4, 9–10) this is displayed clearly in 'base/superstructure' distinctions, in the reduction of socialism to an ideology that has to be grasped, and a fundamental misapprehension of what 'forces' and 'relations' of production *are* during socialist construction. Mauger also (1973: 14–15) reproduces the crippling divisions between 'internal' and 'external' policies which is one clear symptom of the partial

6 *For Mao*

transformation of Bolshevism accomplished by Mao and the CPC.

Paul Sweezy's more recent text (1977a), written after Mao's death, attempts to sketch the contours of 'the Mao period'. Here Sweezy is writing in the light of his debate with Bettelheim and his extended reviews of the latter's major work on class struggle in the USSR (Sweezy, 1971, 1974, 1977b). He sees that the 'most important contribution to the advance of Marxism' of the Mao period 'may well be . . . to break what may be called the tyranny of the Soviet model' (1977a: 1). After reviewing the two foci of this challenge – 'the rejection of the Soviet model of economic development' and the GPCR which 'fundamentally and definitively transformed Marxian political theory' – Sweezy concludes that the 'experience of the Mao period' shows how:

> Post-revolutionary society contains not only contradictions inherited from millennia of class-riven society, it produces and reproduces its own contradictions. The revolution provides no final solutions. It only opens the possibility of moving forward *in the direction* of eliminating classes. (Sweezy, 1977a: 11–12)

It is the purpose of the rest of Part One of our book to try to root this fundamental insight in Mao's theoretical writings.

2 EPISTEMOLOGY: WHERE DO CORRECT IDEAS COME FROM?

In a passage he wrote himself, part of a 'Draft Decision . . . on Certain Problems in Our Present Rural Work' of the CPC/CC, in May 1963, Mao Tse-tung outlines 'the Marxist theory of knowledge'. Correct knowledge involves a source and three 'leaps': the source is social practice. In their social practice, human beings 'engage in various kinds of struggle and gain rich experience, both from their successes and their failures' (1963A: 502). The last clause is *not* an afterthought; we shall highlight 'the necessity for error' below.

The first 'leap' is that of perceptual knowledge – by which 'matter can be transformed into consciousness'; 'such leaps are phenomena of everyday life'. Cognition involves this first 'leap' *and* two others: perceptual knowledge accumulates to become logical and conceptual. Thirdly, 'knowledge makes another leap through the test of practice':

Mao as a Marxist

This leap is more important . . . There is no other way of testing truth. Furthermore, the one and only purpose of the proletariat in knowing the world is to change it. (Mao, 1963A: 503)

Mao had outlined this theory in 1937.[5] But he had had predecessors. Much of Marx's writing is aimed against 'speculative philosophy', against the dominance of the mental over the material, against 'forcible' abstraction:

It must be kept in mind that the new forces of production and relations of production do not develop out of *nothing*, nor drop from the sky, nor from the womb of the self-positing Idea; but from within and in antithesis to the existing development of production and the inherited, traditional relations of property. (Marx, 1858a: 278; Cf. ibid., 706 and *SCMT*, *passim*)

So also argues Mao, in, to repeat, a text that was part of a document on *methods of rural work*:

Where do correct ideas from from? Do they drop from the skies? No. Are they innate in the mind? No. They come from social practice, and from it alone . . . (Mao, 1963A: 502)

The following year, in his 'Talk on Questions of Philosophy', Mao argued, first,

We must take life as our starting-point in discussing the unity of opposites. (1964T: 225)

and, second,

Engels talked about the three categories, but as for me I don't believe in two of those categories . . . The most basic thing is the unity of opposites. The transformation of quality and quantity into one another is the unity of the opposites quality and quantity. There is no such thing as the negation of the negation. (1964T: 226; cf. Mao, 1937J: 315f)

Mao is also thoroughly Marxist when he draws upon the existence of class struggles within philosophy. Much of Marx's work was concerned to expose the partial, inadequate, limited grasp of

8 *For Mao*

social phenomena facilitated by much theorising, even of a classical character. As Lenin[6] summarised:

> One expression of the genius of Marx and Engels was that they despised pedantic playing with new words, erudite terms, and subtle 'isms', and said simply and plainly: there is a materialist line and an idealist line in philosophy, and between them there are various shades of agnosticism. The vain attempts to find a 'new' point of view in philosophy betray the same poverty of mind that is revealed in similar efforts to create a 'new' theory of value, a 'new' theory of rent, and so forth. (1908c: 134)

For Mao there are 'two world outlooks' (1937J: 311f). As he challenged 'intellectuals' in 1964:

> To get some experience of class struggle – that's what I call a university.
> . . .
> If you don't engage in class struggle, then what is this philosophy you're engaged in? (1964T: 213, 215)

It is not that practice is ubiquitous in some metaphysical sense, it is that genuine knowledge cannot be separated from transformation, for 'knowledge is verified only when . . . the anticipated results in the process of social practice (material production, class struggle, or scientific experiment)' are achieved (1937H: 296). Correct ideas

> come from three kinds of social practice, the struggle for production, the class struggle and scientific experiment. (1963A: 502)

Of these three, Mao increasingly stressed 'Never forget class struggle' which was intimately related to correct learning and sound socialist construction (e.g. 1957B: 446, 457–9, 463f, 472f).

None of this downgrades the significance of theoretical knowledge. In 1937 Mao argued

> Perception only solves the problem of phenomena; theory alone can solve the problem of essence. (1937H: 299)

The necessity of the leap from perceptual to logical–conceptual

Mao as a Marxist

knowledge was stressed by Lenin in his discussion of 'understanding' (1916b: 143; cf. ibid., 225f). Although it remains true – and we in this sense have 'leant to one side' in our book – that the dominant tendency in marxist theorising is to downgrade practice and to deny the fruitfulness of error, it would be just as wrong to establish a mystical and reified notion of practice which 'gropes blindly', as Stalin correctly phrased it, because it is ultimately reactive to the phenomenal forms of the world. Without the doubly articulated analysis which marxism offers (a set of fundamental tools of analysis – a method – *and* the concrete analysis of historical situations, see Sayer, 1975a, b; 1977b) historical materialism would never comprehend the essential relations which sustain capitalism as a world market system of production.

This needs saying for another reason. We have indicated that the line of the CPC and of Mao himself is constantly emerging from sustained and extremely complicated struggles (including making and correcting mistakes). We have also mentioned that we do not see Mao, or the CPC, as having completely transformed or overcome Bolshevism. Bolshevism remains present, moreover, not only at the important level of facilitating crippling separations (between internal and external policy, for example) and sustaining the possible 'opening' to bourgeois models of modernisation and rationality, it also permeates the core epistemological areas of the CPC's theory. There are, in sum, elements of a speculative metaphysic within Mao's thought. Just as in Lenin we *frequently* find the formula that X is *the* most important aspect of the revolution, so in Mao there remain certain forms of absolutist thinking.

The concept of contradiction, for example, has been rendered mystical, on the one hand, and been used for the most crude apologetics (in relation to analysis of imperialism and 'hegemony') on the other. Marx and Engels in their long polemics against philosophising (which were not merely a feature of their youthful period) show how all metaphysical concepts can operate to sanctify the crudest forms of special pleading. We can, of course, appreciate that Mao had to sustain a long – and ultimately never completed – revolutionary upsurge to try to transform the dead weight of theoreticians (and, equally, practical bureaucrats) from crippling and distorting socialist construction in China. His emphasis on contradiction, we argue, does not see practice as simply 'the opposite' of theory but shows that the only valid theory is that which engages in practical transformation. There can be no

For Mao

transforming practice that is not theorised in that sense – that sees beyond the phenomenal forms and particular relations which currently constitute itself. Equally, to discuss theory apart from transformation is to retreat into scholasticism which is often a form of time-serving apologetics. 'Contradiction' thus has a crucial double-handed purpose in Mao's thought and it is one which has been largely beneficial. But we cannot sustain it as the universal which it has been made, for it *contradicts* many other elements of Mao's practice.

Indeed, Mao's *political epistemology* is incomprehensible outside his emphasis upon modes of learning. If correct ideas come from social practice, it is wrong to see a correct theory (a collection of strategic ideas) as more universal than, more correct than, social practice. Moreover theory cannot deny the possibility of error. The notion of error-free theory is co-extensive with the bourgeois era, finding its social image in the work of academic-commentators and intellectual-critics. What Raymond Williams has argued for the area of cultural theory is generally true:

> several forms of cultural theory have become, within a privileged situation, privileged practices.
>
> . . .
>
> the concepts *criticism*, *literature* and *art*, in their currently available forms, are all contemporaneous with bourgeois society, and are the theoretical forms of its cultural specialization and control. (R. Williams, 1975: 502, 505)

Indeed, the reference to *culture* is crucial and direct in terms of the overall historical experience of socialist construction in the USSR and the Peoples Republic of China.

Amongst the social relations which make possible particular systems of exploitation and oppression, the social imagery of knowledge (and the knowledgeable) are quite central, especially in the semi-feudal and semi-colonial situations of Imperial Russia, and Imperial and Republican China. In sum, orientations to learning reveal the coherence and the thrust of a Communist Party toward a successful and 'solid' socialist revolution and socialist construction.

From Mao's earliest writings – for example, his report from Hunan on the peasant movement, or his 'On correcting mistaken ideas in the Party' (1929B) – he has been concerned to stress: *the important thing is to be good at learning* (1936D: 186). One face of this

Mao as a Marxist

lifelong campaign by Mao is captured in his little pamphlet 'Oppose Book Worship' (1930B) which has earned him several charges of *empiricism*. This precisely illustrates what we have argued above: such a charge implies a kind of theory that is merely extended (and never transformed) by recognition of error. It has as its core a notion of truth which Lenin criticised, when writing of the need to apply Marx's method in order to extend militant materialism,

> only he who never does anything never makes mistakes. (Lenin, 1922f: 223)

Mao argues

> Reading is learning, but applying is also learning and the more important kind of learning at that. Our chief method is to learn warfare through warfare. (1936D: 189–90)

> It has to be understood that the masses are the real heroes, while we ourselves are often childish and ignorant, and without this understanding it is impossible to acquire even the most rudimentary knowledge. (1941B: 12; cf. 1927A: 54 and 1966D: 251f)

> Nobody should be labelled a 'narrow empiricist' except the 'practical man' who gropes in the dark and lacks perspective and foresight. (1941B: 13)

That year, in the first of his three key texts on this problem (1941F; 1942A, B) Mao argues (as earlier, 1929B: 111f) against subjectivism, which is

> flashy without substance, brittle without solidity. They are always right, they are the Number One authority under Heaven, 'imperial envoys' who rush everywhere. (1941f: 21)

Significantly, we emphasise, subjectivism, for Mao, is marked by poor or peculiar (and partial) historical knowledge – knowing more of 'ancient Greece' than of China. Subjectivism is also marked by a refusal to investigate:

> Our comrades in the Party School should not regard Marxist theory as lifeless dogma. It is necessary to master Marxist theory

12   *For Mao*

and apply it, master it for the sole purpose of applying it. (1942A: 38)

Subjectivism and dogmatism, moreover, has its own style:

> Stereotyped Party writing is a vehicle for filth, a form of expression for subjectivism and sectarianism. It does people harm and damages the revolution, and we must get rid of it completely. (Ibid., 49)

In his text 'Oppose stereotyped Party Writing' are themes to which Mao returns, for example, in many of his comments during the GPCR. He indicts such writing for a number of reasons: 'empty verbiage'; 'it strikes a pose in order to intimidate people'; 'it shoots at random, without considering the audience'; 'its drab language'; it arranges items under a complicated set of headings, as if starting 'a Chinese pharmacy' and 'it is irresponsible and harms people' (1942B: 56f). Above all

> whoever talks glibly about 'tranformation to a mass style' while in fact he is stuck fast in his own small circle had better watch out, or some day one of the masses may bump into him along the road and say, 'What about all this "transformation", sir? can I see a bit of it, please?' and he will be in a fix. (Ibid., 64; cf. Marx's polemics against 'philosophising': 1846a: Part I; 1863a, b, c; 1880)

Mao is also thoroughly marxist in refusing to grant power to concepts, above all those of bourgeois philosophy. He shares his perception of 'freedom' with Marx and Lenin. Marx, in his 'Speech to the Democratic Association on the Question of Free Trade', argued

> Do not be deluded by the abstract word Freedom! whose freedom! Not the freedom of one individual in relation to another, but freedom of Capital to crush the worker. (1848b: 463)

Similarly, in his brilliant comprehension of the theoretical significance of the Commune, Marx describes how

> The working class did not expect miracles from the Commune. They have no ready-made utopias to introduce *par décret du peuple*.

Mao as a Marxist

They know that in order to work out their own emancipation . . . they will have to pass through long struggles . . . (1871a: 73)

Lenin was also clear on the need to discover the class-content of freedom:

Let the liars and the hypocrites, the obtuse and the blind, the bourgeois and their supporters, try to deceive the people with talk about freedom in general, about equality in general, and about democracy in general. We say to the workers and peasants . . . Ask them . . . is there equality of the two sexes? Which nation is the equal of which? *Which class is the equal of which?* . . . Freedom for which class? (1919: 121)[7]

For Mao

Freedom is won by the people through struggle, it is not bestowed by anyone as a favour. (Mao, 1945D: 293)

Those who demand freedom and democracy in the abstract regard democracy as an end and not a means. Democracy sometimes seems to be an end, but it is in fact only a means. (1957B: 388; cf. 1962B).

This too is closely related to Mao's comprehension of historical materialism as the theory and practice of transformation (rather than contemplation):

Engels spoke of moving from the realm of necessity to the realm of freedom, and said that freedom is the understanding of necessity. This sentence is not complete . . . Does merely understanding it make you free? Freedom is the understanding of necessity and the transformation of necessity – one has some work to do too . . . It won't do just to understand necessity, we must also transform things. (1964T: 228)

As Marx argued

The coincidence of the changing of circumstances and of human activity or self-change can be conceived and rationally under-

14   *For Mao*

stood only as *revolutionary practice*. (Theses on Feuerbach, original version, III)

Thus, the theory of this practice entails a new conception of theory (of philosophy) – one grasped by Lenin and by Mao. Marx and Engels argue that for the production 'on a mass scale' of 'communist consciousness', *revolutionary practice* is doubly central

not only because the *ruling* class cannot be overthrown in any other way, but because the class *overthrowing* it can only in a revolution succeed in ridding itself of all the muck of ages and become fitted to found society anew. (Marx, 1846a: 53)

Mao, far more than any previous marxist, has grasped the intimate connection between philosophy and socialist construction, and the need, if materialism is to be truly historical and militant, to

Liberate philosophy from the confines of the philoscphers' lecture rooms and textbooks, and turn it into a sharp weapon in the hands of the masses.

That is, it is essential to prevent (but not by administrative measures) the 'recrystallisation' of a *new* philosophy, with *new* philosophers, amongst Party cadres. In contradistinction to many other interpretations, therefore, we argue that Mao's emphasis upon practice (upon materialism as transformation) is both historically informed and consistently marxist–leninist.

We cannot end this brief exploration without illustrating a general view (quite evident amongst many intellectuals, some of them marxists) that Mao is not quite 'up to the mark' as a philosopher, that we have to be, as it were, 'kind' to him. We shall illustrate from a text by the man who thought Mao obsolete in 1963: S. R. Schram.

The relative mediocrity of Mao Tse-tung as a Marxist *philosopher*, that is to say as a systematic thinker dealing with problems on a high level of abstraction in terms of Marxist categories, can be explained no doubt by the difficulties in assimilating Western thought. But there is certainly more to be said on this. Mao Tse-tung unquestionably has a certain lack of interest in theoretical problems as such. He has a tendency to relate everything to the

Mao as a Marxist

class struggle, and to certain other values: the affirmation by the Chinese people of its own personality, or the mastery of man over nature. These problems he envisages less in philosophical terms, than as aspects of the day-to-day struggle to carry out the revolution. (Schram, 1969: 168; cf. Wittfogel, 1963; Bulkeley, 1977)

In view of what we have said, in view of the manifest accomplishments of peasants and workers in China,[8] it is a useful theoretical exercise to study this quotation in terms of what social relations it makes evident for our inspection. For example, 'high level of abstraction' (whether or not systematically) evidently indicates an epistemological space from 'class struggle' or 'day-to-day struggle'. That space, measurable in capitalist social formations, allows just that 'recrystallisation' of which we spoke; it marks a surplus-extraction at work, justified not by the need for 'experts' to aid the proletariat, but, on the contrary, for the peasants and workers to aid (i.e. pay for) experts. It is for the transformation of those relations (for the overcoming of those spaces) that we commend Mao as a far from mediocre philosopher.

3 PRACTICE

In one of their first sustained *critiques* of 'speculative philosophizing' (a work which Lenin found 'highly characteristic'),[9] *The Holy Family* (Marx, 1844e – the chapter is written by Marx), the founders of historical materialism expose 'The Mystery of Speculative Construction' (ibid., 57f).

> If from real apples, pears, strawberries and almonds I form the general idea '*Fruit*', if I go further and *imagine* that my abstract idea '*Fruit*', derived from real fruit, is an entity existing outside me, is indeed the *true* essence of the pear, the apple, etc., then – in the *language of speculative* philosophy – I am declaring that '*Fruit*' is the '*Substance*' of the pear, the apple, the almond, etc. I am saying, therefore, that to be a pear is not essential to the pear, that to be an apple is not essential to the apple; that what is essential to these things is not their real existence, perceptible to the senses, but the essence that I have abstracted from them and then foisted on them, the essence of my idea – '*Fruit*'. (Marx, 1844e: 57–8)

16 *For Mao*

Alas, continues Marx, reality presents itself as, in fact, 'different real fruits'; speculative philosophy proceeds by claiming 'different ordinary fruits [as] different manifestations of the life of the "*one* Fruit"' (ibid., 59).

> Hence the value of the ordinary fruits, *no longer* consists in their *natural* qualities, but in their *speculative* quality, which gives each of them a definite place in the life-process of '*the* Absolute Fruit'. (Ibid., p. 60)

This 'contempt for the particular' has been recognised by other philosophers[10] and offers a pure metaphysics: a 'speculative construction . . . free from all disturbing accessories' (ibid., 61).

In *The German Ideology*, Marx and Engels argue that the 'whole trick of proving the hegemony of the spirit in history . . . is . . . confined to the following three attempts':

> No. 1 One must separate the ideas of those ruling for empirical reasons, under empirical conditions and as corporal individuals, from those rulers, and thus recognise the rule of ideas or illusions in history.

> No. 2 One must bring an order into this rule of ideas, prove a mystical connection among the successive ruling ideas, which is managed by regarding them as 'forms of self-determination of the concept' . . .

> No. 3 To remove the mystical appearance of this 'self determining concept' it is changed into a person – 'self consciousness' –or, to appear throughly materialistic, into a series of persons, who represent the 'concept' in history, into the 'thinkers', the 'philosophers', the ideologists, who again are understood as manufacturers of history, as the 'council of guardians', as the rulers . . .

> This historical method which reigned in Germany, and especially the reason why, must be explained from its connection with the illusion of ideologists in general, e.g., the illusions of the jurists, politicians (including the practical statesmen), from the dogmatic dreamings and distortions of these fellows; this is explained perfectly easily from their practical position in life, their job, and the division of labour. (Marx, 1846a: 62; cf. Lenin, 1916b: 362–3)

Mao as a Marxist

We agree with Lenin who finds in Marx (best displayed in the latter's analysis of the dialectics of bourgeois society)[11] 'the fundamental philosophical line of materialism (from being to thinking, from matter to sensation)' (1908c: 22). Moreover, in a section significantly entitled 'The criterion of practice in the theory of knowledge', Lenin argues that it is 'a twisted professorial idealism'

> when the criterion of practice, which for every one of us distinguishes illusion from reality, is removed . . . from the realm of science, from the realm of the theory of knowledge. Human practice proves the correctness of the materialist theory of knowledge, said Marx and Engels, who dubbed attempts to solve the fundamental question of epistemology without the aid of practice 'scholastic' and 'philosophical crotchets'.
> . . .
> The standpoint of life, of practice, should be first and fundamental in the theory of knowledge. And it inevitably leads to materialism, sweeping aside the endless fabrications of professorial scholasticism. Of course, we must not forget that the criterion of practice can never, in the nature of things, either confirm or refute any human idea *completely*.
> . . .
> by following the *path* of Marxian theory we shall draw closer and closer to objective truth (without ever exhausting it) . . . (Lenin, 1908c: 139, 142, 143)

In his 1914 'Conspectus of Hegel's *Science of Logic*', Lenin wrote

> *Essentially*, Hegel is completely right as opposed to Kant. Thought proceeding from the concrete to the abstract – provided it is *correct* (N.B.) (and Kant like all philosophers, speaks of correct thought) – does not get away from the truth but comes closer to it. The abstraction of *matter*, of a *law* of nature, the abstraction of *value*, etc., in short *all* scientific (correct, serious, not absurd) abstractions reflect nature more deeply, truly and *completely*. From living perception to abstract thought, *and from this to practice* – such is the dialectical path of the cognition of truth, of the cognition of objective reality. (1916b: 171; cf. ibid., 225f, especially p. 228)

18   *For Mao*

We have to take care that we do not appear to be posing a rigidly *scholastic* materialism – a system – against its idealistic 'equivalent'. In much marxism the element of the *historical*, which we argue means that materialism-in-marxism is transformation (practices), is hidden; and with it, the class specificity of the 'validity'[12] of historical materialism. Marx, towards the end of his life, corrected his own work to take account of a possible over-systematisation of his texts. We are thinking here of the important letters to Russian socialists (especially 1877, 1881a), the writings on the Commune (1871) and the subsequent crucial corrections of the 'political programme' of the *Manifesto* (1872a, 1881b; cf. Lenin, 1917a, b; Balibar, 1972; 1976a, b). But we are also thinking of Marx's response to his (mis)handling by academic writers, his 'Notes on Adolph Wagner' (1880):

> In the first place I do not start out from 'concepts' . . . What I start out from is the simplest social form in which the labour-product is presented in contemporary society, and this is the '*commodity*'. I analyse it, and right from the beginning, in the *form in which it appears*.
>
> . . .
>
> my analytic method, . . . does not start from *man*, but from the economically-given social period, has nothing in common with the academic German method of connecting concepts ('With words we can in heat debate/With words a system designate') . . . (1880: 198, 201, TM translation)

Earlier, in a passage centrally relevant to our argument at this point, Marx had argued that people 'begin with production' (ibid., 190): through social practice people 'learn to distinguish "theoretically" from all other things the external things which serve for the satisfaction of their needs' (ibid). At a certain point such a *class* of things may be categorised linguistically as they have been empirically distinguished, ('*erfahrungsmässig*, i.e. by experience' adds the translator).

> But this linguistic designation only expresses as an idea what repeated corroboration in experience has accomplished, namely, that certain external things serve men already living in a certain social connection (this is a necessary presupposition on account of language) for the satisfaction of their needs. Men assign to these

Mao as a Marxist

things only a particular (generic) name, because they already know [them] . . . (Ibid., 190–1, TM translation)

Thirty-odd years *earlier*, Marx had grasped the same point when he wrote in *The German Ideology*

> The 'mind' is from the outset afflicted with the curse of being 'burdened' with matter, which here makes its appearance in the form of agitated layers of air, sounds, in short, of language. Language is as old as consciousness, language is practical, real consciousness that exists for other men as well, and only therefore does it exist also for me . . . (1846a: 44)

As he had marginally noted earlier in his text

> Language is the language of re[ality]. (Ibid., 38, footnote***)

Consciousness and language are structured and restructured through social practice. But, again, the emphasis could be incomplete without stressing that

> in reality, and for the *practical* materialist, i.e. the *communist*, it is a question of revolutionising the existing world, of coming to grips with and changing the things found in existence. (Ibid., 38–9)

It is because human beings have both an historical nature and natural history, that philosophy turns upon practice, itself understood historico-empirically.

> Empirical observation must in each separate instance bring out empirically, and without any mystification and speculation, the connection of the social and political structure with production. The social structure and the state are continually evolving out of the life-process of definite individuals, however of these individuals, not as they may appear in their own or other people's imagination, but as they *actually* are, i.e. as they act, produce materially . . .
> . . .
> As soon as this active life-process is described, history ceases to be a collection of dead facts, as it is with the empiricists (themselves

20 *For Mao*

still abstract), or an imagined activity of imagined subjects, as with the idealists. (*Ibid.*, 35–6, 37)

Marx stressed this point many times – it is inscribed in the analysis of the *Grundrisse* and of *Capital* – the stress always being on the 'definite historical form' as he argued against Storch, who because he does not conceive material production '*historically* . . . cannot get beyond meaningless general phrases' (1863a: 285).

> from the specific form of material production arises in the first place a specific structure of society, in the second place a specific relation of men to nature. Their State and their spiritual outlook is determined by both. Therefore also the kind of their spiritual production. (Ibid.)

Mao joins Marx in presenting a sustained critique of a false conception of consciousness. It is not the usual receptacles of 'false consciousness' that they point to, the lower orders, workers and peasants with 'wrong ideas'; but, on the contrary, to those whose 'practical position in life' and 'the division of labour' predispose them to sustain a false imagery of consciousness, downgrading material experience – above all through dehistoricising social practice. Dematerialization and dehistoricization recuperate the 'living space' for intellectuals *qua* experts, the donors of 'Correct Ideas' to otherwise (so they argue) falsely conscious workers. This cripples socialist revolution and socialist construction.

Practice for Mao is paramount because he is, to use Marx's term, a '*practical* materialist, i.e. . . . *communist*' for whom 'it is a question of revolutionising the existing world'. But this revolutionising has to 'correctly handle' the major contradiction between objective and subjective through what Marx called 'revolutionary practice': the simultaneous transformation of circumstances and people. This practice is most evident in the great social struggles – for production, between classes and within scientific experiment and artistic creation. Here people see further because both the forms of what confronts them and their norms for its categorisation have been 'pushed back'. We shall argue below, and throughout, that this is ever-present in Mao's theorisations of the problems of politics and production. But Mao's *realism*, his theoretical significance, and the reason why he cannot be reduced to a pragmatist, is displayed in his early work:

Mao as a Marxist

Our practice proves that what is perceived cannot at once be comprehended and that only what is comprehended can be more deeply perceived. Perception only solves the problem of phenomena; theory alone can solve the problem of essence. The solving of both these problems is not separable in the slightest degree from practice. Whoever wants to know a thing has no way of doing so except by coming into contact with it, that is, by living (practising) in its environment. (1937H: 299)

If you want to know a certain thing or a certain class of things directly, you must personally participate in the practical struggle to change reality . . . If you want to know the taste of a pear, you must change the pear by eating it yourself. (Ibid., 299–300)

Of course, as Mao states clearly here, 'most of our knowledge comes from indirect experience'; and, as he also stresses, immediate (perceptual) knowledge is extremely partial – although more accurate than purely 'rationalist' apriorism – and to deny the need for the deepening of the perceptual through cogitation is to 'repeat the historical error of "empiricism"' (ibid., 303). But marxism, Mao argues, is not theoretical in some sense that denies, or downgrades, practical action.

Marxism emphasises the importance of theory precisely and only because it can guide action. (Ibid., 304)

The transformation at the heart of marxism 'must manifest itself in the leap from rational knowledge to revolutionary practice' (ibid.).
Mao is arguing here (characteristically in a text aimed at dogmatism within the CPC) a point which he has generalised in a number of different ways. In the following passage, written in 1957, Mao's strategy is clear:

Over a long period we have developed this concept for the struggle against the enemy: strategically we should despise all our enemies, but tactically we should take them all seriously. This also means that we should despise the enemy with respect to the whole, but that we must take him seriously with respect to each and every concrete question. If we do not despise the enemy with respect to the whole, we shall be committing the error of opportunism . . . But in dealing with concrete problems and

22   *For Mao*

particular enemies we shall be committing the error of adventurism unless we take them seriously. (*Quotations*, 79–80)

As he argued twenty years earlier:

Idealism and mechanical materialism, opportunism and adventurism, are all characterized by the breach between the subjective and the objective, by the separation of knowledge from practice. (1937H: 307)

Mao has argued against this 'separation' through his attack upon superficiality which argues the one-sidedness of phenomena:

In studying a problem, we must shun subjectivity, one-sidedness and superficiality . . . The reason the dogmatist and empiricist comrades in China have made mistakes lies precisely in their subjectivist, one-sided and superficial way of looking at things. To be one-sided and superficial is at the same time to be subjective. (1937J: 323, 324)

Remember here we are talking about death and defeat. Mao recalled this bitterly in 1956 (' . . . this ended in a great defeat' 1956F: 87, cf. 1962B: 172). The following year at the Party Conference on Propaganda Work, Mao argued

One-sidedness means thinking in terms of absolutes, that is, a metaphysical approach to problems. In the appraisal of our work, it is one-sided to regard everything either as all positive or all negative. (1957C: 429)

Mao applied this in his analysis of 'what attitude to adopt in studying our historical experience' (1944B: 163)

Treat all questions analytically; do not negate everything . . . Lacking an analytical approach, many of our comrades do not want to go deeply into complex matters, to analyse and study them over and over again, but like to draw simple conclusions which are either absolutely affirmative or absolutely negative. (1944B: 165; cf. 1944C)

Mao as a Marxist

The Great Proletarian Cultural Revolution was in large measure, a revolution *for* practice *against* dogmatism and subjectivism. This was a method used repeatedly by Mao – his 1920s *Analyses* (1926A, B; 1927A), 1940s *Surveys* and *Problems* (1941B, C; 1942G) and, above all, his *Data* used at the enlarged plenum (1955F, H, J, K); all involve the use of practical experience against dogmatism. A similar consistency is revealed in his use of 'exemplary transformations' – where a given collectivity have done better, faster, by going all out, even though they have 'bad conditions'. But to call upon 'practice' in order to vanquish dogma, is also to stress the centrality of practical experience for making marxism 'solid'. Thus in his speech on Agricultural Co-operation in 1955, Mao outlined three steps toward socialist collectivisation: mutual aid teams, small producer co-operatives, and

> the third step will be to call on the peasants, in accordance with the same principles of voluntary participation and mutual benefit, to unite further . . . and organize large agricultural producers' co-operatives which are fully socialist in nature. These steps make it possible for the peasants gradually to raise their socialist consciousness through their personal experience and gradually to change their mode of life, thus lessening any feeling of abrupt change. (1955F: 409; SR translation)

Commandism, coercion, administrative measures – in sum, *Terror* will not accomplish any real change because, simply, it mistakes people for things and misunderstands transformation as if it were manipulation from above.

> Persuasion, not compulsion, is the only way to convince them. Compulsion will never result in convincing them.
> . . .
> . . . we must not be frightened if people come into contact with erroneous things. It will solve no problem simply to issue administrative orders forbidding people to have any contact with perverse and evil phenomena and with erroneous ideas, or forbidding them to see ghosts and monsters on the stage . . . Even great storms are not to be feared. It is amid great storms that human society progresses. (1957C: 432f)

Finally, Mao's commitment to *practice* follows from his under-

24 *For Mao*

standing of how this 'practical' approach eventuates in more collective and therefore more egalitarian methods of work and forms of organisation.

4 POLITICAL AND CULTURAL RELATIONS

Mao's views upon political and cultural relations follow from the above outline (itself, of course, informed by his experiences of success and error in Party work from the 1920s). Since the above views were formed after bloody errors in Party building and leadership, Mao was similarly anxious to avoid catastrophe in methods of work by the Party amongst the people. He provides a number of admirable sketches of the many two-line struggles that have taken place within the Party, locating them carefully in terms of his overall strategy and political epistemology.[13]

Practice is again salient: 'serving the people' and the mass-line method of Party work is oriented precisely to practical experience, it addresses itself to the relational facet of the same errors that produce elitist dogmatism and idealism. Just as there is perceptual, rational and valid (i.e. practically verified) knowledge, so

> In all the practical work of our Party, all correct leadership is necessarily 'from the masses, to the masses'. This means: take the ideas of the masses (scattered and unsystematic ideas) and concentrate them (through study turn them into concentrated and systematic ideas), go to the masses and propagate and explain those ideas until the masses embrace them as their own, hold fast to them and translate them into action, and test the correctness of these ideas in such action . . . And so on, over and over again in an endless spiral, with the ideas becoming more correct, more vital and richer each time. Such is the Marxist theory of knowledge. (Mao, 1943B: 119)

Cadres who do not carry out investigations tend to be 'crude and careless, to indulge in verbiage, to rest content with a smattering of knowledge' (Mao, 1941F: 18; cf. 1941B). Moreover,

> It is not enough to set tasks, we must also solve the problem of the methods for carrying them out. If our task is to cross a river, we cannot cross it without a bridge or a boat. Unless the bridge or the

Mao as a Marxist

boat problem is solved, it is idle to speak of crossing the river. (Mao, 1934C: 148)

If the situation was difficult under conditions of armed struggle, new problems will arrive with victory:

With victory, certain moods will grow within the Party – arrogance, the airs of a self-styled hero, inertia and unwillingness to make progress, love of pleasure and distaste for continued hard living. (1949J: 374)

Mao also concluded the same March 1949 second plenum of the 7th CC/CPC by discussing 'Methods of work of Party committees'.

10. Pay attention to uniting and working with comrades who differ with you.

11. Guard against arrogance. For anyone in a leading position, this is a matter of principle and an important condition for maintaining unity. Even those who have made no serious mistakes and have achieved very great success in their work should not be arrogant. Celebration of the birthdays of Party leaders is forbidden. Naming places, streets and enterprises after Party leaders is likewise forbidden.

12. Draw two lines of distinction. . . . between revolution and counter-revolution and between achievements and shortcomings . . . To draw these distinctions well, careful study and analysis are of course necessary. Our attitude towards every person and every matter should be one of analysis and study. (1949K: 380–1; notice the *anti*-'personality-cult' injunctions here)

Where there are mistakes and errors, social practice will be seen as the means of correcting mistaken ideas. Errors must be 'corrected by education and not by the crude method of reprimands' (1955F: 390, SR). But what is 'education'? After all

One does not necessarily learn how to do a job just by attending a training class and listening to a lecturer explain a few dozen points. (Ibid.; cf. Mao, 1964F)

26   *For Mao*

Both cadres and peasants will remould themselves in the course of the struggles they themselves experience. (Ibid; cf. 1956D: 20–1, *PR* edn)

In 1957, Mao spoke of 'intellectuals' (in general, not only Party cadres) going 'among the masses, to go to factories and villages . . . We should create an atmosphere in which "getting close to workers and peasants" virtually becomes a habit . . .' (1957C: 485, SR).[14] In the following year's justly famous 'Sixty points on working methods' (1958F; cf. 1958D, E), there is much concerning cadres who are made central to the continuing struggles in a social formation which still has 'classes and class struggle' (1958F, 64). Relations between cadres and people, and political and cultural relations in general, become exactly and precisely central during socialist construction; this is the message of several texts of the 1950s. Slavish adherence to rules, for example, can 'become obstacles to heightening the activism of the masses' (ibid., 66) and 'bureaucratism' prevents reality being firmly grasped. Mistakes and criticism, moreover, are to be expected *and welcomed*.

By 1962 the problem of socialist construction itself is seen as closely 'geared to' the problem of political and cultural relations. Since 'classes do exist in socialist countries and . . . class struggle undoubtedly exists' (Mao, 1962C: 189) struggles within politics and culture are struggles between two classes, lines and roads. Political and cultural relations of production may engender the recrystallisation of bourgeois forces that propagate an anti-socialist line and try to force China along a capitalist road. This fundamental discovery could still be 'attended to' in quite divergent ways, with quite contrasting methods and different orientations towards cadres. Politics could become, in one reaction, *policing*. In other, politics would have to be combined with collective work to constantly challenge the 'spaces' (within political and cultural production) that facilitate a bourgeois line. Metaphysics and arrogance were no longer matters of residual 'error' or 'mistakes'; they were collectively practices of the bourgeoisie, showing the potential capitalist road.

Much of this was already implicit in the experience of the Border Region years and in the practices of collectivisation in the sphere of agricultural production (both analysed in detail in Part Two of our book) of the 1930s and 1950s, respectively; but the explicit statements come after the rallying call of the 10th Plenum of the 8th

Mao as a Marxist

27

CC/CPC: 'Never forget class struggle!'. In two texts of 1963 Mao spelled out a coherent cadre policy – in the 'Note on "The seven well-written documents . . ."' (1963C) and, at greater length, in the Centre's 'Instruction on learning from each other' (1963F). The latter attacks 'conceit' as a manifestation of 'the bourgeois, idealist world view': 'It is individualistic' and overlooks 'the strength of the masses' and their creative energies in 'the history of social development' (ibid., 88–9) Cadres, in contrast, should be modest and have humility. Why?

> As a collectivist, [the cadre] must not discount the merits of the masses.
> . . . work is constructed like a huge machine, with its wheels, screws, steel frames, and other parts of different sizes and shapes, each being indispensable. . . . the scope of an individual view is narrow and limited, whereas the scope of revolutionary work and knowledge is broad and their contents extremely rich and complex. (Ibid., 90–1)

Cadres must study marxism – leninism, and avoid the extreme of 'self-abasement'. They must always *serve the people*.

All of this is summed up in the tenth of Mao's fifteen theses on socialist construction (1964R):

> . . . it is necessary to maintain [N.B.] the system of cadre participation in collective productive labour. The cadres of our Party and state are ordinary workers and not overlords sitting on the backs of the people. By taking part in collective productive labour, the cadres maintain extensive, constant and close ties with the working people. This is a major measure of fundamental importance for a socialist system; it helps to overcome bureaucracy and to prevent revisionism. (Ibid., 68–9)

Speaking to Regional Secretaries and members of the Cultural Revolution Group of the CC in July 1966, Mao argued:

> How can you get by without perceptual knowledge? None of you go down because you are busy with routine matters; but you should go down even if it means neglecting routine matters, in order to get perceptual knowledge. (1966K: 257)[15]

28 *For Mao*

Only a long and sustained political and productive immersion in the experience of workers and peasants can protect a Party from encouraging, within itself, the State and the Army, the 'rationalist' heresy that Mao constantly returns to. This can take 'left' and right forms – it can adopt the metaphysics of complete negation (adventurism) or complete affirmation (opportunism). It might encourage Party work organised round *either* 'All struggle and no unity' *or* 'All unity and no struggle'. It might, particularly in the generation of 'new scholars' who have dogmatically imbibed slogans and texts, encourage *both* the impulse to immediate achievement (without attention to methods of work) *and* (because such commandism leads to failure in the long or the short run) deep failure and despondency. Marx had encountered this in the internal polemics of the Communist League. He accused his enemies of separating the objective and the subjective and basing themselves solely upon the latter.

> *Will* is put forward as the chief factor in revolution, instead of real relationships. We say to the workers: 'You have 15, 20, 50 years of civil war to go through to change the circumstances and fit yourselves for power!' You say instead: 'We must gain power *immediately* or we can go to sleep!' (quoted in Nicolaievski, 1956: 249)

Marx here, as in earlier passages we quoted, is talking about the necessity for a *cultural revolution*. But before we discuss cultural relations it is necessary to clarify some issues relating to class.

Mao, like Marx and Lenin, operates with two contradictory analyses of class – 'positional' and 'relational'. These ambiguities relate to other similar tensions within marxism, for example, over the State, and are connected to the fact that, whilst a social formation without classes or a state is the aim of all practical materialists, a social formation without production relations or contradictions is inconceivable. The situation is further complicated by the two different kinds of social formation being depicted by Lenin and Mao – and Marx in relation to the Paris Commune and various political programmes – capitalist and socialist. We have argued in *SCMT* that the 'positional' view of class (like the reading of 'base/superstructure' metaphors as a social law) is part of the social problematic of Bolshevism. It is also a stage on the road to fully embracing the theory of productive forces. Taking all

Mao as a Marxist

three together we are dealing with a theory that is metaphysical, turns upon an invariant 'contempt for the particular', and emphasises the power of intellectuals, cadres and experts (plus 'technology' and 'economic laws') as against the people.

Given what we have said above, it is hardly surprising that Mao struggled with and against the positional theory of class, base/superstructure language, and the theory of productive forces all his life. The emphasis on social practice was one part of his attempt to sustain the validity of Lenin's grasp of the core of marxism as transformation – as a 'guide to action' which cannot *a priori* dictate and determine.

But we speak here of struggling, not of overcoming. Much of 'Maoism' (in England in particular) refuses to recognise this fact and swings from a Bolshevik theory of productive forces to the purest voluntarism and scripturalism: a theory of productive willpower. Indeed, as we argued in *SCMT*, both the voluntarism and the determinism are facets of the Bolshevik social problematic. Nevertheless Mao points a way forward, and goes partly down that road.

A positional theory of class, broadly speaking, is sociographic in method and entails plotting individuals in terms of (narrowly conceived) relations of production *and* then 'reading off' from those positions (i) the individual's political potential/consciousness and (ii) the social formation's 'revolutionary potential'. Such a theory, for example, (with the UN statistics manuals) can easily tell us that most social formations are not yet ready for revolution since they lack a sufficiently significant (statistically speaking, to be sure) proletariat. The closeness of this to bourgeois social science and Menshevik thought should, we hope, be obvious.

A relational theory of class entails recognition of the multiplicity of formations which sustain/disrupt social individuals. It recognises the significance of Marx's notion of 'mode of life' (1846A: 31f; cf. 1863a: 288; *SCMT*: Ch.1). As Edward Thompson has argued

> in the actual course of historical or sociological (as well as political) analysis it is of great importance to remember that social and cultural phenomena do not trail after the economic at some remote remove; they are, at their source, immersed in the same nexus of relationship. (1965: 356)

That is to say, as he put it three years later, 'class relations and class consciousness are cultural formations' (1968: 937).

30   *For Mao*

The significance of the difference between the two theories of class (and class struggle) is revealed when we consider the following statements by Marx and Lenin.

> What we have to deal with here is a communist society, not as it has *developed* on its own foundations, but, on the contrary, just as it *emerges* from capitalist society; which is thus in every respect, economically, morally and intellectually, still stamped with the birth marks of the old society . . . (1875: 17, MESW, III edn)

> We can (and must) begin to build socialism not with abstract human material, or with human material specially prepared by us, but with the human material bequeathed to us by capitalism. (1920b: 50)

What is here recognised is that the social relations of the capitalist mode of production are constituted through frameworks, codes, and images which stamp individuals and mark them in specific ways. Hence, to repeat an earlier presentation, the paramount need for *simultaneous* challenges to, and eventual transformation of, circumstances *and* selves which Marx (and Mao) regarded as revolutionising practice.

It follows from this that only a cultural revolution (not 'separated from' or 'consequent upon', but *simultaneous with* revolutionising the forces of production) carries forward, safeguards, and, eventually, completes the tasks of socialist revolution and socialist construction. This is Lenin's argument in 'Tasks of the Youth Leagues' (1920c) and in his 'Our Revolution' (1923c). Following Lenin, Mao has added to this a stress upon the ubiquity of class struggle during the whole historical epoch of socialist construction.

Mao recognised the cultural revolution first when he himself 'went down' and saw how the Peasant Associations enabled people to *stand up* (1927 A). In his analysis of 'New Democracy' there are sections analysing China's Cultural Revolution (1940A: XII – XV) combined with sections of Bolshevik analysis (ibid., III); a tension already evident in 'On Contradiction' where Mao argues against the 'mechanical materialist conception'.

> True, the productive forces, practice and the economic base generally play the principal and decisive role; whoever denies this is not a materialist. But it must also be admitted that in certain

Mao as a Marxist

conditions, such aspects as the relations of production, theory and the superstructure in turn manifest themselves in the principal and decisive role. (1937J: 336)

By the early 1960s – largely, as is clear from his 1950s writings (e.g. 1955J), in his recognition of the permanent lessons of the Border Region years – Mao had recognised how the promotion of a flourishing socialist proletarian culture entails 'a protracted and fierce class struggle' (to use his ninth thesis, 1964R: 68). That is to say:

> The socialist revolution on the economic front (in the ownership of the means of production) is insufficient by itself and cannot be consolidated. There must also be a thorough socialist revolution on the political and ideological fronts. Here a very long time is needed to decide 'who will win'. (second thesis, ibid., 65)

Cultural Revolutions (the plural is important) are needed because without them cadres and the whole Party cannot continue along the socialist road. In February 1967, Mao explained

> In the past we waged struggles in rural areas, in factories, in the cultural field, and we carried out the socialist education movement. But all this failed to solve the problem because we did not find a form, a method, to arouse the broad masses to expose our dark aspect openly, in an all round way and from below.[16]

The GPCR was seen to be that 'form'. In January 1967, Mao declared of it: 'This is one class overthrowing another'. (1967B: 274). The first resolution of the 11th Plenum (8th CC/CPC) in August 1966, recalled Mao's comments from the 10th Plenum in 1962, and argued

> Although the bourgeoisie has been overthrown, it is still trying to use the old ideas, culture, customs and habits of the exploiting classes to corrupt the masses, capture their minds and endeavour to stage a come-back. The proletariat must do just the opposite: it must meet head-on every challenge of the bourgeoisie in the ideological field and use the new ideas, culture, customs and habits of the proletariat to change the mental outlook of the whole of society. (1966P: 117–18; cf. 1962C; 1966I, S)

32 *For Mao*

It is in this context (and, we submit, this context only) that we can comprehend Mao's cultural theories and practices. First, to counter a common prejudice,[17] Mao never collapses cultural relations into political relations:

> Politics cannot be equated with art, nor can a general world outlook be equated with a method of artistic creation and criticism. We deny not only that there is an abstract and absolutely unchangeable political criterion, but also that there is an abstract and absolutely unchangeable artistic criterion; each class in every class society has its own political and artistic criteria. (1942C: 89)

Indeed, entirely congruent with our general outline, Mao rejects apriorism and dogmatism in cultural as in all socialist relations:

> In the field of arts we should also learn this lesson and take good care not to let dogmatism get the better of us. To study foreign things does not mean importing everything . . . We must accept things critically . . .
>
> . . .
>
> In short, art must have independent creative qualities . . . we should not shun experimentation . . . Uniformity leads to writing to formulae . . .(1956F: 87f. Cf. 1944A; 1951D; 1954E; 1963E; 1964O)

In 1938 Mao had argued: 'Foreign stereotypes must be abolished, there must be less singing of empty, abstract tunes, and dogmatism must be laid to rest . . .' (1938D: 209f; quoted in Mao, 1942B: 67).

In sum, cultural relations (the norms and forms of cultural production and reproduction) *are* an integral component of the class struggle that is central to the whole epoch of socialist construction. Involved are forces and powers which can restrict, hamper and harm the people's well-being, and forces and powers which can assist in the emancipation of labour, in attacking the 'three great differences' and making the construction of socialism easier. The latter forces and powers have to be realised through struggles to overcome difficulties; they cannot, emphatically, be donated by Party or State 'from above'. The work of Party and State is to hold back the forces and powers that aim to: restrict socialism, enlarge bourgeois rights and sustain the increasing possibility of capitalist restoration.

Mao as a Marxist

Mao here refers to culture in its widest reference (the whole 'ways of life' of socialism, equivalent, for example, to the 'culture' in horticulture or, even, Neolithic culture) and 'Culture' meaning aesthetic objects and their modes of production and reception. In either case, the key question is always: Does this (form or norm) encourage further emancipation of human beings from necessity, demonstrating that 'objective facts' are ever relative and that new 'subjective being' is ever attainable? Does it show a class capable of transforming the world, or does it show a passive, inert mass, led (and misled) by intellectuals and experts, by metaphysics and mysticism?

It is rarely true, if we examine historical experience, that it is the objective situation that *really* prevents (i.e. totally halts) the emancipation of human beings; it is far more usually subjective limitations enforced by class power. As Mao explained in his 'Preface' to that fine collection of case-studies of socialist culture: *Socialist Upsurge in China's Countryside*

> The problem today is that rightist conservatism is still causing trouble in many fields and preventing the work in those fields from keeping pace with the development of the objective situation. The present problem is that many people consider impossible things which could be done if they exerted themselves. It is entirely necessary, therefore, to keep criticizing these rightist conservative ideas, which still actually exist. (1955J: 10; cf. 1955, C–E)

Eight years later, he opined:

> Isn't it absurd that many Communists are enthusiastic about promoting feudal and capitalist art, but not socialist art? (1963E: 11)

Central to that socialist culture must be an understanding of how the world is to be transformed:

> The struggle to reshape the world by the proletariat and the revolutionary peoples consists of these tasks: to reshape the objective world and also to reshape their own subjective world. (Mao, Instruction, 12 January 1968, quoted in Ch'en, 1970: 151)

34 *For Mao*

5 PRODUCTION

Mao has been most consistently misunderstood in relation to production. He has been clear, from the 1930s if not before, that socialist construction *has* to solve two fundamental questions: What is production? How shall it be increased? There are capitalist and socialist answers to *both* questions. As we have argued in *SCMT*, Bolshevism does not give coherently and consistently socialist responses.

It is as well to recall, at the start of this section, the fourteenth point of the famous Sixteen Articles:

> The aim of the great proletarian Cultural Revolution is to revolutionize people's ideology and as a consequence to achieve greater, faster, better and more economical results in all fields of work.
> . . .
> The great proletarian Cultural Revolution is a powerful motive force for the development of the social productive forces in our country. Any idea of counterposing the great cultural revolution against the development of production is incorrect. (Mao, 1966P: 125–6)

In January 1967, Mao said to the Cultural Revolution Group:

> We must speak of grasping revolution and promoting production. We must not make revolution in isolation from production. The conservative faction [N.B.] do not grasp production. This is a class struggle. (1967A: 276).

That is to say, Mao was compelled to rethink orthodoxies in the matter of production problems from the 'fourteen deeds' of the Peasant Associations (1927) onwards. Above all, *before* the Long March, Mao was worried that

> Unless the Party in the border area can find proper ways to deal with economic problems, the independent regime will have great difficulties during the comparatively long period in which the enemy's rule will remain stable. (1928A: 70; cf. 1928B: 73f)

Mao as a Marxist

The message is often repeated: 'Pay attention to economic work' (1933A); 'Our economic policy' (1934B); and, 'Be concerned with the well-being of the masses, pay attention to methods of work' (1934C). In the first of these, Mao argues against the common view that phenomena normally thought separate *are separable*:

> We must bring about the continued growth of the people's economy, greatly improve the livelihood of the masses and substantially increase our public revenue, thus laying firm material foundations for the revolutionary war and for economic construction. (1933A: 132; cf. 1940L: 445f).

> . . . economic construction today is inseparable not only from the general task of the war but from other tasks as well. (1933A: 135; cf. 1934B: 141; 1934C: 149; 1945B, E)

In all of this the co-operatives were crucial agencies of socialist construction as we discuss in our first section of Part Two below. After the Long March, Mao argued

> . . . it is imperative for the revolutionary ranks to turn the backward villages into advanced, consolidated base areas, into great military, political, economic and cultural bastions of the revolution . . . (1939M: 316–17)

It was in this text that Mao first outlined his concept of 'New Democracy' which some, possibly including Liu Shao-chi, sought to sustain against socialist construction (see Mao, 1953E, F, H–K; 1955F; 1964T: 216). In the full outline of 'New Democracy' (1940A), section VI concerns 'The Economy of New Democracy', a text which bears close comparison with similar programmatic statements of Marx, Engels, Lenin and Stalin. In contrast with the two latter's admiration for the 'American path' and 'American efficiency', Mao is clear:

> we must never establish a capitalist society of the European – American type or allow the old semi-feudal society to survive. Whoever dares to go counter to this line of advance will certainly not succeed but will run into a brick wall. (1940A: 353–4; cf. 1947H: 167f; 1949J: Sect. IV)

36 *For Mao*

Fundamentally – and again the contrast with Bolshevism is exact – Mao throws back the gibe of the dogmatists: *yes*, he affirms,

> We are now living in a time when the 'principle of going up into the hills' applies; meetings, work, classes, newspaper publication, the writing of books, theatrical performances – everything is done up in the hills, and all essentially for the sake of the peasants . . . As every schoolboy knows, 80 per cent of China's population are peasants. So the peasant problem becomes the basic problem . . . (1940A: 366, 367; cf. 1956D: 15, Peking Review edn)

And, contrary to many accounts, 'New Democracy' never meant ignoring the second part of the production problem ('How is it to be increased?'). Such a view ignores the real situation. Struggles for rent reduction, to increase production, to support the Army, were class struggles. There were equally important struggles within the Party, as we outlined above, for example, over 'better troops and simpler administration' (Mao, 1942D; cf. 1942G: 115f) in the base areas.

At the end of 1942, Mao repeated his advice of ten years earlier:

> We shall simply be resigning ourselves to extinction unless we develop both the private and the public sectors of the economy. Financial difficulties can be overcome only by down-to-earth and effective economic development. (1942G: 111)

But – note again – rent reduction and increased production must be achieved by the peasants through class struggle, 'otherwise the results will not be solid' (1934D: 131; cf. 1945S: 72). To labour heroes of 1943, Mao repeated his call of sixteen years earlier (1927A: 24): 'Get organized!' (1943F).[18] This text is a major condensation of much we have argued thus far in our book, in so far as it relates – concretely – Mao's political epistemology, and his views on political and cultural relations, to the two questions with which we began this section. The task for Communists is 'to organize the strength of the masses' (1943F: 155; cf. 1945S, T).

Speaking to labour heroes in 1945, Mao summed up how far he had come to answering the production problem (and how far he had overcome the orthodox 'obvious' answers):

Mao as a Marxist

If instead of coercion and commandism, which are self-defeating because of their quest for quick results, we adopt a policy of patiently persuading people by setting them good examples, then it will be possible for the majority of the peasants to be organized into mutual-aid groups for agricultural and handicraft production in the next few years. Once such production groups become the usual practice, not only will output increase and all kinds of innovations emerge, but there will also be political progress, a higher educational level, progress in hygiene, a remoulding of loafers and a change in social customs, and it will not take too long before the implements of production will be improved, too. With all this happening, our rural society will gradually be rebuilt on new foundations. (1945A: 241-2)

Later, in a specific comment moreover upon 'labour-exchange teams', Mao synthesised his experience of the 1930s and 1940s thus:

In the last analysis, the impact, good or bad, great or small, of the policy and practice of any Chinese political party upon the people depends on whether and how much it helps to develop their productive forces, and on whether it fetters or liberates those forces. (1945D: 301)

What is being said here? How does the formulation 'organize the strength of the masses' relate to what we have been arguing? First, notice how it is being set against *commandism* and *coercion*. Second, consider that the means of organisation cannot be that of hierarchy and obeying explicit rules because this would defeat the achievement of desired ends by the people themselves; only in that way can the achievements be *solid*. Thirdly, the sequence of the 'spiral' mentioned in Mao's two addresses to labour heroes is fundamentally significant; the passage quoted *ends with* the improvement of the 'implements'.

We are arguing that all the struggles of the years since 1949 are available for inspection in the strategy for understanding and solving the production problem displayed during the Border Region years. This is not to say that those years provided a dogmatic 'code', a kind of 'Left' equivalent to the huge rule books beloved of managerialism. On the contrary it provided a deep suspicion of codification *per se*. By relying on local efforts, by exemplary transformations (which offer not a rigid sequence *to copy* but a set of

38 *For Mao*

principles *to apply*), by preventing the Party and State from becoming new overlords it proved possible, to take the most dramatic example, for everyone in China to have enough to eat.[19]

As texts published during the GPCR made clear,[20] there was a bitter struggle waged over the production problem between a conventional view of classes and productive forces and those who saw the experience of the Border Region years as offering a more secure General Line. Mao's speech on Agricultural Co-operation (1955F) and the High Tide materials (1955J) are part of that struggle. These texts show that Mao is not the idealist, utopian, moralist and so on that many have designated him; it is because he is concerned that everyone should have enough to eat that he attacks (over and over again) *forms of social relations* which prevent, disrupt, cripple, restrain or in any way limit the increasing enthusiastic self-emancipation of the workers and peasants of new China by their own efforts. The main enemy here is precisely models of Development that turn upon 'The Plan' and other codes of pacification. Another enemy is those who complain that the speed of socialist transformation is *too fast*:

> Excessive criticism, inappropriate complaints, endless anxiety, and the erection of countless taboos – they believe this is the proper way to guide the socialist mass movement in the rural areas. (1955F: 389, SR edn; cf. SW, V: 184)

Pace is crucial. Slowness (1949 onwards) had led to 'capitalism . . . steadily growing in the countryside' (1955F: 411, *SR* edn). Many of his editorial comments in the High Tide collection show that the problem of pace is only a facet – if the more evident one – of the methods (or social form) involved in socialist construction. Some of the comments also have their targets within the CPC, within the Central Committee itself as much as at local cadre level. Indeed the (still implicit) critique of Bolshevism is at its sharpest here. Cadres, State officials, Party chiefs share with rich and middle peasants a suspicion of novelty and a disbelief in the destitute and poor being able, in fact, to run things – *not only well but better than their 'betters'*.

> Socialism is something new. A severe struggle must be waged against the old ways before socialism can be brought about. (1955J: 128)

Mao as a Marxist

Mao's views are very clearly expressed in the famous discussion 'Who says a chicken feather can't fly up to heaven?' (ibid., 136–9). *Who* says it? Well, of course, it is obvious, isn't it?:

> In thousands of years has anyone ever seen one that could? The impossibility of such a feat has practically become a truism. (Ibid., 137)

> The poor want to remake their lives. The old system is dying. A new system is being born. Chicken feathers really are flying up to heaven. In the Soviet Union they have already got there. In China they've started their flight. (Ibid., 138)

From the High Tide to the Great Leap Forward – smashed and diverted far more ideologically and organizationally than technologically – the message is the same: 'Don't lose touch with the people; be adept at recognising their enthusiasm . . . '(ibid., 151)

> The relationship between the party and the masses is comparable to that between fish and water. Unless this relationship is properly forged, the socialist system can neither be established nor consolidated. (1957I: 56, *Ch'en* edn)

By the mid-1950s Mao was arguing for a concept of a General *Line* complementing (and later being more important than) successive detailed Five Year *Plans*. This took the form of a slogan: 'building socialism with greater, faster, better and more economical results'. By this time, also, Mao had reversed the normal sequence of events in 'Development' and 'Modernization' which puts all emphasis upon heavy industry, upon the cities, upon building up a proletariat (defined as the factory workers). Although the line of taking agriculture as the foundation (and grain production as the cornerstone of that foundation) was not fully issued until the 10th Plenum of the 8th CC/CPC in 1962, it is evident in many earlier texts (e.g. 1955F: 405f, MTSR). His speech to the Politburo on 25 April 1956, 'The Ten Great Relationships', brings out this, along with many other matters, with exceptional clarity. It places production before procurement and both before the accumulation of capital. It redefines production to focus upon, *first*, the daily needs of the people. Like other texts it draws attention to the significance of different production collectivities increasing their

40 *For Mao*

overall production and conceptualising that increase (which will eventuate in an increased standard of living for each family) as the result of definite, new, socialist methods of work and new ideas. Here, to anticipate a theme which is present in the second and third Parts of our book, there is an explicit criticism of the Soviet Union's production strategy.[21]

A good example of a text which has been misread is 'On the correct handling of contradictions' (1957B), which has a number of sections specifically devoted to socialist construction and the production problem. In one of these Mao suggests that by encouraging agricultural, and thus light industrial, production heavy industry will also be increased. He makes a specific prediction concerning steel production, that it 'can be raised to 20,000,000 tons or more' in 'three five-year plans or perhaps a little longer' (1957B: 419–20). A year later, at Chengtu, Mao expressed himself doubtful about the possibility of this (1958H: 109–10). But, in fact, according to the *Times* (21 March 1973) steel output was 21m tons in 1971 and 23m tons in 1972.

Although doubtful at Chengtu, Mao was clear on how the 'line for building socialism' was 'being created'; 'it reflects the creations of the masses in their struggles. This is a law' (1958H: 111, 112). Although against 'blind faith' and rigid copying, this does not mean that Mao lacks a production strategy.

> Unless we despise the old system and the old reactionary productive relationships, what do we think we are doing? If we do not have faith in socialism and communism, what do we think we are doing? (Ibid., 121)[22]

In the 'Sixty points' (1958F) and other documents of that time – not least because he was simultaneously engaged upon study of Stalin's economic strategy and current events within the USSR – Mao stresses precisely why politics must be in command, if production is to be increased and consolidated. This is not *commandism* (by the Party) nor, especially, a policy of the 'cadres decide everything'. All the deviations which he castigates (including his own self-criticisms) come from, he argues, the distance between cadres and officials and the day-to-day struggles of production. Pure voluntarism (petit-bourgeois fanaticism or adventurism) ignores the dull facticity of real tasks that have to be done little by little. Pure materialism (elitist dogmatism, world-weariness) ignores historical materialism;

Mao as a Marxist 41

ignores, that is, exactly what production constantly accomplishes: the transformation of matter, the overcoming of necessity.

Again and again, in those detailed accounts which so many experts (amongst them, many marxists) refuse to consider as theoretically significant, there is much delight taken in showing how although this or that expert declared it to be impossible that various kinds of production could take place – look, they have been accomplished! Water flows, crops grow, people are now different, the world has been changed. Far too many texts are also taken in their ethereal forms, or, at best, politicised. In fact, Mao's famous reduction and summing up of Marxism, 'it is right to rebel against reactionaries', for example, is extraordinarily apposite within situations of complex production problems. Similarly, 'Dare to struggle, dare to win'. Nobody is going to construct the Red Flag Canal,[23] for example, unless they are collectively and consciously armed with a most rebellious spirit!

Describing China's Great Leap Forward in 1964, Mao and Chou En-lai[24] argued

We cannot follow the old paths of technical development of every other country in the world and crawl step by step behind the others. We must smash conventions, do our utmost to adopt advanced techniques, and within not too long a period of history, build our country up into a powerful modern socialist state.

. . . From a poor and blank start haven't we through fifteen years of endeavour reached an appreciable level of development in all aspects of socialist revolution and socialist construction. (1964X: 231)

6 CONCLUSION

We shall try now to summarise what we have been arguing thus far, without too greatly anticipating the necessary detailed exposition which follows in Part Two. A more final summary will be found in Part Three.

Above all we have argued against a 'reading' (to use an expression that our 'new scholars' will understand) of Mao and of historical experience in China which sustains the very separations (enforced by bourgeois categories) that historical materialism has to cast away, as illusions, in order to make possible the long, extremely

42   *For Mao*

complex, many-sided and tortuous struggles through which ordinary people can demonstrate how they are transforming the
objective and subjective world. Mao's marxism is thus at one with
that of Lenin and Marx in being primarily *methodological*. If it is
dogmatic, it is through its 'militant negativism'; its proscription
applies solely to methods of thought and work which restrain or
delimit the *increasingly* confident enthusiasm of the majority that *they*
can transform necessity and increase *their* opportunities to emancipate labour. Our references to other marxists seek to demonstrate this thematic continuity which forms one strand of
historical materialism.

Lenin, in a speech he gave despite his illness,[25] explained the only
secure way that 'NEP Russia will become socialist Russia'.

> we must not approach socialism as if it were an icon painted in
> festive colours. We need to take the right direction, we need to see
> that everything is checked, that the masses, the entire population,
> check the path we follow and say: 'Yes, this is better than the old
> system'. That is the task we have set ourselves . . .
>
> We must remake things in such a way that the great majority of
> the masses, the peasants and workers, will say: 'It is not you who
> praise yourselves, but we. We say that you have achieved
> splendid results, after which no intelligent person will ever dream
> of returning to the old'. (1922d: 442)

Three months later, in his famous 'Our Revolution' (1923c),[26]
Lenin speaks against 'impossibly pedantic' marxists, with their
'infinitely stereotyped' notions about the 'development of the
productive forces', their 'cowardice', their 'slavish imitation of the
past' and their 'purely theoretical point of view'.

Much of Mao's theory and practice is oriented against the latter
kind of marxism, toward the former secularisation and genuine
democratisation of socialism which is either to be made by the
people or not at all (it cannot, except in short spurts sustained by
enormously expensive apparatus, be made *for* them). The force of
the word 'dream' in the quotation from Lenin's speech would be
appreciated by Mao who was always fully aware that within mass
movements which seemed (phenomenally) socialist, there may well
be much capitalist greed and individualism, such as an emphasis on
the communes as redistributive agencies[27] rather than new social
forms of production, distribution and exchange.

Mao as a Marxist 43

This, to reiterate, is why there is the sustained emphasis upon political and cultural relations – above all upon, on the one hand, 'philosophy' and, on the other, 'social practice'. Lin Tien-hsi explained this succinctly to Maria Macciocchi:

> Philosophy is participating in the class struggle on the level of production. (Macciocchi, 1971: 142)

The methodology here, as we have argued at length previously,[28] inverts the normal and obvious. Judgements as to the 'socialist' qualities of social phenomena have to grasp the latter as experienced/constructed by the working population. Do they indicate the accomplishment or the suppression of 'great facts' of the kind Marx referred to in 1864 and 1871?

The social practice and the philosophy are thus indissolubly intertwined, forming the front and back (to use a philosophical figure from Mao) of a socialist construction that will be solid in so far as what is transformed is as much the evaluative and cognitive categories as the particular production problem. Mao suggests that historical materialism has two outstanding characteristics: 'its class nature' (serving the proletariat), and 'its practicality' ('objective results in social practice') (1937H: 297). Mao's methodology here (as consistently also with Marx)[29] is *empirical*: time and again, Mao stresses not simply the need to investigate, but conducts detailed investigations himself. Indeed, the cumulated evidence of such investigations, by Mao and others, has been used against dogmatists and pragmatists alike at various turning points in the extended struggle between two lines, two roads and two classes since the formation of the CPC.

But most centrally Mao's emphasis upon practical theory relates internally to his emphasis (shared totally by Marx)[30] that the emancipation of the working population of the world must be their own accomplishment. As the Sixteen Articles of 1966 stress:

> In the great proletarian Cultural Revolution, the only method is for the masses to liberate themselves, and any method of doing things on their behalf must not be used.
>
> Trust the masses, rely on them and respect their initiative. Cast out fear. Don't be afraid of disorder. (1966P: 120)

A few days before, talking to members of the Central Committee

44   *For Mao*

and others, Mao offered an analysis (philosophical and practical; at
once economic, political and cultural) with which we close Part
One. We invite readers to return to it, and indeed to Part One as a
whole, in the light of the more detailed, more concrete and more
materialist and more historical studies sketched in Part Two.

We believe in the masses. To become teachers[31] of the masses we
must first be the students of the masses. The present great
Cultural Revolution is a heaven-and-earth-shaking event. Can
we, dare we, cross the pass into socialism? This pass leads to the
final destruction of classes, and the reduction of the three great
differences.[32]

To oppose, especially to oppose 'authoritative' bourgeois
ideology, is to destroy. Without this destruction, socialism cannot
be established nor can we carry out first struggle, second
criticism, third transformation. Sitting in offices listening to
reports is no good. The only way is to rely on the masses, trust the
masses, struggle to the end. We must be prepared for the
revolution to be turned against us. The Party and government
leadership and responsible Party comrades should be prepared
for this. If you now want to carry the revolution through to the
end, you must discipline yourself, reform yourself in order to
keep up with it. Otherwise you can only keep out of it. (1966J:
254)

Part Two
On Practice: Four Studies

The four essays which follow are not *historical* studies in the conventional sense, for this we direct attention to existing publications. What is being attempted here is the provision of what we regard as a crucial location for many of Mao's major theoretical discoveries. These are both context for, and in some measure the content of, the cumulative marxism we have analysed in Part One. They also show the internal relation between historical experience (of specific classes in particular struggles involving definite political, cultural *and* production strategies) and theory which we have argued is a distinctive mark of historical materialism.

The first essay examines the Border Region years of 1937 to 1946 since we see this as the crucial inception of Mao's long struggle with and partial transformation of Bolshevism, following on from that great 'manifesto': the Long March. Next, an essay focuses on a much shorter time-period – that of the mid-1950s – and argues the general practical and theoretical lessons contained in the famous collection *The High Tide of Socialism in the Chinese Countryside*. A third essay analyses the Great Proletarian Cultural Revolution of the mid-1960s which was, as Rossanda has remarked, an event of international significance. Our last essay compares the work of Mao and Gramsci, arguing for the latter's materialism against a general idealistic interpretation which is increasingly current.

1 THE BORDER REGION YEARS

In this essay we are writing about that period *after* the Long March and *before* the complete victory of the Communist forces. For convenience we can use the dates when Yenan was the capital of People's China, 1937–1946. For a full history, apart from reading Mao's own work (contained in the first four volumes of his *Selected*

45

Works) of this period, there are four writers whose work is crucial – for the start of the period: Edgar Snow and Agnes Smedley; for the later part and beyond: Jack Belden and William Hinton.[1] All of these, and others,[2] will also provide some account of the significance of the Long March.[3]

It is essential to be realistic in any assessment of the Long March (as Mao, 1935A, stresses). The destruction was immense: in the case of the Army, about two-thirds (Wolf, 1969: 152); in the case of the Party, far more than two-thirds, leaving a Party numbering about 30–40,000 (ibid., 150).[4] The Border Region of Shansi-Kansu-Ninghsia was also considerably poorer and more rugged than that of the Kiangsi Soviet.[5]

But, not in spite of but *because of* the immensity of the suffering, it remains true to declare, with Mao,

> the Long March is the first of its kind in the annals of history, . . . it is a manifesto, a propaganda force, a seeding-machine . . . It has announced to some 200 million people in eleven provinces that the road of the Red Army is their only road to liberation. Without the Long March, how could the broad masses have learned so quickly about the existence of the great truth which the Red Army embodies? (1935A: 160)

Here Mao summarises both the external and the internal (for the Party, for the Army) lessons of the Long March through his stress upon an exemplary transformation (of defeat into victory, of encirclement into creation of a new headquarters).

Mao's military theory and practice[6] drew upon the lessons of the Long March; but in 1928 he had already stressed how internally related were military and political matters (e.g. 1928B: 81f), again this reference was not only external (the Army as an example to the People) but internal:

> the reason why the Red Army has been able to carry on in spite of such poor material conditions and such frequent engagements is its practice of democracy. (Ibid., 83)

It was at this time that Mao issued the first version of the 'Three main rules of discipline and eight points for attention';[7] these were slightly revised in 1929. The version issued by General HQ of the People's Liberation Army in 1947 reads:

On Practice: Four Studies

(1) Obey orders in all your actions (2) Don't take a single needle or a piece of thread from the masses (3) Turn in everything captured.

These are the 'rules of discipline'; the 'points for attention' are:

(1) Speak politely; (2) Pay fairly for what you buy; (3) Return everything you borrow; (4) Pay for anything you damage; (5) Don't hit or swear at people; (6) Don't damage crops; (7) Don't take liberties with women; (8) Don't ill-treat captives. (1947G: 155).

These may seem thoroughly unorthodox in their repudiation of treating troops like animals or machines to anyone who has been 'occupied' by soldiers. They are as realistic as all Mao's other views. No army that was a burden upon the People could be truly popular. They also attracted recruits to the army and encouraged peasants to return to their villages which were now seen as 'protected' rather than 'occupied'.

But Mao's strategy does not stop at the level of understanding how to fight effectively. Any strategy must grasp, coherently and consistently, who is the main enemy. By mid-1935, Mao argued that the main enemy was Japan and that the CPC should try to work with the KMT for a national united front against Japanese invasion. The Japanese armies had been steadily invading China since the incident of 18 September 1931; they extended their territory from 1934 and launched a more general invasion in July 1937. Up until the Sian incident of December 1936, when Chiang Kai-shek was detained by some of his own officers until he agreed to join the CPC's fight against the Japanese, KMT resistance had been weak toward the Japanese invasion, ferocious toward the CPC. This follows from Chiang Kai-shek's own analysis of the CPC as 'Red bandits' who were a disease of China's soul; the Japanese were merely a disease of the skin; the soul must be cleansed before the skin. This analysis is entirely congruent with Chiang's reintroduction of Confucianism as the 'official' religion of China in 1934.

The most concise analysis by Mao, amongst his many military and political writings on the subject, is that entitled 'The tasks of the Communist Party of China in the period of resistance of Japan' (1937D). Therein, Mao argues that the contradiction between

48   *For Mao*

'China and Japanese imperialism' is now principal and that this would have internal and international consequences. He dates this change from December 1935.[8] The later Japanese strategy of 'Loot all! Kill all!! Burn all!!!' and the obvious (i.e. visible) complicity of KMT officials with Japanese imperialism; the accumulation of landed and capitalist wealth[9] and the covariation of political power; and the relations within the KMT army; justified Mao's call and the CPC/Red Army practice.

The call – along with the external and internal relations of the Red Army – was also part of a much larger movement which is normally summarised as 'the mass line' or the Yenan Way.[10] This entailed a direct attack upon (and eventual destruction of) the social relations (in imagery and actuality) of semi-colonial, semi-feudal China which have as their central apparent dichotomy the 'Scholar' and the 'Peasant'. The former embodies all wisdom and no work; the latter reverses these qualities and is, above all else, *passive*. Several visitors – for example Agnes Smedley and Edgar Snow – stressed this in many sketches in their works (e.g. Smedley, 1938: 281–2; Snow, 1937: 216f, 1961: 214f on the famine). Mao, from the 1920s, had *known* that this appearance of sullen but constant passivity was simply that, an *appearance* which concealed the potential for turning the world upside-down. That is why the CPC

> movement aimed first of all at the political and moral liberation of the peasants, without which it would have been fruitless to propose a radical reform of the system of economic exploitation. (Chesneaux, 1973: 160)

To transform passivity into activity there seem to be various methods – payment by results, coercion, fear, and self-oriented activity. In a territory which faced three enemies – the Japanese and KMT armies plus 'defeatism' – production resulted from an admixture of all this. What was central to the Border Region years was a particular form of organisation; or, more generally, a new orientation to organisation, toward the whole range of social relations (again, of imagery and actuality). This was linked (as we stressed in Part One above) to solving the problem of learning. A wrong *method* of learning would produce coercion and commandism, keep Party and Army exterior to the people, *and lose the war*. Being 'bad at learning' might mean taking a far too general view (Mao, 1936D:

On Practice: Four Studies 49

180) or far too specific a view. Mao criticised this 'slavish attitude to foreign ideas' and 'blind faith' many times: Some

> say it is enough merely to study the experience of revolutionary war in Russia, or, to put it more concretely, that it is enough merely to follow the laws by which the civil war in the Soviet Union was directed and the military manuals published by Soviet military organizations. They do not see that these laws and manuals embody the specific characteristics of the civil war and the Red Army in the Soviet Union, and that if we copy and apply them without allowing any change, we shall also be 'cutting the feet to fit the shoes' *and be defeated*. (Ibid., 181, our emphasis)

Several commentators remark this new kind of organisation.[11] Snow noted as 'rather typical of the intensity of soviet efforts were the methods used to increase production and utilize great areas of wasteland' (1937: 225; 1961: 221) and he goes on to analyse the 28 January 1936 *Order of Instruction* of the Land Commission (Wayapao, Shensi) which stresses the twin features of great importance: (i) making the Red Army as productively useful as possible, and (ii) bringing into production the whole population.

> But how did the peasants feel about this? The Chinese peasant is supposed to hate organization, discipline, and any social activity beyond his own family. Well, the Reds simply laugh at you when you tell them that. They say that no Chinese peasant dislikes organization or social activity if he is working for himself and not the . . . landlord or the tax-collector. (1937: 226; 1961: 222)

Israel Epstein reported in the *New York Times* in 1937:

> The tax burden of the peasantry is reduced because garrison troops, the personnel of government institutions, university students and other similar groups have all been given waste land to cultivate, and produce at least a part of their food themselves, lessening the dependence on the grain levy, An Eighth Army brigade which we visited had reclaimed 25,000 acres and was growing more than twice the amount of food and cotton it required. (quoted in Chesneaux, 1973: 135)

What these witnesses report is properly characterised as a social

50 *For Mao*

revolution in a quite directly materialist sense.[12] They were witnessing the challenge to expert notions of the possible through a change in 'natural facts'. Stressing how 'the medium of civilization' mediates the physical and the human (as Marx and Engels clarify in *The German Ideology*), Buchanan has rightly remarked that

> it cannot be overemphasised that . . . vulnerability to disease and to calamities such as drought or flood is not a constant, that it varies according to the degree of organisation, the technology and the resources of the human groups concerned . . . (1970: 116f)

Mark Selden's formulations seem insufficiently to have grasped this fundamentally materialist point; the emphasis is placed too greatly upon the ideational and visionary.

> Out of the ashes of military strife which enveloped China and Vietnam in protracted wars of liberation emerged a radically new vision of man and society and a concrete approach to development. Built on foundations of participation and community action which challenged elite domination, this approach offers hope of more *humane* forms of development . . .
>
> [People's War] forges new bonds of unity in which the very definitions of leader and led are recast and the beginnings of a new social basis are created. (Selden, 1970: 374, 375 reprint pagination)

In fact the unity (of *specific* human groups, moreover) is forged through polarisation against old and new enemies and through solidarity on behalf of class-specific, truly popular objectives. Much of the knowledge (that practical materialists have to be good at learning) is quite literally embodied within the way that productive groups work *together*. These are the only sure (that is fully emancipatory) resources for socialist construction.

This understanding is central to Mao's philosophy of this period (as we stressed in Part One above), in his writings on the Army and the Party, and in his stress on how increasing production was (a) part and parcel of good Communist work (b) inseparable from winning the war against the Japanese and exposing the true nature of the KMT and *its* social base. In what many regard as Mao's most 'capitulationist' text (the adjective is, of course, farcical given the

On Practice: Four Studies 51

course of historical events), on the tasks of the CPC in the period of resistance to Japan, there occurs a strong insistence upon maximal democracy in the base areas so that region becomes 'a model of resistance and democracy'. Moreover,

> Essential economic construction should be conducted in this area and the livelihood of the people should be improved. Essential cultural work should be carried out. (Mao, 1937D: 273; cf. 1938B, C, D, E, F; 1939M)

In all the work of the Party in the Border Region it was essential to draw a clear distinction between themselves and the various enemies of the people. This meant not reproducing 'new Communist scholars and imperial envoys' to replace the old Confucian elite. It also meant using the principles of voluntary participation and mutual benefit in the new forms of productive enterprise. Thus, in the 1936 *Order of Instruction* (mentioned above), analysed by Snow, the emphasis is upon

> widespread propaganda to induce the masses to participate voluntarily, without involving any form of compulsory command. (quoted in Snow 1937: 225; 1961: 222)

Mao's writings during the period covered by this essay stress similar themes repeatedly, offering thereby a sustained critique not only of the methods of old China but of their potential replication within Party work. Above all the critique exposes the conditions which make possible the normal separations (fighting a war *or* growing crops, for example) which sustain particular modes of production that turn upon the pumping of surplus value from majorities to benefit minorities. The 'cultural revolution' attempted is, of course, paradigmatic for any successful socialist construction (which begins long before the particular benchmark of a military victory). Like Marx, Mao recognises that

> men's minds are liable to be fettered by circumstance and habit from which even revolutionaries cannot always escape. (1942D: 101)

It is entirely to the point to stress that this remark occurs within a discussion of the policy of 'better troops and simple administration'

52   *For Mao*

which entailed, *inter alia*, making Army, Party and State administration more productively self-sufficient, thus reducing its parasitic nature and the amount of public taxation which was needed. This view pervades Mao's general taxation policy also:

> many of our comrades place a one-sided stress on public finance and do not understand the importance of the economy as a whole . . . The reason is that an outmoded and conservative notion is doing mischief in their minds. They do not know that while a good or bad financial policy affects the economy, it is the economy that determines finance . . . To neglect economic development and the opening up of sources of finance, and instead to hope for the solution of financial difficulties by curtailing indispensable expenditures, is a conservative notion which cannot solve any problem. (Mao, 1942G: 111–12)

It is perhaps worth stressing the relevance of this strategy to certain persistent crises within social democracy's outlook on capitalism since the 1960s in the capitalist social formations. Note further,

> In the financial and economic field, the Party and government personnel at the county and district levels should devote nine-tenths of their energy to helping the peasants increase production, and only one-tenth to collecting taxes from them. If pains are taken with the first task, the second will be easy. (Mao, 1943D: 132)

Selden argues

> The co-operative unit was in fact a microcosm of the society envisioned by war-time leadership, embodying not only a promethean vision of man actively striving to control nature, but confronting the full scope of rural problems. (1970: 383–4, reprint pagination)

But (aside from ignoring one-half of China's population) this again down-values what was specific to the co-operative movement. There is an excellent account in Snow's chapter 'The anatomy of money' (1937/1961: Part 6, Ch. 5). The CPC, he writes there,[13]

> defined the co-operative 'as an instrument to resist private

On Practice: Four Studies   53

capitalism and develop a new economic system', and they listed its five main functions as follows: 'to combat the exploitation of the masses by the merchants; to combat the enemy's blockade; to develop the national economy of the Soviet districts; to raise the economic-political level of the masses; and to prepare the conditions for Socialist construction'. (Snow, 1937: 232; 1961: 227–8)[14]

Snow here is quoting from the Department of National Economy's *Outline for Co-operative Development* (1935, Wayapao, Shensi). It is as well to stress a point he makes in a later chapter on 'Soviet industries' that although the KMT had tried to copy the CPC system in parts of South China,

> results thus far suggest that it is extremely difficult, if not impossible, to operate such co-operatives under a strictly *laissez-faire* capitalism. (Snow, 1937: 253; 1961: 247)

These go some way to qualify the claims of Jack Gray that

> the Yenan industrial co-operatives were part of the wider Chinese Industrial Co-operatives movement of the war period; indeed they owed more to Indusco than to Communist ideas of co-operative organization. The existing bureaucratic Party co-operatives were abolished in 1943, and the only industrial co-ops which remained to act as models for a new co-operative movement were those which had been set up with Indusco help for which Mao Tse-tung expressed his gratitude. (Gray, 1973b: 125)

As Gray goes on to stress, the best account is given in Snow's book *Scorched Earth* where he writes:

> In July, 1938, when the Government appointed Rewi Alley chief technical adviser of the Chinese Industrial Co-operatives, the organization did not own a single factory, lathe or even a chisel – while Alley himself was its only staff (1941: 191)

By October 1940 an 'army of 300,000' people was directly involved in Indusco work (ibid., 192). In 1940, according to Gray (1973b: 125) Indusco ran 2,300 co-ops of which 80 were in the Border

54 *For Mao*

region; by 1945 there were 882 in a much larger Communist area. Snow (1941: 216, 218) cites some Indusco slogans:

Industrial co-operatives are *really* the workers shops!

Industrial co-operatives are the method of boycotting Japan!

If we are bombed once we shall rebuild once. If we are bombed ten times we will rebuild ten times.

Asking Rewi Alley what had been the most memorable experience of the first two years of Indusco work, Snow was told

> One winter morning we were leaving a little village on the edge of Mongolia, when we heard tinkling bells, and stepped aside as a long caravan of camels came out of the mist, their breath turning to frost in the bitter air. As they went by we were amazed to see the lead camel carrying the huge silk banner of Indusco, and our red triangle emblazoned on the big boxes of freight. It was a camel-puller's transport co-op, hauling guerrilla products. The men with me, who had come up from the warm South, suddenly realized they were part of something that covered a whole nation. How they cheered those camels as they snorted past into the dawn! (Snow, 1941: 1956)

Mao recognised the significance of co-operation in 1927 in his 'Investigations' (1927A: 54). By 1943 – in the central text of this period, 'Get organized!' – he argued

> The co-operatives are now the most important form of mass organization in the economic field. (1943F: 155)

He argued, furthermore, that all 'the productive activities of the masses in our army, our government and other organisations and our schools' entailing mutual help and joint labour 'are co-operatives of a sort' (ibid., 156). He recognised that various forms of co-operation ('methods of collective mutual aid') 'are the inventions of the masses themselves' and began the vast liberation of peasant production from the shackles of 'individual economy' which 'keeps the peasants in perpetual poverty' (ibid.). He saw 'mutual aid groups' as forms of co-operative for agrarian production

On Practice: Four Studies 55

which, along with multi-purpose co-operatives, transport co-operatives, and handicraft co-operatives, were

> four kinds of co-operatives among the masses and the collective labour co-operatives in the army, the schools and the government and other organizations, [with which the CPC] . . . can organize all the forces of the people into a great army of labour. This is the only road to liberation for the people, the only road from poverty to prosperity and the only road to victory in the War of Resistance. (1943F: 157)

Methods of work were, again, crucial.

> It is wrong to regard the co-operatives as money-making concerns run for the benefit of the small number of functionaries or as stores run by the government and not economic organizations run by and for the masses. (1943D: 133)

The major method should be to encourage by example, to *demonstrate* the effectiveness of particular methods, and to *widen* the involvement in production (1943D: 134; 1943F: 157). Without the mass-line, there will be defeat – military defeat, political defeat, total defeat (starvation and disease) – because there will be no clear line dividing the enemy from ourselves.

> Another mistake is 'draining the pond to catch the fish', that is, making endless demands on the people, disregarding their hardships and considering only the needs of the government and the army. That is a Kuomintang mode of thinking which we must never adopt. (1942G: 114)

> Whether it is the tendency towards bureaucracy in local work or towards warlordism in army work, the fault is of the same nature, namely, isolation from the masses. (1943F: 159)

Of course, as we stressed above, this was not simply a co-operative *tactic*; the strategy is quite general:

> Our culture is a people's culture; our cultural workers must serve the people with great enthusiasm and devotion, and they must link themselves with the masses, not divorce themselves from the

56 *For Mao*

masses . . . . All work done for the masses must start from their needs . . . .

Unless they are conscious and willing, any kind of work that requires their participation will turn out to be a mere formality and will fail . . . There are two principles here: one is the actual needs of the masses rather than what we fancy they need, and the other is the wishes of the masses, who must make up their own minds instead of our making up their minds for them. (1944F: 236–7)

Statements like this text ('The United Front in cultural work') have encouraged a particular interpretation of Mao during the years before 1949 (and *beyond*, since it is claimed that Mao strengthened and defended 'New Democracy' for several decades).[15] Chesneaux demonstrates the falsity of this view. First, the 'policy of rent and interest reduction was pursued with vigour, with the deliberate intention of reducing the economic power of the landlords' (1973: 132). Secondly, peasants were armed and trained in guerrilla warfare – lessons they would not forget. Thirdly, there were the two aspects of the line between the CPC and the enemy: (i) in 'the final analysis the term "collaborator" has as much a class significance as a patriotic one' (ibid., 133) and (ii) Yenan operated (along with the CPC and the Red Army) as a 'social model'.

Furthermore, as we noted above, Mao stressed repeatedly that

Rent reduction must be the result of mass struggle, not a favour bestowed by the government. (1945S: 72)

To bestow rent reduction as a favour instead of arousing the masses to achieve it by their own action is wrong, and the results will not be solid. (1943D: 131; a view repeated in Mao, 1955J: *passim*)

The rectification campaigns of these years had the same strategy as later struggles *against* the opportunism and dogmatism of those who argued that the agrarian revolution could be entirely postponed, in order to fight a 'good' military war and *against* the adventurism and voluntarism of those who thought it useful to emulate the Japanese policy of 'kill all!' with regard to landlords and rich peasants; a policy which would have curtailed production.

Again the text 'Get organized' refutes directly any theory of 'Mao

On Practice: Four Studies 57

as moderate'. It celebrates (and the word is entirely appropriate) the success of an implicit critique of Bolshevism – placing production before procurement, putting provision of daily necessities ahead of capital accumulation. This text urges the taking of the mass-line, not because of some vision of Prometheus but because only by doing that would the Japanese be defeated *in such a way* that rapid mobilization against the KMT and (eventually) both comprador and national, industrial, fiscal, merchant and agrarian *capitalists*, would be *swift and decisive*. Because the party, army, schools and government produce their own food and cotton and have workshops for simple necessities

> less is taken in taxation from the people, who can therefore enjoy more of the fruits of their labour. (1943F: 154).

There is only one correct policy: to organise the strength of the masses, not through coercion, commandism or fiscal or administrative measures but by believing that those masses possess the resources to be (and have) more than they are (and do). Mao was quite explicit that this learning had a future reference – learning now would be applied later:

> We must exert ourselves and learn, because China depends on us for her reconstruction. (1945A: 245)

> War is not only a military and political contest but also an economic contest. (1945B: 250; cf. 1945E)

The story of Mao's long fight against the 'Bolsheviks' (and, in some ways more crucial, his implicit critique of Bolshevism *tout court*)[16] has been sketched by us elsewhere. It is still an area of maximum polemic;[17] we examine some general features of this in our Part Three below. We have noted above Mao's criticism of those who wish to apply mechanically what they saw as the lessons and methods of the Great October Socialist Revolution and subsequent events in the USSR. Some of this was very evident by the end of the period here examined (e.g. Mao, 1944B, C) or implicit during it (e.g. Mao, 1937H, J; 1939M); but recently Mao has made it clear that some of his writings were directly concerned with Comintern policy:

58 *For Mao*

Speaking generally, it is we Chinese who have achieved understanding of the objective world of China, not the comrades concerned with Chinese questions in the Communist International. These comrades ... simply did not understand Chinese society, the Chinese nation, or the Chinese revolution. For a long time even we did not have a clear understanding of the objective world of China, let alone the foreign comrades! (1962B: 172)

Even before the dissolution of the Third International [i.e. 1943], we did not obey the orders of the Third International. At the Tsunyi Conference [1935] we didn't obey, and afterwards, for a period of ten years ... we didn't obey them at all. Those dogmatists utterly failed to study China's peculiarities ... (1964T: 218–19)

The Chinese revolution won victory by acting contrary to Stalin's will ... If we had followed Wang Ming's, or in other words Stalin's, methods the Chinese revolution couldn't have succeeded. When our revolution succeeded, Stalin said it was a fake. (1958H: 102–3; cf. 1956F: 87; 1964T: 217)

In the famous editorials of the *People's Daily* in 1956, we find similar passages:

> ... there was a time – the ten years of civil war from 1927 to 1936 – when some of our comrades crudely applied this formula [direct the main blow at the middle-of-the-road] of Stalin's to China's revolution ... the result was that, instead of isolating the real enemy, we isolated ourselves and suffered losses to the advantage of the real enemy. (Mao, 1956C: 15)

As the CC/CPC noted in 1963 'Long ago the Chinese Communists had first-hand experience of some of his [Stalin's] mistakes' (*On the Question of Stalin*, p. 8).[18]

Our main point here is that the struggle against Comintern errors was part and parcel of the struggle *for* socialist construction *against* dogmatism and commandism. This is no more evidence for Mao's 'nationalism' (or his sinification of Marxism) than is Lenin's (or the more general Bolshevik) critique of, and break with, Kautskyism and the Second International. It represents learning from the

On Practice: Four Studies 59

examples of previous social practices and historical experience of attempting socialist construction. It does not apply a rigid model (neither does it generate one) but demonstrates a consistent methodology. All successful socialist revolutions will be compelled to adopt the same methodology; to be as 'nationalistic' and as 'sinified', if they do not then they shall be crippled and deformed, never more so if they believe that Mao's theory is mantra-like, to be chanted in the streets of a different social formation to make the walls fall down! Adoption of any methodology, moreover, does not *guarantee* success since the world is constantly changing and new analyses (in which marxism is applied and extended; through which historical materialism becomes enriched) and social practices are constantly to be undertaken.

Nevertheless, we must not swing to the other extreme and declare the experience of the Chinese people in these Border Region years to be 'inscrutable' and so heavily imbedded within their circumstances that we can simply study them at a distance. This would be to make them religious statuettes and closed archives. When Mao argued in April 1945 that there were two possible destinies for China, we believe he was making a general statement about the alternatives which confront the majority of the people of the world and which are, more clearly now in the 1970s than when he spoke to the 7th Congress of the CPC in 1945, very relevant to the current situation and future prospects of England, Wales, Scotland, and Ireland. Indeed for all Europe, there is

> a destiny of light and a destiny of darkness . . . A China which is independent, free, democratic, united, prosperous and strong . . . a new China whose people have won liberation, or a China which is semi-colonial, semi-feudal, divided, poor and weak, that is, the old China. (1945C: 251)

Jack Gray has outlined the longer-term implications of the Border Region years for the theory and practice of the CPC (and, we might add, for the many two-line struggles within the CPC *and* for the polemic between the CPC and the CPSU).

> The border region experience gave the Chinese very low expectations from centralised planning . . . The border regions were in the poorest parts of China, so the Chinese became experts at substituting labour for capital, in organising large masses of

60   *For Mao*

people, more or less voluntarily, to undertake co-operative production. (Gray, 1973a)

The production drive [of 1942] involved two main types of operation, one in agriculture and the other in industry. In agriculture, mutual aid methods were used to increase the cultivated area,[19] and within it the irrigated area. Central to this undertaking was the resettlement of refugees from the Japanese-held areas through co-operative land reclamation. This experience was the source of Mao's confidence that the collectivisation of Chinese agriculture could be achieved through the benefits of co-operative labour-intensive construction, based on mutual-aid teams – one of the key controversies of the mid-fifties. In industry, co-operatives were created using simple or improvised technologies; and these co-operatives were pregnant for the whole future of China, for within them are the seeds of the Great Leap, the Communes, and much of the strategy of rural economic development which emerged in 1958. (1973b: 125; cf. Gray, 1965; 1966; 1972a, b).

As Gray pointed out: these choices are not 'politically neutral' (1973a); but neither are political and cultural relations without direct relevance for *which* productive strategy is best suited. We are, in fact, dealing with a spiral that takes as its starting point the 'fact' (following upon experience and investigation) that there *are* resources unused within existing methods and production relations which, if successfully unleashed, will both solve the pressing political and production problems of the moment and transform the people, production relations and implements used. The wager on the people is a wager on concealed forms of energy, illumination, knowledge, and strength which can only be made visible through a new form of organisation. This must not replicate the suppressive and coercive features of existing social relations, for it is they which keep the real resources hidden (they sustain passivity and poverty); the new organisation must be, in one sense, militantly negative. It must prevent exterior and interior enemies of the people from preventing the latter's full emancipation through their own efforts to change the objective world and thereby throw off the habits of mind and custom which hold them down. The new socialist form of organisation cannot be parasitic upon the people, demanding their

On Practice: Four Studies

conformity to a dogmatic image of capitalist development in which experts (State officials, Party cadres, military officers) have to be sustained by the productive activity of others, in which what is best is always 'foreign' and what is worst is always 'native', and in which machines are more important than people, and capital more important than both.

These are the lessons, implicit[20] and explicit, which we think can be drawn from Mao's theory and practice during the Border Region years. They are very relevant to a study of socialist construction in several countries, not least in China in the 1970s.

2 THE MASS-LINE AT WORK: THE HIGH TIDE OF SOCIALISM IN THE CHINESE COUNTRYSIDE

Readers of *The Times* will be familiar with the contours of class struggle in China; they lie (as of course they do everywhere else) between romantic, idealistic 'extremists' on the one side and rational, pragmatic 'moderates' on the other. Readers of *Pravda* unfortunately receive a similar message; in this version, the 'Mao gang' are described, in suitable marxist jargon but with the same connotations, as subjectivist, petit-bourgeois adventurists.[1] There is a superficial rationale to these charges, for Mao undoubtedly does insist on politics before economics, and 'redness' before expertise. But what is persistently misunderstood in such formulations is the sense of 'before': as far as Mao is concerned, if you sincerely want to promote production, you will grasp revolution. For we are not dealing here with either/or dichotomies, but with relations; and relations, moreover, which are at the same time contradictions. 'Politics', for Mao, is what makes 'economic' *practices* possible – and *makes* them of one type rather than another. Therefore there can never be a purely and politically neutral 'economic' strategy.

In the words of his 'Sixty points concerning working methods',

> Ideological and political work is the guarantee for the completion of economic technological work and it serves the economic base. Ideology and politics are, moreover, the commanders, the 'soul'. A slight relaxation in our ideological and political work will lead our economic and technological work astray (1958F: 64).

In this essay we shall pursue this apparent paradox. We will attempt

62   *For Mao*

particularly to show, in the context of the struggles over agricultural co-operation in the mid-1950s, just how false is the orthodox picture of Mao who, precisely at his most 'idealist', 'utopian', and 'extreme', is profoundly (and dialectically) a materialist.

MAO'S 'ECONOMICS'

Jack Gray (all cited texts) has set out what he terms 'the economics of Maoism' in some detail and we need not rehearse his arguments in full here.[2] But the preponderance of commentaries from the right (and the untransformed Bolshevism of most assessments from the left)[3] oblige us to spend some time initially establishing that Mao does have a coherent productive strategy, and a strategy solidly based in empirical realities and learned through long years of practical experience. He formulates it most clearly in two seminal documents from the nineteen-fifties: 'On the question of agricultural co-operation', and 'On the Ten Great Relationships' (1955F; 1956D; cf. 1955G, 1957B, section XII). It will be advantageous to outline this strategy against the background of Bolshevik assumptions as elaborated in *SCMT*, and as followed, in part at least, in China during the first years of the People's Republic (see 1958H).

For the Bolsheviks, and for Mao, the critical problem for a Communist Party and one heightened in a so-called 'backward'[4] country, is to secure rapid and accelerating development in the forces of production. Such development is the material (experiential) basis for socialism; only thus can the people be fed, housed, clothed. But Bolshevism, we have argued, understood this key tenet of historical materialism in a very restricted way. Forces of production were equated with industrial technology *per se*, and the capitalist industry of the West was viewed as providing the paradigm for their development. This perspective sustained a variety of policies designed to transfer resources from agriculture to heavy industry, the assumption being that subsequently agrarian production could in turn be 'modernised', and its social relations eventually transformed, on a suitably 'advanced' industrial base; it was axiomatic, within this perspective, that mechanisation must precede co-operation. It is here that Mao takes issue. 'In agriculture, with conditions as they are in our country', he wrote in 1955, 'co-operation must precede the use of big machinery (in capitalist countries agriculture develops in a capitalist way)' (1955F: 406, SR trans.). This marks far more than a merely tactical reversal of

On Practice: Four Studies 63

Bolshevik priorities. Accelerating co-operation is the keynote of Mao's entire strategy. Contrary to what is usually assumed, Mao is adamant that 'heavy industry is the core of China's economic construction' (1957B: 419), and hence aims at rapid capital accumulation. It is at just this point – and for just this reason – that he rejects the Bolshevik (and capitalist) option of plundering agricultural producers in order to generate that capital:

> If your desire [to develop heavy industry] is genuine or strong, then you will attach importance to agriculture and light industry so that there will be more grain and more raw materials for light industry and a greater accumulation of capital. And there will be more funds in the future to invest in heavy industry. (1956D: 286)

> As agriculture and light industry develop, heavy industry, assured of its market and its funds, will grow faster. Hence what may seem to be a slower pace of industrialisation will actually not be so slow, and indeed may even be faster. (1957B: 419)

The point is a simple but critical one. If, in order to finance heavy industry, agrarian production is leeched of its resources, industry itself will finally be harmed. Not only will it undermine further funding from agricultural surpluses, it will also deprive itself of the market through which it aims eventually to generate its own capital. This is, as Mao once observed of Soviet agriculture, a case of 'draining the pond to catch the fish' (quoted in Gray, 1969a: 262). If, on the other hand, resources are put into agriculture and the light industry that serves it, the result will be a living standard rising fast enough ultimately to sustain funds and markets for heavy industry. Developing agricultural production must therefore take precedence over procurement – for the sake, so Mao asserts, of industry itself. It is here that his challenge to the Bolshevik ranking of technical before social revolution becomes significant.

Within the Bolshevik problematic the reasoning we have just outlined would be regarded as flawed, in so far as the possibility of substantial increases in agricultural output in the absence of prior mechanisation would be viewed with considerable scepticism[5]. Mao, however, sees co-operation (and the class struggle to achieve and sustain it) as a productive force in its own right, and its progressive acceleration as the key to his strategy. It is, in sum, the best 'social form' for the emancipation of labour. In outline,

64 *For Mao*

through co-operation, labour can be used for construction projects. These increase production capacity and create a demand for labour-saving light industrial products, whilst at the same time generating the funds to purchase products, and thus finance light industry[6]. The utilisation of these goods frees more labour; co-operation is extended (in the nineteen-fifties, from Mutual Aid Teams, via lower and higher APCs, to People's Communes), allowing ever more ambitious construction; capacity, demand and incomes increase correspondingly in a widening spiral. For Mao the spiral is potentially infinite, with burgeoning agricultural production demanding and funding light industry and with light industry in turn, through its needs for means of production, supporting heavy industry. Gray argues the pertinence of 'under-employment' in traditional Chinese agriculture to this strategy. We would rather stress, with Mao, the productive benefits of people co-operating, and the critical question of whose politics are in command. This will bring us to the very heart of Mao's alleged 'idealism'.

SOCIALIST UPSURGE IN CHINA'S COUNTRYSIDE

In 1955, a book was published in China: *The High Tide of Socialism in China's Countryside*. It is an extremely important historical document, for two reasons. First, it had a crucial bearing on the course of the struggles within the CPC in the mid-nineteen-fifties over the direction and the speed of agricultural co-operation and thus of the whole strategy sketched out above (for details, see Han Suyin, 1976, Part I, Ch. 2; Gray, 1970). Second, and of more direct importance here, because, rather than in spite, of its saturation with empirical detail, it represents a seminal statement of Mao's theory. The *High Tide* consists of 176 articles from the provincial and national press, interviews, Party Committee and work team reports, and so on, on experiences of the struggle to establish APCs in China; 44 of these are translated in the English edition (1955J). The collection as a whole is introduced by Mao, who also offers his comments on individual pieces. The scope of the book is apparent even in its greatly abridged translation; the reports (and Mao's comments) range through APCs differing widely in geographic conditions, social make-up, and historical experience, with varying successes and problems, and at all stages of development. The sum is a graphic and comprehensive picture of what no reader can doubt

On Practice: Four Studies 65

was an acute class struggle. But through the *High Tide*, and emerging from the experiences it describes, run a number of consistent themes. It is on these that we shall focus. In doing so, we hope to indicate both why and how socialist politics must be in command, for the productive strategy we have outlined above to succeed.

In Part One, we spent a lot of time dealing with Mao's epistemology, and its relation to his mass-line understanding of socialist politics. Nowhere is that relation displayed more effectively than in the *High Tide*[7]. To begin with, we should note this in the very existence of such a collection of reports on what are, in fact, exemplary transformations. The *High Tide* practices what Mao preaches within its pages:

> Let him walk awhile among the people, learn what they are thinking, see what they are doing – that is how to cure his ailment. Let him get some advanced experience from them and publicise it. That is the medicine for rightist obtuseness. (1955J: 45; all subsequent page numbers *cited alone* refer to this text)

The point is underlined when we recall that the reports in the *High Tide* were Mao's weapons in the struggle in the CC/CPC that raged through 1955 (150 – 1, 159 – 60; see also Han Suyin, 1976; Gray, 1970). It is worth quoting some of the charges made by Mao's opponents as he himself lists them:

> For instance they had thought that the people's demand that the whole countryside go co-operative within three years was an idle dream; that co-operation in the [old-liberated] north could be achieved more quickly than in the [new-liberated] south; that it was impossible to run co-ops in the backward areas, in the mountain regions, in the national minority areas, in areas stricken by natural calamities; that it was easy to form a co-op but hard to make it strong; that the peasants were too poor and had no way of raising funds; that the peasants were uneducated and so lacked people who could act as book-keepers; that the greater the number of co-operatives, the more blunders they would make; that co-operatives were growing too rapidly for the political consciousness of the people and the level of experience of the

66   *For Mao*

. officials; that the Party's policy of unified purchase and supply of grain and its policy on co-operatives were causing the peasants to lose enthusiasm for work; that unless the Party immediately backed down on the question of co-operation, the worker – peasant alliance would be endangered; that the spread of co-operation would produce a vast pool of surplus labour for which there would be no outlet; and so on. Many more similar ideas could be cited–illusions, every one. (150–1)

Most of these, of course, are real problems, and acknowledged as such, in empirical detail, in the *High Tide*; but Mao has a simple answer to those who see in such problems 'laws' before which we must cringe: 'Don't lose touch with the people; be adept at recognising their enthusiasm from its very essence' (ibid.). Virtually every one of these purportedly insuperable obstacles is shown in the *High Tide* (again with a wealth of detail)[8] to have been conquered on at least one occasion by ordinary people. Mao's comment is the obvious one: 'If this place could do it, why can't others?' (12).

The *High Tide*, in short, is itself pre-eminently a learning exercise, in the tradition of Mao's 1927 *Investigation* and 1941 *Surveys*, epitomising a political strategy based on the premise that correct ideas come from and must be tested in social practice. And the same theme informs and is the constant refrain of the individual studies within it. Time and again we are shown how solutions did so emerge, and the nuts and bolts of the methods of work within which the mass-line could operate are a central preoccupation. We cannot exemplify here as fully as we might wish, for the *High Tide* emphases on exchange of experience within and between co-ops are legion. But what follows will, we hope, more than adequately demonstrate this point.

CLASS STRUGGLE

Stalin once described collectivisation in the USSR by the phrase 'pacification of the villages' (see *SCMT*, Ch. 3). For Mao, by contrast, fanning class struggle in the villages was the key to establishing APCs and making them solid. Rather than being seen simply as a 'sea of enemies' (and a source of funds for the 'material base' of their future proletarianisation), the peasants, in Mao's perspective, are regarded as embodying contradictions; those

On Practice: Four Studies 67

'contradictions amongst the people' Mao rightly accused Stalin (though the charge is relevant to Bolshevism as such) of being unable to 'handle' (1957B; cf. 1956C). It is the case for Mao that as Lenin put it (in a passage frequently quoted in China) 'small production *engenders* capitalism and the bourgeoisie continuously, daily, hourly, spontaneously, and on a mass scale' (Lenin 1920b: 24). Indeed this is one reason for the haste on Mao's part so deplored by his opponents on the right. On the other hand, Mao does not equate 'small production' with the 'rural sector', and he is equally emphatic in his insistence that the mass of the people have within them the collective knowledge, skills, and enthusiasm to build socialism. It is this he relies on (and to this that the *High Tide* bears eloquent witness); the people are urged to upturn their social relations in order to liberate that potential and harness it to improving their lives through increased production. But that liberation is always a struggle; a struggle that Mao sees in class terms, because for him what fetters the emancipation of labour is above all the enduring power of the old ruling class, as exercised in a multitude of ways inside every productive community and every man and woman within it.

Let us illustrate, from the *High Tide*. To begin with, outright and open resistance to the APC movement, by rich peasants, former landlords and KMT officials and so on, is richly documented. This takes many forms; one case cited (the figures are for a District) lists

> poisoning of draught animals, twice; the destruction of water conservancy works, once; the undermining of production plans, four times; the destruction of compost, once; theft, nine times; corruption, three times; creating rumours, four times; the murder of a functionary, once. (337)

As damaging (and no less a form of class war) is the scorn of the well-heeled for the 'co-op' with 'no draught animals except a three-quarter share in the ownership of a donkey' (69; cf. Wang Kuo-fan) and the educated for upstart 'book-keepers' who cannot even read. In the teeth of their opposition many an APC was built.[9] But the greatest problems lie within the co-ops.

Rich peasants, former landlords, and the like were from the beginning excluded from the APCs;[10] co-operation was to be the task of poor and middle peasants, the former taking the leading role. Nonetheless there remained a good deal of tension between these

68 *For Mao*

class fractions, on which, again, the *High Tide* pulls no punches.[11] From their side, middle peasants fear (and many articles make it plain that their fears are not without foundation) being dragged into co-ops merely for their tools and animals, having these abused and neglected by the collective, losing income by having to subsidise their poorer neighbours, and so forth. A common response is to 'hedge their bets' by, say, diverting their savings, labour, or simply concern, into private sidelines as an insurance against the co-ops failing; which is an understandable strategy maybe, but a strategy liable to produce just what it aims to guard against. The poor peasants on the other hand, are worried that they may end up being used as cheap labour within APCs dominated by and run for middle peasants; many disputes over how workpoints for different tasks are to be evaluated, or shares of land and labour as respective determinants of income, come back to this issue. Again, the *High Tide* reports make it very clear that their fears too are far from groundless.

The 'petit-bourgeois mentality' that Bolshevik demonology ascribes to all peasants, then, is not absent from the Chinese countryside. Indeed, the *High Tide* regards it as an extremely serious problem, and is arguably more sensitive to its productive implications than anything which has come out of the Bolshevik literature. Mao dwells on this in several of his comments (128, 136–9, 219–20, 228–9, 235–9, 302–3). Importantly, though, Mao as ever is aware of contradiction. Middle peasants are not seen as 'agents of capitalism' pure and simple; the possibility of their being persuaded of the benefits of socialism through experience is accepted and worked for. And in the same way the poor peasants are not viewed uncritically as an unsullied fount of socialist wisdom. Mao urges their leading role on the grounds of their present socio-economic position and their past experience (236–7) but this does not blind him to the fact that they too bear the scars of class, and hence need to transform themselves.

The peasants' doubts concerning what their co-operation can achieve are founded on more than just 'petit-bourgeois aspirations'. Throughout the *High Tide* we meet attitudes of resignation, of fatalism, of disbelieving cynicism, and of what appears to be simple apathy. 'Dragons in the sky, insects in the paddies, there is nothing unnatural in that' (295), 'You can't feed a hen in the morning and expect it to lay in the afternoon . . . It's not worth the bother' (428) and 'Every year you want us to find tricks and tap the

On Practice: Four Studies 69

potential . . . It's like adding oil to fat. It's utterly impossible!' (391) are not at all untypically dismissive responses to activists' proposals to solve problems of (respectively) natural calamities, shortages of literate personnel, and surplus labour, through collective mobilisation. In much the same way we find a frequent tendency among the peasants and local cadres to want to rely on 'expert' help from outside (higher Party committees, work teams, trained technical personnel) to solve local problems, and to despair if such assistance is not forthcoming; 'If more people are made available "from above" . . . we'll set up more co-ops. If we can't get any, we won't set up so many' (180) is one such instance. A Bolshevik, maybe, would see here the proverbial 'dull-wittedness of the *muzhik*' (the phrase is Trotsky's),[12] a confirmation of the peasants' inability to play more than a passive part in changing their own conditions of production. Mao thinks differently.

Like Fanon[13] Mao believes that the most enduring legacy of oppression lies in the self-images of the oppressed. And like Marx[14] he is acutely aware of the class foundation of such images. As we have emphasised elsewhere (*SCMT*, Ch. 1; Sayer, 1975a), class involves far more than relations of ownership; to define a specific form of property 'is nothing else than to give an exposition of *all* the social relations of . . . production' (Marx, 1847b: 154, our emphasis). Central to all class dictatorships[15] (though epitomised perhaps in the mandarin culture of old China) is the emasculation of the direct producers by the division of labour. The peasant attitudes we have summated above spring from a specific experience of powerlessness which is just as much a constituent of the class rule of landlord and capitalist as is the appropriation of the means of production. Major effects of capital's production relations are those that disguise the creative power of the producers as 'hidden attributes of a trained caste' (Marx, 1871b: 170). It is these relations Mao sees as underlying what others analyse as peasant 'stupidity'. The concept of class struggle in the *High Tide* is therefore capacious, but it is not sloppy. It accurately grasps how extensive is the ensemble of social relations (that is, ways and modes of having, thinking, feeling, acting, seeing, being) which forms a ruling class's social power, and thus maps the full dimensions of the struggle to overthrow that power. A mode of production, as Marx long ago realised, is not just 'the reproduction of the physical existence of . . . individuals'; it is 'a definite *mode of life* on their part' (Marx, 1846a: 32).

70   *For Mao*

POLITICS IN COMMAND

Mao's famous dictum, 'Political work is the life-blood of all economic work' (302, quoted more fully above, p. 2), dates from his *High Tide* comments. By now, the statement itself hardly needs further justification; if the (socialist) development of their productive forces depends upon the people's transformation of their production relations, and if this is in every sense a class struggle, then politics are supremely salient. There is a good deal more to be said, however, on what kind of 'politics' Mao has in mind. We may begin with some 'methods of·work' which are definitely not to his liking:

> Many cadres . . . would rather see ten mutual-aid teams go down than let a single co-op fail. For this reason, a number of small mutual-aid teams ran their production less satisfactorily than they ought to . . . Theoretically arrangements have been made for the co-op to keep contact with the teams, but such contact is more apparent than real. The officials on the spot have not done enough to educate the team members patiently or to give them wholehearted help. In directing the work of the team they are hot-tempered and arrogant . . .. (225)

> In order to complete its task, the county Party committee hastily turned two mutual-aid teams with only two Youth League members in them into the Tungsheng Co-op . . . But once Tungsheng Co-op was formed, neither the local Party branch nor the cadres tried to understand what was really the matter, they simply passively acknowledged that the key personnel of the co-op was not as capable as that of others . . . On top of all this, certain abuses in the grain policy led to *a lessening of the members' desire to make the land yield more.* [Members said] 'We know that a co-op is a good thing. But when we set one up, nobody bothered about us . . . They haven't been here even once, perhaps because they don't think much of our poor little village, where they can't get good food and accommodation . . .' (269, 272–3).

> When some achievements had been made, the cadres became smug about increased yields, and didn't think it necessary to make any further efforts. They grew haughty and priggish,

On Practice: Four Studies 71

unwilling to tolerate any supervision by the membership. They put on airs and went so low as to help themselves to public funds . . . Not only had the way of carrying out Party and government policy been rash and extreme, but the cadres of this co-op were utterly corrupt . . . The person sent subsequently by the [County Party] committee to investigate the case stayed a couple of days in the co-op, replaced the chairman with someone else and thought his duty of checking was thereby fulfilled. But actually the main trouble remained untouched. *It was understandable that the co-op members were not enthusiastic to do any more work than was necessary.* (433-5 our emphasis throughout)

Less spectacular, but similarly debilitating in its productive implications, is the catalogue of 'departmentalism, reluctance to rely on the poor peasants, struggles for more active peasants and better-off households, and unprincipled disputes' (381) reported of the 'vanguard' in Talichuang township.

In such cases Mao does not mince words over where the blame lies:

> Because all co-operative members are working peasants, although various strata among them may disagree on many things, they can all ultimately be made to understand. At times, some co-ops fall into a really terrible state. The *sole* reason for this is that they cannot get the Party to lead them . . .. (266, our emphasis; cf. 27,138, 159, 168, 187, 206-7)

This is thoroughly consonant with the perspectives elaborated above. 'The poor want to remake their lives' (138); they therefore have a potentially boundless enthusiasm for socialism (27, 44-5, 159, 168). This is Mao's touchstone (and it finds ample confirmation in the *High Tide*). But equally, to deny that the producers are burdened with the 'muck of ages' (Marx, 1846a: 87), 'old ideas reflecting the old system' (302), and that these impede this remaking, is utopian. Correct leadership, for Mao, is all about handling this contradiction. His recommendations for doing so in the *High Tide* are both practical and detailed. Most generally (and insistently), he urges adherence to the principles of voluntary participation and mutual benefit. Thus,

Don't force them[middle peasants] to join before they are willing

For Mao

just for the sake of obtaining the use of their draught oxen and farm implements . . . as to the guiding principles of co-operation, we must carry out a policy of mutual benefit to both poor and middle peasants; no-one should be allowed to suffer a loss. (238; cf. Gray, 1972a)

Mao is not just being 'nice' (and still less 'liberal') here. He is acutely aware that to infringe these principles would (quite literally) be counter-productive. The consequences of policies of commandism and coercion, as well as being documented in some of the *High Tide* articles themselves, are writ large in the Soviet Union; in the wholesale slaughter of livestock which followed collectivisation, or, more revealingly still, in the comparable figures for production on the *kolkhozi* and the peasants' private plots.[16] Hence Mao opposes 'leftist' precipitateness as vigorously as he does rightist 'tail-ending', urging a very different form of 'persuasion':

> Here we had a struggle between two alternatives – socialism and capitalism. . . .
> *Let us see who increases production* in a two or three year period: Is it the well-to-do middle peasants working alone? Or is it the poor peasants and the lower middle peasants working together in co-operatives . . . Most of the poor peasants and lower middle peasants are still watching from the sidelines. At this stage both sides are still fighting for adherents . . . . (136–7, our emphasis)

> The important thing is to create examples to show the peasants. When they see that large and advanced co-ops are better than small and elementary co-ops, they will want to combine their co-operatives and organise advanced co-ops. (313)

The crucial thing, for Mao, is that the peasants experience their co-operation as having and being more. This is more than a crude *realpolitik* (though it certainly speaks volumes for Mao's realism). It is central to the struggle against the class-bound self-images we spoke of earlier. Peasants are experiencing what they themselves can collectively do. To put it another way, they are discovering themselves as a productive force. Mao's politics are directed to just this end (see 1945D: 301, quoted above, p. 37).

As with policy, so with methods of work. Throughout the *High Tide* Mao loses no opportunity to stress class struggle, and there with

On Practice: Four Studies 73

the critical importance of painstaking and sustained political and ideological work:

> The agricultural co-operative movement, from the very beginning, has been a severe ideological and struggle. No co-op can be established without going through such a struggle . . . Old ideas reflecting the old system invariably remain in people's minds for a long time . . ..(302)

> To bring our more than 500 million peasants through socialist transformation is a project which cannot possibly be achieved in an atmosphere of calm seas and gentle breezes. It demands of us Communists that we patiently educate the great mass of the peasants – who are still burdened with many of the habits and ideas of the old society . . ..(253)

But at the same time, he constantly sees this struggle as above all a matter of helping people discover and develop their own collective resources, and advocates methods geared to this. Again experience is paramount:

> This line – of going deeply into problems of one place, then applying the experience gained there in all other places . . . is none other than the famous Marxist – Leninist line which our Party has long adhered to and which has proved so effective in all its work among the people. (60)

> . . . taking the peasants' own experiences and analysing them in detail – now there is a method that is really effective. (254)

Nor is this merely abstract sloganising; individual reports in the *High Tide* abound with discussions of practices (highlighting of exemplary cases, review meetings, setting up of demonstration plots, shock brigade activities, establishing of local co-op and mutual aid networks, etc.) through which this 'mass line' can become a reality. In similar vein Mao stresses the importance of the peasants' consent for extensions of co-operation (460–1, 477–8) and urges sensitivity to variations in local conditions (219–20, 313).

Relatedly, he insists that

74 *For Mao*

> Ideological and political education . . . must be based on the life and experience of the peasants and be conducted in a very practical manner with careful attention to detail . . . It should be conducted not in isolation from our economic measures, but in conjunction with them. (303)

This is not condescension; rather, it is precisely the condescension of the cadre and the expert for the people which Mao consistently opposes. 'Neither bluster nor oversimplification will do' (ibid.);

> . . . the incompetent teachers . . . oversimplify the problem with such so-called slogans as 'Either you follow the road of the Communist Party or you follow the road of Chiang Kai-Shek'. This is just labelling people to cow them into compliance . . ..(254)

> . . . as long as the Party does not merely issue orders or oversimplify matters when rousing the people to join co-operatives, but instead reasons with them, helps them to analyse the situation, and relies entirely on their understanding and willingness, there certainly will not be much difficulty in establishing co-operatives everywhere *and, what is more, increasing output.* (27)

Mao follows the latter comment with the remark: 'The "pointing out of difficulties" method used in this village is worth our special attention' (28). The same objectives lie behind his (very funny) polemic against 'that Party jargon which gives us such a headache' (329), and his insistence on the principles of Party policy being 'publicly proclaimed to the masses' (237).

CONCLUSION

Trotsky once summed up a widespread Bolshevik attitude when he opined that after 'the' revolution,

> nothing remains for the peasantry to do but to rally to the regime of workers' democracy. It will not matter much even if the peasantry does this with a degree of consciousness not larger than that with which it usually rallies to the bourgeois regime. (Trotsky, 1906: 205; see *SCMT*, Ch. 3)

On Practice: Four Studies

Mao takes exactly the contrary view. For him the 'degree of consciousness' is the decisive factor, and the correctness or otherwise of methods of work depends on whether or not they help raise it. For (to get back to where we began) the people's increasingly conscious co-operation is the key to a socialist upsurge in their productive forces. And (to underline a point we have never left)

> The main indicator by which all co-operatives should measure their health is – *is production increasing, and how fast?* (28, our emphasis)

3 BOMBARDING THE HEADQUARTERS: THE GREAT PROLETARIAN CULTURAL REVOLUTION

There is no shortage of discussions of the Great Proletarian Cultural Revolution in China, nor of Mao's role therein.[1] We are heavily invested – not to say infested – with detail and with judgements. Yet there is a disappointing if familiar absence of analysis. Almost without exception these discussions embark on evaluation with premises based in preconception, rather than concrete evidence and an attempt to penetrate beyond the appearances that evidence encapsulates (to paraphrase Mao's own critique of a Soviet textbook on political economy).[2]

Thus, some interpreters, particularly 'Friends of China', have adopted stances of uncritical admiration quite alien to Mao's own practice and his insistence on the method of criticism and self-criticism as 'a method of resolving contradictions among the people', and moreover 'the only method' (1962B: 163). Mao's emphasis was equally as much on learning as on teaching, and he responded as follows to Lin Piao's attempts to construct a living icon of him:

> As for the question of genius, we both have discussed this and must still study the question of standing on the side of idealism or materialism; of whether history is made by genius or by slaves.[3]

For most critics, on the other hand – and here bourgeois and Trotskyist observers are close bedfellows – the GPCR was either a spasm of ideological fervour or a cynical power-struggle at which

76   *For Mao*

Mao proved the most adept. The latter is a good example of dealing only in surface appearances, since:

> It is not that the social struggle is a reflection of the Party Central Committee. Rather the struggle within the Party Central Committee is a reflection of social struggle. (1968A: 480).

The former view of Mao as a zealot was for a time displaced by a grudging acknowledgement of the practical benefits of the GPCR by bourgeois economists. In the process, they substituted an imputation of economism for that of voluntarism, a view equally false and indicative only of their own ideological straitjacket.

The chief aim of this essay is to offer an appreciation of Mao's part in the Cultural Revolution, and of what it adds to our comprehension of Mao himself, by an analysis of selected themes and their interconnection within a coherent and materialist theory and strategy. Class struggle, politics in command and production, democracy and centralism, and the processes and problems of identifying a correct mass-line are the strands we shall trace. It will become apparent that many themes recur here from earlier discussion, and yet that amidst this continuity and application of lessons learned in previous experience they retain a dynamic through ongoing learning and experimentation in the face of new problems. Mao is prepared to admit mistakes, and this conscious fallibility may be his greatest virtue, since it enables him to try and put them to constructive purposes. This, too, is initially a question of method:

> Proletarian Marxist philosophy, of course, must all the more closely serve present-day politics . . . Marx, Engels, Lenin and Stalin must be read. . . But Communist Party members and proletarian thinkers of every country must create new theories, publish new works, and produce their own ideologies to serve present-day politics. (1962A: 305)

> One must not be restricted. Lenin refused to be restricted by Marx . . . one must not be superstitious . . . one must have new interpretations, new viewpoints and creativity. (1966F: 380)[4]

Four months after this last quotation, in the midst of the Cultural Revolution, Mao is equally insistent on direct application of this:

On Practice: Four Studies 77

Political material, directives of the Centre, and newspaper editorials are all guidance for the masses which are not to be regarded as dogmas. (1966K)[5]

It is conventional to picture the Cultural Revolution as a clearly defined and unprecedented episode, commencing late in 1965,[6] climaxing through the years 1966 and 1967, and effectively concluding with the Ninth National Congress of the CPC in April 1969. Whilst these dates serve as useful initial guidelines, any closer examination reveals continuities before and after the designated period that blur the boundaries and give a fuller picture of the context and content of the struggles that took place. Thus the GPCR followed in the footsteps of the Great Leap Forward, and reactivated many ideas which had been partially submerged or left unelaborated, such as the Anshan charter for democratic organisation in industry or the slogan 'grasp revolution and promote production'. It was the culmination of struggle between two lines that had been visible and intensifying throughout the Socialist Education Movement (SEM). In that year Mao launched his scathing attack on cadres who overvalued themselves, feared criticism and distanced themselves from the people (1962B), though the basis of this and of the GPCR strategy itself was in principle to be found in writings from the Yenan years onwards. Mao later put the GPCR in context as the tenth major struggle within the CPC since its inception (1971A).

The experience of the successes of the Great Leap Forward (GLF) and SEM were important, but so too were the failures, and the major sources of these. Both had been misapplied in many places. The GLF was often treated as an instruction to be enforced from above rather than a call to mass participation and innovation, whilst the SEM in many cases saw the call for a politicised 'clean-up' movement involving broad-based criticism and self-criticism channelled into a petty persecution of local cadres' errors, driving them in turn further into commandism as self-protection. This is the backdrop to Mao's observation, in one of the opening shots of the GPCR, that to carry out directives blindly and to the letter was in fact to sabotage them.[7] Mao, as we shall discover, believed that Party organisation was essential to protect the revolution, yet he did not reify this into an assumption that the Party produces the correct line automatically, for the Party is also pervaded by the struggle between two classes, roads and lines. The root of the problem for

78 *For Mao*

Mao, as he had seen in the 1930s, was the growing bureaucratism and even elitism in the Party itself, such that it was no longer responsive to the people and thereby was also unable to reform itself to become so.

Mao had often defied or passively resisted official party policy even in the years before the long March and had spent at least as much time effectively in opposition as in command.[8] The *High Tide* revealed Mao's preparedness, well after 1949, to 'bombard the headquarters', to call for enlarged plenums and generally to encourage the widest possible criticism of the Party CC. Nonetheless, as a project mounted within an apparently victorious revolutionary organisation which in Bolshevik (CPSU and much of CPC) orthodoxy could be regarded as secure, and in which his personal position could be as comfortable as he wished, the GPCR was a quite remarkable conception. Mao's role should not be deified: 'The Cultural Revolution can only be the emancipation of the masses by the masses' (6 November 1967).[9] But it remains gargantuan.

The justification of the need for a tidal wave of mass criticism emerges from Mao's analysis of classes and class struggle within socialism. His rejection of the ideas of peaceful transition and of socialism as a 'state of the whole people' was made fully extant in the polemic with Khrushchev and the CPSU after 1963.[10] This clearly lent impetus and confidence to his application of the arguments advanced in the polemic to the internal situation in China. He continued with growing force to elaborate his view that class struggle remained the key factor in the transition to socialism. Thus in 1964 he argued:

> At present the task of the revolution has not been completed, it has not yet been finally determined who, in the end, will overthrow whom. (1964Q: 243)[11]

Mao was optimistic that counter-revolutionaries could win no final victory in China, but never deterministically so even after the GPCR victory. Hence his repeated stress in these years on the need to treat class struggle as a central component of education, and not just the bookish theory of it either.[12]

The nature of Mao's understanding of class struggle in this period explains much about the conduct of the GPCR. Many Western observers have referred in confusion or scorn to the absence of any

On Practice: Four Studies 79

visible alternative class to struggle against, and have suggested that all that is happening is a scapegoating of some Party cadres who are labelled as bourgeois for propaganda purposes. Friends of China have all-too-often offered a defence that also treats the issue as belligerence against identifiable individuals (whether landlords or 'those in authority taking the capitalist road') and no more. It would be apologism to deny that within China the enemy has often been over-personalised and externalised as agents of the bourgeoisie (as in the Lin Piao affair),[13] thus diverting attention from the struggle between two roads and two lines.

Despite this, the predominant stance of Mao himself on these matters throughout the SEM and GPCR was against false exorcism through persecution of individuals, in conscious contrast to Stalin's policies[14] or those of the right in the CPC. He repeatedly emphasised the essentially positive nature of most errants[15] and thus encouraged the method of constructive criticism. On errors both in policy and in methods of work Mao is to be found frequently reiterating the theme that 'It is difficult to avoid mistakes, the point is to correct them honestly'.[16]

These two policy aspects – on the one hand that those who lend support to what are actually capitalist policies may still be socialist and so deserve tolerance, on the other the uncompromising view of class conflict – may seem at odds. In fact they are quite consistent within Mao's perception of the nature of people, and of the purpose of cultural revolution. The emphasis on struggle, criticism and self-criticism as the means to transformation of outlook arises from a belief that in socialism class exists not as some convenient social mapping of categories of people, but in and through the struggle between capitalist and socialist relations and lines. This anticipates the rediscovery, in recent years, of Marx's analysis of ideology as an aspect of the structure of reality itself.[17] Thus Mao argued in the GPCR for a recognition of the 'dual nature' of people. To externalise failings altogether onto others is to evade the struggle against bourgeois tendencies in oneself:

> To use the excuse of distinguishing between 'inner' and 'outer' is to fear revolution . . . There are some comrades who struggle fiercely against others, but cannot struggle against themselves. In this way, they will never be able to cross the pass. (1966J: 254)

Marx's *Capital* started with the analysis of the dual nature of

80 *For Mao*

commodities. Our commodities also have a dual nature . . . our comrades likewise have a dual nature, correct and incorrect. Don't you have a dual nature? I know I have. (1965H: 239)[18]

Policies must also be adopted which are two-edged in this perspective. This is the basis of Mao's reference to commodities. There is no means of magically altering reality and so evading this. There is a need for continual struggle against the counter-socialist elements that are constantly regenerated, within the Party, in agriculture, industry, education and all aspects of society (Mao also laid great stress on the arts, for instance). This struggle, of which the GPCR was to be only a more energetic phase, required the destruction of surviving capitalist and creation of socialist relations of production. Only thus could the people simultaneously transform themselves and their material circumstances. The continuing centrality of production to Mao's politics is thus evident throughout, and we shall return to this point shortly.

First, however, a further misapprehension needs to be corrected. There are some *aficionados* of the Cultural Revolution who see it as an exercise in participative democracy in the liberal sense of that term. Mass involvement and debate in preference to commandism and coercion were indeed elements of the GPCR, but Mao is not thereby departing from the principles of 'Combat liberalism' (1937L). As with the 'blooming and contending' of Hundred Flowers-type campaigns, engagement of the largest possible number of people is itself a reinforcement of the dictatorship of the proletariat. It is true that Mao had deemed purges to be destructive and counter-productive rather than militant (being, once again, an externalisation of blame), but this rejection from a socialist viewpoint is utterly alien from any move to embrace some sinified 'Eurocommunism'.[19]

The 11th Plenum of the CC/CPC in August 1966 thus reiterated in its resolutions a theme long propounded by Mao:

A strict distinction must be made between the two different types of contradictions: those among the people and those between ourselves and the enemy (1966P).

Disagreements among the people are normal, unavoidable and, moreover, if correctly expressed and used, are 'necessary and beneficial'. But in 1965 Mao had argued that freedom of speech was

On Practice: Four Studies 81

'the exclusive right of the people', and justified this by observing that capitalist dictatorship reversed the process and suppressed criticism by the people of the minority in power. He thus rejected the relevance of the bourgeois notion of 'democracy', and in consequence he is also to be found in the early months of the GPCR rejecting the principle of 'natural rights of man' proposed by bourgeois philosophers:

> Is there such a thing as rights bestowed by nature? Isn't it man who bestows rights on man? Were the rights we enjoy bestowed by nature? Our rights were bestowed by the people, and primarily by the working class and lower-middle peasants. (1965H: 235)

For Mao the GPCR remains 'a revolution under the dictatorship of the proletariat' (1967E).[20] If freedom of criticism amongst the people themselves is held down, under whatever slogan, the result is the opposite of socialist politics.

> Even under a proletarian dictatorship, the masses should be allowed to petition, demonstrate and litigate . . . Judging from this act [limiting places where *tatzebao* could be published] of suppressing the Great Cultural Revolution of the students, I don't believe there is genuine democracy and genuine Marxism. It is a case of standing on the side of the bourgeoisie to oppose the Great Proletarian Cultural Revolution. (1966N)

The GPCR is, then, an exercise in asserting the rights of the masses against any attempt to prevent those rights being used. Even if such attempts have their origins in the highest Party circles, for Mao they can only be a representation of the attack of one class on another. The analysis of class struggle is thus reinforced, and the duality of dictatorship and democracy seen as a necessary unity in socialist society. If the proletariat do not enforce control, and impose their political economy, then it is certain the bourgeoisie will:

> . . . either the East wind prevails over the West wind or the West wind prevails over the East wind, and there is absolutely no such thing as equality. (1966I: 108)[21]

82 *For Mao*

In the early months of the GPCR the Left had indeed been partly thwarted in their efforts by the 'Group of Five' led by Peng Chen who headed the Party's Cultural Revolution committee. In April 1966 Mao intervened to endorse attacks on this group's attempts to confine the scope of criticism sufficiently to 'philosophical' or other 'theoretical' issues as to prevent an explosion of mass criticism of concrete policies.[22] The 16 May circular, from which the last quotation above is taken, confirmed this and elaborated the reasons for it, relaunching the Cultural Revolution on a more Left basis. This was further marked in June by the change of adjective in the name of the movement itself from 'Socialist' to 'Proletarian'.

The 16 May circular emphasised that construction arises precisely out of the struggle to destroy bourgeois ideology and its manifestations, and insists that 'all class struggles are political struggles'. Since class struggle is seen as taking place in all social spheres, politics is all-pervasive.

Mao's greatest concern remained that of promoting learning. At the same time, however, he incessantly stresses the need to avoid the danger that education becomes merely academic. Throughout the GPCR he is to be found scorning bookwork – even reading 'too much' Marx.[23] This is directed against the tendencies towards elitism of the 'educated' and so to regeneration of the division of labour. Mao does not decry study, but rather returns with fresh vigour to the old theme of the need to go out and experience reality directly, since books can convey only parts of it and in a stereotyped form. As Mao had indicated in a new Preface (1961B) to 'Oppose book worship' (1930B), he regarded book worship and dogmatism as synonymous. It is in opposition to dogmatism above all that Mao directs his attacks. From this came the decision to encourage and eventually require all students to 'go down' to the countryside for a period, to learn far more than to teach:

> To get some experience of class struggle – that's what I call a university. They argue about which university is better, Peking University or People's University. For my part I am a graduate of the university of the greenwoods, I learned a bit there. (1964T: 213).

Those who view education as the acquisition of productive skill, and whose conception of production is conventionally blinkered, could only be appalled by the assertion that 'For our youth, the major

On Practice: Four Studies

subject of study is class struggle' (2 August 1966, Ch'en, 1970: 116).[24]

For a time, in mid-1966, Liu Shao-chi (as during the SEM) ordered work-teams into the universities and other centres of unrest. The ability of such teams to successfully isolate the Left as 'unruly' elements in many cases is disturbing. The tide of criticism was strong, but use of residual authority and trivialisation of Left slogans could still hold it back a while. Whether the dam would have burst from the pressure from below is not known, since Mao himself took a dramatic step: On 16 July he went for a now legendary swim in the Yangtze, symbolically announcing his personal immersion in the GPCR also.[25]

At a work conference on 21 July, Mao then criticised those who continued to suppress rather than mobilise the student movement. The great majority of rebels were good, not bad:

> What are you afraid of? when bad people are involved you prove that they are bad. What do you fear about good people? You should replace the word 'fear' by the word 'dare' . . . You must put politics in command, go among the masses and be at one with them. (1966J: 255)

Then, on 5 August, Mao made his attack on the conservatives fully public by publishing a wall-poster of his own, *Bombard the Headquarters*, in a similar vein.[26] The emphasis was on the right of the masses to rebel against revisionism, which could develop – and had done so – at the very core of the Party itself.

Those who polarise this supposedly 'ideological' (in the pejorative sense) campaign to put 'politics in command' and a concern for order, stability and production are again exposed for the ideologists they themselves are by a closer examination of Mao's words and policies during the GPCR. Not only does politics in command emerge as itself a *productive* strategy, but the criticisms of both ultra-Left (see below) and of conservatives are voiced as a reproach of their treatment of production. Our last essay showed this clearly, and there is no relapse in the Cultural Revolution.

The period preceding the GPCR had witnessed a widespread acceptance among policy makers of Yang Hsien-chen's arguments for a long period of balanced, steady construction of a 'synthesized economic base'.[27] This was implicitly contrasted to the supposed idealism of 'Maoist' views which allegedly called for a revolutionis-

84 *For Mao*

ing of ideas as a condition for changing the material world. Yang's views were, significantly, a development from his philosophical confrontation with Mao in which he argued for an inherent tendency to unity ('two combine into one') rather than contradiction ('one divides into two'). The latter was an expression of Mao's belief in struggle as the motive force of society, and Yang's opposition to it must be evaluated in this light. Yang's ideas on 'economics' were later to yield something closer to fully-fledged Libermanism (profits and economistic material incentives in command) in the work of Sun Yeh-fang, denounced during the GPCR.

Mao had always opposed this narrow, mechanical version of materialism, equally as he opposed the idealist notion that one could somehow magically call on a change of consciousness among the people that would then sweep all obstacles before it. He saw the revolutionising of ideas as inseparable from the transformation of the material world of which they were an integral part.[28] Similarly, it was metaphysics to think that new machinery could somehow alter people by itself. Mao argued his case not only from direct experience of the Socialist Upsurge and Great Leap (and further back to Yenan) but also by reference to Soviet history. He refuted Bolshevik orthodoxy by pointing out that collectivisation was a political act there also, preceding and making possible subsequent mechanisation.[29]

Idealism in Mao's eyes entailed not recognising that there were limits to the rate of transformation, regardless of enthusiasm, to go beyond which was to court disillusion. This was to an extent a lesson of the Great Leap:

Judging from the present, socialist construction cannot be too fast; we have to stress wavelike advances. (1961A: 244)[30]

Mao's definition of freedom encapsulates well the profoundly materialist perspective in which he formulated his policies (to recall a text quoted p. 13 above, here in its temporal context):

Freedom is the understanding of necessity *and* the transformation of necessity – one has some work to do too. (1964T: 228)

The conservative 'theory of productive forces' subverted marxism

On Practice: Four Studies 85

by its distortion of the 'material' in 'materialism', leaving out the people themselves as a material force.[31] This lack of belief in the people led to them being seen as unreliable, and so disorder being viewed as antithetical to production. It was cadres of this persuasion that Mao had taunted in 1962:

> There are some comrades who cannot bear to listen to ideas contrary to their own, and cannot bear to be criticised . . . You think that nobody will really dare to touch the arse of tigers like you? They damn well will! (1962B: 166–7)[32]

In 1966 Mao encouraged the reverse side of this, that production was in fact enhanced by the promotion of revolution and criticism.[33] In January 1967 he expressed the theme succinctly:

> We must speak of grasping revolution and promoting production. We must not make revolution in isolation from production. *The conservative faction do not grasp production*. This is a class struggle. (1967B: 276, our emphasis)

This is a two-edged argument. On the one hand revolutionary activity enhances production – 'Revolution is the emancipation of productive force'.[34] On the other, production advances most effectively not through stable, orderly, obedient labour and importation of technology, but through the commitment and motivation of the producers:

> Should we attach more importance to men, to things or to both? Some comrades think only things, not men, are important. In fact, if we do our work on men well, we shall have things as well. (1964I)

The GPCR was aimed, in the most determined and extensive fashion yet, at resolving the gamut of political problems and so unfettering productive potential.

Mao had distinguished three areas of struggle: production, scientific experiment, and class struggle.[35] These became known as the three directives, but it is important to note that the last of the three was regarded as the key to the others. It was on this issue amongst others that Teng Hsiao-ping was denounced after his

86 *For Mao*

second fall in 1976, for having ranked the three as equally important.[36] But this is not to rob the other two of importance in their own right, the essential point being the interdependence of all three:

> Class struggle, the struggle for production and scientific experimentation must be linked up. Only carrying out the struggle for production and scientific experimentation but not grasping class struggle cannot kindle the spirit and enthusiasm of the people, nor can the struggle for production or scientific experimentation be done well . . . To only carry out class struggle . . . and to say 'support the General Line' are meaningless. (1964G: 342)

As the Cultural Revolution proceeded, so Mao perceived more clearly some of the problems in the forms of struggle adopted. The encouragement of the Red Guards had involved the young, and especially the students, but the debate took more time to have its impact in industry and in the countryside. Once it did encompass the labouring people the productive and political ramifications were far more deeply felt,[37] and the movement took on its full significance. We have discussed these productive benefits ourselves in *SCMT*.

The trade unions and many local Party committees were disbanded because of their economism, commandism and bureaucratism and replaced on an expanding scale by 'three-in-one' revolutionary committees.[38] These were to be organs of an unprecedented extension of mass democracy. But first there had to be consolidation of success, and inevitably perhaps the GPCR had generated many sorts of excess. The tasks that faced Mao were to maintain the impetus and direction of revolution, forestalling any suppression of criticism, whilst ensuring that the 95 per cent or more of essentially good cadres were not swept out in the flood. It was also, as we have seen, necessary to prevent the tide of revolution becoming 'anarchistic' in the productive sphere and so losing sight of production itself, and this must have limited the relative speed with which workers and peasants involved themselves all-out in the struggle.

In 1966 Mao's emphasis is, for the most part, found to fall on the fruitful yield of disruption that was really far less chaotic than it seemed to the doubting. Thus the fourth of the 16 Articles announces:

On Practice: Four Studies 87

Don't be afraid of disorder ... Chairman Mao has told us revolution cannot be so very refined, so temperate, kind, courteous, restrained and magnanimous. (1966P: 120)[39]

At the Central Work Conference of October 1966 Mao continued to defend the need for the GPCR, arguing that disorder was unavoidable in the early stages of a venture which represented a new stage in revolutionary activity, the means of handling which were still being learnt. 'Since it was I who caused the havoc, it is understandable if you have some bitter words for me' (1966T: 271). Yet he was adamant that only if cadres encouraged change rather than sought to defend the *status quo* would matters improve (p. 273) and he went on to make the attack on conservatives for not understanding production quoted above. Mao also admitted to having lost his confidence somewhat in the first upsurge of the GPCR (p. 271) and celebrated its restoration. The remainder of 1966 saw the emergence of the GPCR in industry also, culminating in the 'January storm' and the declaration of the Shanghai people's commune at the start of 1967.

On 23 January Mao called on the People's Liberation Army to intervene on the side of the Left. This, however, helped to arouse in some areas a 'February Adverse Current' in which many of the Left were again depicted as ultra-Left. This resurgence of counter-revolutionary forces probably led Mao to rein back on his criticism of Leftist excesses and accompanying call for a return to unity for a time.

Nevertheless, Mao was increasingly concerned with a danger of which he had always been aware (as witness his germane criticisms of 'ultra-democracy' and related deviations in 1929B), and yet whose strength and extent seems to have caught him a little by surprise. Few attempts have been offered to seriously analyse this phenomenon of the ultra-Left.[40] Pro-China writers are inclined to dismiss them as if the description coined by Mao 'left in appearance, right in essence' were sufficient; bourgeois ideologists have consistently preferred a pragmatist/fanatic dichotomy in which all of the Left are irrational. Yet the emergence of ultra-Leftism provides the only context in which Mao's policies can be properly comprehended and evaluated, as the delineation of major tasks above or the discussion of democracy and centralism below exemplifies. It makes precarious the construction of a correct line, for this must wrestle to maintain a balance between confidence in the people and en-

88 *For Mao*

couragement of criticism, and over-zealous, unrealistic demands for change. This, above all, explains the reason for policy shifts, uncertainty and errors within Mao's overall strategy. Some of the strains this imposed on him show through clearly in the dialogues reproduced in the Red Guards' collection (see 1968A). A judgement had to be made on when temporary production stoppages in the cause of long-term advances became 'squabbles' which could solve no political problems; or when vital criticism deteriorated too widely into mere accusation, or was sweepingly used in ways that seemed Left-inspired yet left an anarchic vacuum fertile only for revisionist takeover (probably to the temporary relief of the majority). Events at any one time were a tangle of positive and negative activities, almost all proclaimed as being in the name of revolution. The task was to decide when the positive no longer predominated, knowing that to quell unrest was sure to have undesired repercussions for many who continued to make justified criticisms.

With whatever misgivings, from the second half of 1967 Mao leaned more towards the restoration of unity:

> The two factions should talk less of each other's weaknesses and mistakes. Let the others talk about their own weaknesses and mistakes. Each side ought to do more self-criticism – seeking general agreement and leaving minor differences intact. (*People's Daily*, 22 December 1967)[41]

Reform was to be concentrated within the organised operation of factories and rural communes. The emphasis on the need for a vigorous and permanent extension of mass participation, for Redness and a key element of expertise considered as a *practical* resource, and on the continual need to check the tendency to bureaucracy continued. The first plenum of the 9th CC/CPC in 1969 thus dwells on the question of unity, but at the same time stresses the need to continue the struggle in many places where the GPCR still required to be carried out (see 1969C).

It was the forms taken by criticism, and the directing of some of the onslaught on characters such as Chou En-lai in whom Mao retained implicit trust, which had finally convinced him of the need to move towards containment. Unjustified persecution was later referred to by Mao as one of the most undesirable features of the Cultural Revolution, in his interview with Edgar Snow in 1970.

On Practice: Four Studies

Such phenomena were a by-product of a belief that all unwanted elements of society could be abolished at one leap. In practice, this attitude produces disdain for and excoriation of anyone who harboured doubts (the great majority) and even those who had 'poor class backgrounds'.[42]

Again for Mao the key distinction is that between idealism or subjectivism and what could actually be achieved – and what, therefore, such ideals would actually lead to in terms of re-volutionary practice. The resultant limits placed on action can with little effort be portrayed as a lack of genuine desire for thoroughgo-ing revolution by armchair activists.[43] For the materialist, however, the principles are inescapable. One must not pay obeisance to appearances of limits to change (and this conservatives excel in) but one must not be blind to the existence of limits either.

This may clarify the concept of ultra-Left a little, but it does not solve the problem of judgement of what is ultra-Leftism. Brugger suggests (1977: 310) that ultra-Leftism is going beyond what the people will accept at any given time, and it therefore varies with the consciousness of the people. But if one allows that all Leftists seek to change experience, then the question becomes instead a matter of how great a change can be realistically expected. Indeed, just as it is necessary to view the Right – Left struggle as taking place within each individual, so externalisation of ultra-Leftist tendencies must also be avoided. Meanwhile, as we have seen in the GPCR and since, it is all too easy to use the broad brush of 'ultra-Left' as an excuse to paint out many genuinely Left elements, and so resort effectively to a conservative policy of order and stability.

Mao's opposition to ultra-Leftism, together with his concern for policy proven in practice and not just attractive in theory, led to his decision to oppose the moves in Shanghai and elsewhere to reconstruct government on the model of the Paris Commune.[44] He advocated instead the institutionalisation of criticism, elections and mass democracy through the compromise formula of the re-volutionary committee, but allied to the rebuilding also of the Party and of centralism.

In assessing the Cultural Revolution, and the application and tempering of Mao's theories within it, no issue is more appropriate for consideration than that of democracy. The model adopted asserted firstly the rights of the working class over the bourgeoisie, and rejected the liberal/democratic model on those grounds, as we

90 *For Mao*

have seen. For the masses themselves, however, there was already a well-rooted tradition of participation arising out of the Yenan years (in both the extensive co-operative movement and the mutual aid teams) and from the extent of work-group autonomy in many Chinese factories even before 1949.[45] So too the requirement that cadres should participate in labour had become established, and throughout the years leading up to and during the GPCR Mao continued to attach great importance to it:

> If cadres do not participate in labour they inevitably must become divorced from the labouring masses and revisionism must inevitably arise. (1963G: 322)

> Management is a form of socialist education. If managerial staff do not go to the lathe shop to work on the 'three sames' [food, accommodation, work as ordinary workers] and to look for teachers from whom they can learn one or two crafts, then they will live in a state of class conflict with the workers (29 January 1965)[46]

It is, moreover, apparent that the degree to which cadres seriously implement this stipulation in any period serves as a reliable index of the strength of the socialist line in that period over the years from 1949.

The policies of the CPC had implanted greater commitment to autonomy and democracy than that implied by the narrower interpretations of 'workers' control'. The resultant communal democracy had however still to be reconciled, Mao recognised, with co-ordination, organisation and so central control of some sort. On the face of it the two were opposed, and in most socialist theory they are treated as such. Mao realised well the potential conflicts, as his earlier speeches had shown, but he sought nonetheless to creatively combine them. His speech 'On democratic centralism', to which several references have already been made, was devoted above all to this question:

> Without democracy there cannot be any correct centralism because people's ideas differ, and if their understanding of things lacks unity then centralism cannot be established. What is centralism? First of all it is a centralization of correct ideas . . .

On Practice: Four Studies

Without democracy, you have no understanding of what is happening down below . . .. (1962B: 163–4)

The purpose of centralisation is thus associated above all with the role of the Party and the socialist state, expressed in a theory of learning: assimilate from the masses and construct from their achievements a correct general line for their use. 'The only way is to rely on the masses and then centralize' (1966J, version in Ch'en, 1970: 31), in Mao's own words. The aim is not under any circumstances to build a vast state apparatus to be borne on the back of the people – and Mao on several occasions had called for a drastic reduction in the size of the State and so of this form of centralisation.[47] The GPCR took some steps towards this, though not definitive ones by any means. The unified planning system[48] was, for instance, developed and successfully implemented.

The ultimate source of truth was thus, in Mao's view, the masses themselves:

If we really arouse the masses, they can determine who are the good and bad elements. (1961A: 241)

The *Selected Works of Mao*, how much of it is mine? . . . [the major lessons in *SW*] were taught to us by the masses and paid for with blood sacrifices. (1964G: 340)

He further felt that production was not to be achieved by some magical appropriate instruction from above, but through the knowledge and incentive of those who produce. The important thing was that people should know what is socially necessary; they will attain it if the political line is correct and so attracts their full support. 'To have all things united under the central government and strictly controlled is not a good method' (1966C). It is a poor method because it not only neglects local initiative but also it entails a bureaucratic line designed to generate apathy and disaffection in the process.

However, this clearly is not a manifesto for the abolition of the centre. This latter was an error of the anarchistic views which arose in some quarters during the GPCR:

The danger of ultra-democracy lies in the fact that it damages or even completely wrecks the Party organisation and weakens or

92   *For Mao*

even completely undermines the Party's fighting capacity . . .
thereby causing the defeat of the revolution. (Quoted from *Red
Flag*, no. 4, 1967, in Han Suyin 1976: 295)

Mao's own *tatzebao* had invoked a willingness and right to rebel
against the centre if justified, and the restitution of the Party's role
from 1967 did not herald an abrogation of this democratic
imperative. The Anshan constitution, replacing one-man management with greater worker control, had first been endorsed by Mao
in 1960, but only by continuing pressure from 1967 onwards did it
gain country-wide ratification. The source of power was still
proclaimed as the people themselves.[49]

At the same time Mao was aware, unlike those who continually
assay the concoction of some definitive formula for democracy, that
no institution provides the answer in itself. Any formal structure or
terminology can decay into bureaucracy and elitism beneath its
surface formula. It is the substance of relations that counts. Mao also
believed, however, in the continuing role of leadership, the essential
issue being whether this leadership left initiative to the masses,
carried out learning and teaching correctly and continued to
participate in manual labour.

The slogan of 'Doubt everything and overthrow everything' is
reactionary. The Shanghai People's Committee demanded that
the Premier of the State Council should do away with all heads.
This is extreme anarchism, it is most reactionary. If instead of
calling someone the 'head' of something we call him 'orderly' or
'assistant', this would really be only a formal change. In reality
there will still always be heads. It is the content which matters.
(1967D: 277)[50]

This does not seek to negate the right to rebel, but to pinpoint the
extent and limits of what it can achieve. Mao knew not only of past
struggles, but also that others would follow. Han Suyin quotes a
letter to Chiang Ching, written in July 1966, which voices a theme
he often repeated in the years before his death: 'In seven or eight
years one will have to launch another movement to clean
up . . . And this will have to be repeated many times' (Han Suyin,
1976: 268).

In May 1967 a *People's Daily* editorial quoted Mao's statement
that the possibility of capitalist restoration always remained, and

On Practice: Four Studies 93

that further cultural revolutions would be required.[51] Mao seems from some asides to have been optimistic that the strength of the people would decide matters in favour of socialism eventually, but only after many generations of struggle. Continuing campaigns, most prominently that against Lin Piao and Confucius, were launched before 1976.

The Great Proletarian Cultural Revolution still has much to teach us. Lenin said of revolutionary leaders:

> After their death, attempts are made to convert them into harmless icons, to canonize them, so to say, and to surround their *names* with a certain halo for the 'consolation' of the oppressed classes and with the object of duping the latter, while at the same time emasculating the *essence* of the revolutionary teaching, blunting its revolutionary edge and vulgarizing it. (Lenin 1917B: 390)

This, and the other essays in this book, seek to oppose any such vulgarisation of Mao in the soft glow of a sarcophagus. A detailed appreciation of his contribution to the GPCR offers a guide to the conflicts and contradictions involved therein, and to Mao's methods in seeking to find means to resolve them.

4 GRAMSCI AND MAO

A comparison between the treatment of Gramsci and Mao as marxists emphasises the validity of our remarks in the 'Introduction'. It is after all Gramsci that has 'produced' so much literature, his own[1] and that of epigones, devotees, enemies and commentators[2], in English in the last ten or so years. It is Gramsci who is hailed, not least by those who otherwise renounce marxism *tout court*, thus:

> If, in the history of Marxism, the period from the Erfurt program to 1914 can be characterized as the age of the Second International, from 1916 to the middle 1920s that of Leninism, from 1924 to early 1950s that of Stalinism, and from the late 1950s to early 1970s that of Maoism, the 1980s are likely to usher in what may be called a new phase of 'Gramscism'. This is a result of an international situation wherein both Russian and Chinese communism have exhausted themselves [sic] and have found accomo-

94 *For Mao*

dation [sic] within a world order still under a U.S. hegemony [n.b.], based on new and not yet fully developed imperialist relations stronger than earlier versions and immune to traditional challenges. (Piccone, 1976: 485; cf. ibid., 487, 506)[3]

Guiseppe Fiori and *The Times* can agree to hail Gramsci as 'This century's most original Marxist thinker' (Fiori, 1975: IV). In Anderson's 'Papal' declaration:

Today, no Marxist thinker after the classical epoch is so universally [n.b.] respected in the West as Antonio Gramsci. (Anderson, 1977: 5)

Keeping to this framework, Hobsbawm agrees:

Gramsci has become part of our intellectual universe. His stature as an original marxist thinker – in my view the most original such thinker produced in the west since 1917 – is pretty generally admitted. (Hobsbawm, 1977: 206)

The contrast to be drawn is not only with the treatment of Mao alone, but to the lack of comparative treatment between them. There are a few texts that begin such an analysis: George Thomson's comments on the first English versions of Gramsci texts (1957; cf. 1971, 1973); remarks implicit within the work of Althusser or Bettelheim; or more developed essays (e.g. Todd, 1974). But the fullest recognition comes from the author of a work, *Pour Gramsci*, close to our own in spirit, who recognised how

Gramsci should be reread in the light of the Cultural Revolution. The manner in which he poses the theoretical problem of class hegemony provides a key to the interpretation of the thought of Mao Tse-tung during the Cultural Revolution, especially with regard to the transformation of class hegemony into proletarian democracy and the limitation of the repressive aspect of the state. (Macciocchi, 1971: 471)[4]

The comparison suggested here also illuminates particular, and extremely widespread, systematic (i.e. not accidental) misreadings of *both* the texts of Antonio Gramsci *and* the actions of the Great Proletarian Cultural Revolution. As the latter has been used to

On Practice: Four Studies

justify the most extraordinary *blind faith* and *copying from abroad*, so the former has been used to fuel the extensive 'intellectualisation' of marxism, its conversion into a species of that speculative metaphysics which Marx, Engels, Lenin, Stalin and Mao identified as the 'life-philosophy' (the operating code) of anti-socialist experts. Within Italy, Timpanaro noted this in 1966 when he wrote (in contrast to all the 'marxists' rushing to prove how profoundly dialectical they were!)

> the struggle within bourgeois culture is – to put it very schematically – between two idealisms: a historicist and humanist idealism and an empiro-criticist and pragmatic idealism . . . The victory of the second is the victory of modern technocracy over the antiquated humanism characteristic of backward bourgeois classes. (1966: 5)[5]

Gwyn Williams, in a criticism of his own adherence to this reading of Gramsci in his 1960 article, has noted how

> Great tracts of Gramsci's writing, particularly from the Prison Notebooks, assumed a crucial instrumental significance for a wide range of thinkers, Marxist and non-Marxist. Gramsci registered as an altogether congenial fellow who could be put to all manner of good works, particularly by people with an almost physiological *hunger* for a 'liberal' or 'democratic' or indeed, simply *intelligent* communism. (1974c: 12; cf. Davidson, 1977)

Antonio Gramsci (1891–1937), it should be recalled with some force, was only given a brief time of political activity, and some of that marred by ill-health. He was imprisoned from 1926 until his death. The Communist Party of Italy was founded in January 1921 (the CPC itself was founded in July of the same year) and for one and a half years of the period between that momentous event and his imprisonment, Gramsci was in Moscow (some of the time benefiting from the Soviet health services), and for a further six months in Vienna. Gramsci warned, in his own notebooks written in prison, against a possible misreading of his own work. In a section 'Questions of method' he establishes the proper way of studying conceptions which have 'never been systematically expounded by its founder', and warns

96 *For Mao*

These observations are all the more valid the more the thinker in question is endowed with a violent impetus, had a polemical character and is lacking in *esprit de système* . . . (1948: 383)

A work can never be identified with the raw material collected for its compilation. (Ibid., 385)

In his letters (which, in the above text, Gramsci warned had to be read 'with certain precautions', ibid.) he several times indicates his worry about his words being taken too 'literally' (e.g. 1947, II 28 March 1932) or that his style is being made too pedantic by 'prisonitis' (e.g. 1947, II 5 January 1937).

A number of writers have linked Gramsci and Lukács. We could have chosen Lukács to compare with Mao since the former (even more than Gramsci) has had precisely that critical attention so markedly absent from the study of Mao. But Gramsci shares certain of what Lenin might call 'historical peculiarities' which make the comparison with Mao fruitful. There is, to begin with, their shared biographical experiences – the one from Sardinia, the other from Hunan – neither losing their particular ways of speaking and styles of writing from that early formation. Both suffered for their poor backgrounds at school. Gramsci recalled

What was it that stopped me from turning into a stuffed shirt? It was an instinct of rebellion, awakened by the fact that I, who got ten out of ten in everything, could not go on studying, while the butcher's boy, the chemist's boy, the draper's boy, all the rich men's sons were able to. (quoted in Fiori, 1965: 25, n. 3; slightly different translation, quoted in Fiori, 1975: IV)

A similar spirit informs Mao's account to Edgar Snow of his own schooling (Snow 1937: 125f; 1961: 129f; cf. Han Suyin, 1972: Ch. 2). Biographies of both also report their voracious reading – not simply the amount, but its breadth; they demonstrate that autodidacts (despite the patronage of so many scholars) can often make more of their education, can use it – above all – to open questions and extend (or, better, transform) boundaries.

There is their shared demand that historical materialism be understood as a practice, that marxism is a guide to action and not a dogma, that we should learn it through applying it to the resolution of problems, for the transformation of circumstances. They both

On Practice: Four Studies 97

stress the specificity of particular social formations, and of conjunctures within them, resisting (although differently) the dogmatic Bolshevisation of socialist construction. They both, like Marx and Lenin, emphasise the significance of the cultural relations of production and the need for a sustained cultural revolution as constitutive of socialist construction against the dull compulsion of habit and the steady coercion of the obvious. For this reason they both study intellectuals.[6] They both see (again differently) the political importance of agrarian production – above all peasant collectivities – within their different social formations. They both, finally, offer novel explanations of political and military strategy and tactics. John Merrington's conclusion captures their shared project:

> The underlying thematic of Gramsci's Marxism . . . finds its unity and coherence in his creative confrontation of the social and historical realities of his world. His renewal of Marxism was never the detached work of a 'scientist' but rather the product of a lifetime of political struggle . . . The result was a Marxism adapted to the actual problems and needs of the Italian struggle. (1968: 169)

Another prisoner noted at the same time

> the immense merit of Gramsci is that he took as the central node and strategic junction of his analyses the unity, the welding together of theory and praxis . . . Gramsci is the man who asks himself how theory can make the *transition* into history. (Debray, 1969: 49)

Since our whole book concerns Mao, and since we do not have the space to establish a similar situation and examination of Gramsci, we propose to examine briefly some areas within which both Gramsci and Mao have made major contributions to historical materialism. We shall mainly present the views of Gramsci, enabling readers to make comparison with the words and views of Mao presented elsewhere in this book.

Like *any* creative thinker, Gramsci (as Mao) has a complicated relationship with the constituent parts of the theoretical materials beyond which his own thought has moved. We allude here to the

98   *For Mao*

debate as to whether or not Gramsci was a (good) leninist.[7] There remains the problem – one of the themes counterpointed in our own work *(SCMT)* – of what the adjective 'leninist' means in the complicated histories of both marxism and, equally, of Bolshevism as a social problematic. Illustrative of all these problems are the well-documented 'misunderstandings', whether by Gramsci of what Lenin's views were (Davidson, 1974: 128f); or, almost a mirror-image, Lenin's grasp of the 'correctness' of the *L'Ordine Nuovo* group's views (ibid., 135; cf. Fiori, 1965: Ch. 14). Indeed, within this unitary misunderstanding – the one reading somewhat dogmatic views on the Party as if they celebrated the creative strength of the self-organisation of the masses, the other reading somewhat syndicalist views as if they celebrated the flexible organisational forms necessary for a successful Party – we find precisely what Davidson argues.

> Reading Lenin from the point of view of contemporary revolutionary thought, that is, from the point of view of Gramsci, shows that the significant development in his thought is a movement away from the positivist, fatalist views of the Second International towards a philosophy of praxis: towards the point, where, if we may be permitted the image, he hands the baton on to Gramsci. (Davidson, 1974: 142; cf. 145–6)

We must, of course, interject: Lenin handed that baton (which is also a burden) on to many people. It would be ludicrous (and fundamentally a retreat into monasticism) to see Gramsci as the sole *bearer* of that task. But the point is well made, especially when Davidson suggests that both Lenin and Gramsci (and, as we have examined in our first Part, Mao also) focus upon *organisation. How* the party is to be built. *How* socialist construction is accomplished. *How* education is to be engendered. These are fundamental to the canon of Gramsci and of Mao. For that reason, Gramsci's bold declaration of 24 December 1917 'The Revolution against "Capital"'(*L'Avanti*; 1977a: 34f), is *fundamentally* correct. The Great October Socialist Revolution was 'the revolution against Karl Marx's *Capital*' (ibid., 34) for that had been taken (and is still taken) as giving an invariant universal path that all people are fated to tread with a set of sequences declaring, in sum, the violence of things over people and the acquiescence of some Communists in that process.

On Practice: Four Studies 99

Besides we must perhaps 'deepen' Davidson's account by recalling that Gramsci's activist theory was geared to socialist construction. In an article of 18 May 1918 which correctly stressed that 'Class struggle is not a puerile dream – it is an act that is freely determined upon and an inner necessity of the social order' (1977a: 46), Gramsci argued that the Italian Socialist Party

> is not a sectional, but a class organization: its morphology is quite different from that of any other party. It can only view the State, the network of bourgeois class power, as its antagonistic likeness. It cannot enter into direct or indirect competition for the conquest of the State without committing suicide, without losing its nature, without becoming a mere political faction that is estranged from the historical activity of the proletariat . . . The Socialist Party does not conquer the State, it replaces it; it replaces the regime, abolishes party government and replaces free competition by the organization of production and exchange. (*Il Grido del Popolo*; 1977a: 40)

Despite the militant absolutism here ('all struggle and no unity' as Mao might opine), this is an early combative *proletarian* Gramsci which will be, perhaps, a little less 'digestible' than the confined and necessarily speculative Gramsci of the *Notebooks*. Moreover, as Gwyn Williams has shown extensively, these early thoughts are not isolated: three articles in *L'Ordine Nuovo* in 1920 are entirely congruent with both the views on the Party *and* on the State indicated in the above. In all three the *cultural* intention of socialism is also manifest: 'Governing party and governing class' (1977a: Text 38), 'Two revolutions' (Text 56), and 'The Communist Party' (Text 61).

Gramsci's commitment to practice, that his Communism *was* a practical materialism, has been obscured by the impact of the *Notebooks* (although, as we shall indicate, they have been 'enjoyed' in a certain way!). By commitment to practice we do not mean any simplistic anti-theory stance, nor do we mean the application of unthought (and thus unrealised) 'laws of revolution' – we hope our work to date shows our distance from both. Study (being 'good at learning') is a significant practice for any communist militant. Lenin's remarks to the Third and Fourth Comintern Congresses – texts which would have been known to Gramsci (and to Mao) – are relevant here.

100 *For Mao*

What is essential now [1921] is a fundamental preparation of the revolution and a profound study of its concrete development in the principal capitalist countries. (quoted in Carr, 1953: 383)

I am convinced [in 1922, Lenin's penultimate public speech] that we must say in this matter not only to our Russian but to our foreign comrades that the most important task in the period now beginning is to study. We are learning in a general sense. They must learn in a special sense in order really to achieve organisation, structure, method, and content of revolutionary work. (quoted in Carr, 1953: 440)

Moreover, not only (as with Mao) did Gramsci attack the unhistorical study of ideologies (1948: 376) but, in his extended critique of Bukharin's *Historical Materialism*, (1921) he shares positions found in both Mao's critique of dogmatism and Lukács's earlier critique of Bukharin's textbook (Lukács, 1925). Both Lukács and Gramsci criticise Bukharin's dogmatism, above all his attempt to *scientise* historical materialism which they both recognise as a speculative metaphysics. There are many passages in both, but especially in Gramsci's commentary, which can be compared point for point with Mao's writings of 1937, both 'On contradiction' and 'On practice' (cf. Mao, 1964T).

It is not perhaps surprising to find Lukács in 1925 quoting Lenin's remarks to the Second Congress of the Comintern which argue against absolutism, dogmatism and mechanical materialism, concluding 'Practice alone can serve as real 'proof' in this and similar questions' (quoted Lukács, 1925: 142). For the same writer had recognised the year before, in his sketch which tried to signify Lenin's greatness, both that 'Historical materialism is the theory of the proletarian revolution' (1924: 9) and that

It was left to Lenin to make the step from theory to practice; a step which is simultaneously – and this should never be forgotten – *a theoretical advance*. For it is a step from the abstract to the concrete. (Lukács, 1924: 47)

The same dialectic is grasped by Gramsci:

The proposition contained in the 'Preface to a Contribution to the Critique of Political Economy' to the effect that men acquire

On Practice: Four Studies

101

consciousness of structural conflicts on the level of ideologies should be considered as an affirmation of epistemological and not simply psychological and moral value. From this, it follows that the theoretical – practical principle of hegemony has also epistemological significance, and it is here that Ilich [Lenin]'s greatest theoretical contribution . . . should be sought. In those terms one could say that Ilich advanced philosophy as philosophy in so far as he advanced political doctrine and practice. (1948: 365)

The point is driven home in several passages where the reality of the world is shown to be *constructed*. Thus, Gramsci argues (recalling not only Mao's whole project, but Marx's remarks about the inception of real (human) history) that the struggle to understand and grasp objective reality is inseparable from the political struggle to make *that* possible. Real objectivity is only knowable when humanity is no longer riven by 'internal contradictions', when there exists the social basis for a more collective, conscious, egalitarian grasp of the real world (e.g. 1948: 444f).

There is no space here to rehearse the tortuous history of Gramsci's part in PCI and Comintern struggles which is in any case well displayed in other texts we have cited and in Carr's model analyses (1953: Chapters 30, 31; 1964: Chapter 28(d) and 31(d)). What that history displays is that Gramsci had to learn (but the PCI did not learn in time) crucial lessons of flexibility well caught in the resolutions of the Third Congress of the Comintern in 1921: 'Revolution always was, and still is, a struggle of living forms on given historical foundations' (quoted in Carr, 1953: 383). Looking back in 1926, Gramsci offers a theory of the United Front not dissimilar to that learned by Mao in his long struggles against Left and Right deviations, against Social Democratic and Fascist treachery, *and* against Comintern 'assistance' and 'expertise':

Lenin summed up what should have been the meaning of the split when he said to comrade Serrati: 'Separate yourselves from Turati, and then form an alliance with him'. We should have adopted this formula to the split which took place, in a form different from the one foreseen by Lenin. That is, we should certainly have separated ourselves from reformism, and from maximalism . . . But afterwards, and without giving up our ideological and organisational struggle against them, we should

102   *For Mao*

have attempted to build an alliance against reaction. To the
leadership of our Party,[8] however, every attempt by the International to make us adopt this line appeared as an implicit
disavowal of the Livorno split [when the P.C.d'I. had formed
from the much larger P.S.I. in 1921].[9] (quoted in Fiori, 1965:
153)

But, it is time to emphasise, the PCI failed to divert Fascism.
There was no socialist construction begun within Italy which
eventuated in that 'break' – creating material, cultural, political
and epistemological spaces. There was no revolution. Reasons for
this are inscribed in that history of party building, and Comintern
assistance, to which we have referred. But a large measure of
difference between Gramsci (and the PCI) and Mao (and the CPC)
must be found in their analyses of agrarian production. Gramsci, as
is well known, recognised the 'Southern question' but his conception of it had two qualities which need emphasis. First, the
'staging' of the impact of socialist construction: from the workers to
the peasants, from the Towns to the Country, from the North to the
South:

> What is indisputable is that only the working class, by seizing
> political and economic power from the hands of the bankers and
> capitalists, is in a position to resolve the central problem of
> national life in Italy – the Southern problem. (*L'Ordine Nuovo*, 13
> January 1921; 1977a: 375)

Secondly – and this is not a matter of an instance here or an instance
there – there is the neutralised imagery of the Risorgimento claimed
by so many diverse groups as a legitimating rhetoric. The next
sentence to the above, for example, reads

> What is indisputable is that only the working class can bring the
> painful task of unification that the Risorgimento began to a
> successful conclusion.

The previous year, in his reflections on various discussions on land
reform, 'Workers and peasants' (cf. Lenin, 1917e), Gramsci
expressed his limited views of the peasantry even more graphically,
through, moreover, a false understanding of the similarity between

On Practice: Four Studies   103

factory and agrarian production. He thinks the parliamentary debates to have been useful if they

> have served to let the broad masses of the peasants in the *whole* of Italy know that the solution to the agricultural problem lies SOLELY in the hands of the urban workers in Northern Italy, and that the solution will be put into effect only by a dictatorship of the proletariat. (*L'Ordine Nuovo*, 3 January 1920; 1977a: 148;[10] our capitals; his emphasis)

There are of course other tendencies within Gramsci's writing – just as we stressed this to be so with Lenin (*SCMT*: Chapters 2 and 3). In an analysis written with Palmiro Togliatti, a sketch, oriented to the events of December 1919, of 'what the Italian revolution should be like' is given:

> On the one side the proletariat, in the strict sense of the word, i.e. the workers in industry and industrialized agriculture; on the other, the poor peasants: these are the two wings of the revolutionary army. (*L'Ordine Nuovo*, December 1919; 1977 a: 139

Here, indeed, the necessarily *collective* force of the poor peasants is given that recognition so central to Mao's texts of 1927. From these forces will come 'organs for collective control over production':

> These organs of control, the peasants' Councils, despite the fact that they will leave intermediate forms of private land ownership (small holdings) in existence will have to carry out a psychological and technical transformation of the countryside and become the basis of a new communal life-style; centres through which the revolutionary elements will be able to enforce their will in a continuous and concrete fashion. (Ibid., 140)

The motive force of the Soviet revolution is correctly grasped in the consequences of the *experience* (cf. Mao) of common struggle by workers and peasants.

> both become convinced through experience that they would never liberate themselves from the oppression of the bosses, unless they gave their own organization of conquest a form that enabled

104 *For Mao*

them to eliminate the exploiter directly from the sphere of production. (Ibid., 140–1)

But in many of his *Notebooks* the remarks on 'the South', or the peasantry, betray a distance which was caught neatly by Mao when he proclaimed the positive achievements of those whom the 'gentlemen' scholars had called '*riff-raff*' (cf. Gramsci, 1948: 272f – a note written in 1930 – and Mao, 1927A).

There are similar difficulties and ambiguities with Gramsci's writings on military and political strategy and tactics. Indeed here – as with the equally famous writings on the State – we find a remarkably sustained exploration of a set of *metaphorical alternatives*, notably 'wars of position' versus 'wars of manoeuvre'. This is, of course, hardly surprising given the conditions under which Gramsci laboured; indeed, in those very *Notebooks*, he stresses

that comparisons between military art and politics, if made, should always be taken *cum grano salis* [with a pinch of salt] – in other words, as stimuli to thought, or as terms in a *reductio ad absurdum*. (1948: 231)

He also makes two other points which ought to be better known: 'in political struggle, there also exist other forms of warfare' besides 'war of movement' or 'war of position' and he goes on to talk about commandos, which includes 'the art of organising sudden sorties and surprise attacks with picked men' (1948: 232). Secondly,

Another point to be kept in mind is that in political struggle one should not ape the methods of the ruling classes, or one will fall into easy ambushes. (1948: 232)

Anderson (1977: 55f) has indicated some possibly unknown precursors of the dichotomies that Gramsci examined, in the debates amongst Kautsky, Luxemburg, Martov, Marchlewski, and Lenin. These, as other debates examined there (and in other literature) on such alternatives at work within the Comintern, all show the fallacy of speculative universalisms – the confusion between strategy and tactics which has done more to deform socialist construction than any other confusion, as many struggles in China have shown. What would it mean about marxism if it did actually generate universalisms of the kind which are constantly and

On Practice: Four Studies   105

dogmatically generated and enforced as 'the correct line' when they are the reified and abstracted instances of a partly understood historical moment? This is forcible abstraction with a vengeance! There is all the difference in the world (between worlds, in fact): compare a general line such as 'Going all out . . . '; such strategic constants as 'Never forget class struggle . . . '; or methodological constants as 'The mass-line . . . '. In contrast consider: '*Because* capitalism is now stabilised, all wars *will* be wars of . . . '; '*Because* (as a noted "retreat") NEP was introduced, NEP-measures form a constituent of *all* socialist construction after the revolutionary defeat of the bourgeois ruling class . . . '; or, '*Because* (as invariant constants independent of the human will) of "the laws of world economy" and "the international division of labour" socialist formations *must* . . . '.

Not only, as we have indicated, does Gramsci provide such examples of absolutism but his work has been quarried precisely to abstract this or that tactical aphorism, metaphorical aside, half-completed remark, in order to render it as holy writ, as *strategy*. For comparison with the problem of critical interpretation think that Lenin had completed only the *Notebooks* for *State and Revolution* and then been assassinated! More to the point, although it is notable how silent Gramsci is on such matters, imagine simply that Lenin had left only his *Notebooks* on Agrarian questions and never come to power.

The fragments left by Gramsci[11] – on military and political questions – are full of insights, causing a useful (if sometimes only momentary) hesitation with regard to particular renderings of historical materialism. But it is very far from being the kind of book of texts that it is treated as in the recent literature; think only of the glaring absences in the literature which Gramsci knew – which nobody writing in the 1930s could know – which we now know today. But, more to the point, think of the historical experience. Imagine, again, what it would have meant had Gramsci been able to read the *Grundrisse, The German Ideology* or, more to our present point, Mao's philosophical writings. Generally speaking, where Gramsci does say something of strategic significance it is already present within the historical materialism that is *now* available to us, not least that established by the practical materialism of the working people of the USSR and of China.

Unsurprisingly Anderson uses Gramsci as a foil to illustrate (again) the 'wonder that is Trotsky':

106 *For Mao*

> it was above all Trotsky who provided the working-class movement, East or West, with a scientific critique of both the ideas of 'war of manoeuvre' and 'war of position', in the field where they really obtained – military strategy proper. (1977: 73)

Really? Actually 'above all'? One would have thought, if the historical text is to accord somewhat more accurately with historical experience, that some aside or footnote might have indicated Mao Tse-tung or Chu Teh as being involved in the strategy and tactics of warfare from the 1920s until 1949 and beyond. Mao did, after all, provide military writings and we do have historical accounts of his practice.[12]

The non-mention of Mao is, of course, a major reason for our own essays here; but this specific absence is revealing as to a more general absence from the work of Gramsci (and Anderson). Neither understands production. For them the problem of military or political strategy can be thought of without reference to 'costs'; they therefore do not understand the singularity of the State (its real coercion) as felt by the working classes under capitalist domination: it has to be paid for by the diversion of funds from their collective labour. Not only is it not their State, but they bear its inflation. We have noted above how Mao stresses that if the People's Liberation Army (and before that the Red Army) was to be truly popular it would have to be part of the wider army of labour without which the war against both the Japanese and the KMT could not be won. This popularity meant that *this* army would give more to the production collectivities within which it resided than it took away – the Army would not only grow its own food and other daily necessities, it would aid (through early forms of mutual aid teams, hospitals, schools) the peasants in their own struggle for production.

Internally, Mao – from the 1920s – stresses that the Red Army must be democratic (e.g. 1928B: 83) because the 'Chinese Red Army is an armed body for carrying out the political tasks of the revolution' (1929B: 106). Mao's strategy and tactics is normally read as 'guerrilla-ism' – but in 1929 he attacks both 'the ideology of roving rebel bands' and 'the remnants of putschism' (1929B: 114). But, as we have argued, this is only a fragment of a much wider strategy on Mao's part – to refuse to erect *any* absolutes which restrict the investigation of the empirical present situation. Hence his remarks concerning those who urged 'all struggle and no unity' and others who sought 'all unity and no struggle' – deviations

On Practice: Four Studies 107

present within the CPC from its foundation. Hence also his long struggles against 'cutting the feet to fit the shoes', against blind faith and mechanical copying, which he applied to military affairs (1963D: 180f; 1959O). It was, after all, in the context of discussing strategy for China's revolutionary war, that he first emphasised, '*The important thing is to be good at learning*' (1936D: 186; cf. 1957B: 420f; 1958H: 96f).

In his military methods proper Mao had to argue against 'marxists' (especially those who believed there could never be any marxism in the mountains, 1936D: 214) in order to keep flexibility in the face of invariant methods such as 'seizing key cities' and 'don't give up an inch of territory'. As we noted above he also argued against 'guerrilla-ism' (1936D: 243f; 1938B, C). The point is often made that

> Epistemologically speaking, the source of all erroneous views on war lies in idealist and mechanistic tendencies on the question. People with such tendencies are subjective and one-sided in their approach to problems. (1938C: 121)

Regarding methods of war, Mao is insistent that a clear line be easily visible between the methods of really popular forces and the enemy's forces. Here his arguments against commandism (against 'draining the pond to catch the fish') are aimed at Left adventurism which may achieve victories but at a cost of making those 'victories' *donations* to the people. It was also necessary to keep clearly separate from the Japanese policy of three atrocities – looting, burning and killing all – which related to the CPC policy on prisoners: treating all wounded properly; releasing back to the enemy side those who wished to go; recruiting all who wished to stay, subject to political vigilance against spies and agents.

Finally, since, as with Gramsci (in part), Mao's work is known (if at all) as aphorisms and slogans, it is as well to close this discussion by quoting the full passage from which a particular remark has often been taken.

> It is very difficult for the labouring people, who have been deceived and intimidated by the reactionary ruling classes for thousands of years, to awaken to the importance of having guns in their own hands. Now that Japanese imperialist oppression and

108   *For Mao*

the nation-wide resistance to it have pushed our labouring people into the arena of war, Communists should prove themselves the most politically conscious leaders in this war. Every Communist must grasp the truth, 'Political power grows out of the barrel of a gun'. Our principle is that the Party commands the gun, and the gun must never be allowed to command the Party. Yet, having guns, we can create Party organizations, as witness the powerful Party organizations which the Eighth Route Army has created in northern China. We can also create cadres, create schools, create culture, create mass movements. (Mao, 1938F: 224–5)

In their discussions of political and cultural relations there is more apparent similarity in the work of Gramsci and Mao. Both, for example, recognise that public opinion is constructed. Gramsci argued:

Public opinion is strictly linked to political hegemony. It is the point of contact between civil society and political society, between consensus and force. The state, when it wants to initiate an unpopular action, preventively creates the adequate public opinion; that is, it organizes and concentrates certain elements of civil society. (quoted in Bates, 1975: 363; cf. Gramsci, 1948: 170, n. 71)[13]

In 1962, at the 10th Plenum CC/CPC (a fact recalled in the sixteen articles of the 11th Plenum CC/CPC, 8 August 1966), Mao said

Writing novels is popular these days, isn't it? The use of novels for anti-Party activity is a great invention. Anyone wanting to overthrow a political regime must create public opinion and do some preparatory ideological work. This applies to counter-revolutionary as well as to revolutionary classes. (1962C: 195; cf. 1966P: 117f)

But there are major differences between the two on these questions. Anderson, unwittingly, brings one to our attention in his text mentioned above. There he considers one of the 'more serious consequences' of Gramsci's reflections upon military strategy to have been his welcome for the dictatorship of the proletariat (which Marx, Lenin, Stalin and Mao have also pointed to) as the key

On Practice: Four Studies 109

means to facilitate more rapid, more complete, more 'solid', socialist construction and thus cultural revolution.[14] What Anderson is pointing to here is also a curious conundrum concerning Gramsci's analysis of the State – where it is revolutionary it is Bolshevik, where it is non-Bolshevik it is also, alas, non-revolutionary.

First, given the clamour surrounding 'hegemony', it is necessary to illustrate at some length the alternative dictatorship-of-the-proletariat view in Gramsci's work. We can begin by agreeing entirely with Gramsci's unremarkable (in terms of the historical materialism available to us *now*) point that analyses

> cannot and must not be ends in themselves (unless the intention is merely to write a chapter of past history), but acquire significance only if they serve to justify a particular practical activity. (1948: 185)

What was the passage which so alarmed Anderson? It is Gramsci's gloss upon both the stabilisation which the Comintern detected after 1924 and the consequent likelihood of maximal continuing isolation for the USSR.

> The war of position demands enormous sacrifices by infinite masses of people. So an unprecedented concentration of hegemony is necessary, and hence a more 'interventionist' government, which will take the offensive more openly against the oppositionists and organise permanently the 'impossibility' of internal disintegration – with controls of every kind. (1948: 238–9)

The need for dictatorship is also stressed again:

> For some social groups, which before their ascent to autonomous State life have not had a long independent period of cultural and moral development on their own . . . a period of statolatry is necessary and indeed opportune. (1948: 268)

Although he correctly warns that both 'theoretical fanaticism' and permanent 'government of the functionaries' must be avoided, in a third passage, Gramsci (largely because, it must be noted with vigour, the intellectuals who develop marxism are not linked to the

110 *For Mao*

people) makes the above theses paradigmatic for the development of new proletarian culture:

> Only after the creation of the new State does the cultural problem impose itself in all its complexity and tend towards a coherent solution. In any case the attitude to be taken up before the formation of the new State can only be critico-polemical, never dogmatic. (1948: 398; cf. Lenin, 1920c; 1923a, b, c, d).

Taken with his published writings' endorsement of proletarian dictatorship and class rule (e.g. 1977a: Texts 13, 38, 56, 61) we can see here a coherent alternative to that Gramsci so much in vogue amongst intellectuals, the theorist of hegemony.

But whether we take the hegemony approach (whose ambiguities are outlined by Anderson, 1977) with its emphasis upon cultural activity by intellectuals of a new type *before* the revolution, or the 'modern Prince' view, with *its* emphasis upon the State as an instrument, Gramsci (and those who echo him) fails to transcend base/superstructure metaphor. He does not, as we have said, understand production. As with the military writings, so generally: he cannot grasp momentary instances as contradictory unities in opposition. Paradigmatically he cannot grasp coercion and consent as facets of that unitary regulation by which capital rules. Indeed both his instrumentalism and his intellectualism are, to be sure, complementary – not too surprising perhaps in the writings of a man locked in a prison. The machine view or the mental view of the State (relation) obscures its particular class nature. Of the construction, incoherence and – it must be repeatedly stressed – permeable fragility of the State, Anderson remains ignorant in his *analyses of the present* although he has, of course, displayed the history for us. The central 'image' of the State (relation) for Gramsci (one taken without query by Anderson, 1977, *and* Hobsbawm, 1977) is a distinctly superstructural agency which can be 'handled' and 'directed' by the masses, but is not theirs and cannot become theirs. This is Gramsci's Bolshevism (a feature which, as we have noted, recurs in much language and some of the practices of Mao also). Both this, and his emphasis upon the possibility of creating a cultural offensive which would lead to the 'capture of the State' (to the possibility of using it as an agency of transformation), divert attention from the real resources which practical materialists should assist in making conscious and simultaneously unleashing. Those

On Practice: Four Studies   111

'real resources' are the productive powers and energies of the creators of wealth which are currently constrained and hampered by the crippling restrictions of the division of labour, socially, technically and culturally.

Law, for example, is 'perfectly' a mixture of consent and coercion – in short, moral regulation, that reveals the whole dichotomous imagery of base/superstructure to be dangerously misleading. The State (and thus moral, political, and legal relations) comprises relations of production in a particular social form (analogous precisely to the market form) of a historically determinate mode of production. As a former Lord Chancellor correctly remarks: 'Law is about compulsion, the coercion of men and women to do what would otherwise never have been their choice' (Hailsham, 1977: 374; cf. Thompson, 1975: 258f)[15]. Marx's long struggles against Hegelian notions of Law, as well as absolutely clear formulations in *Capital* (1863a: 201, 284f; 1865a: 339f), show the errors of an analysis which *begins* with the legal (or, more generally, State) relations and 'forgets' class structure and production relations. This does not deny that much of Gramsci (e.g. 1948: 246f) provides an excellent 'reminder', as it were, that these resources *are* within historical materialism. Another emphasis needs making against all those today who think (often claiming Gramsci to their aid) capitalism capable of self-regulation. Gramsci shows that the *fully* regulated, just as the fully *ethical*, 'State' awaits conditions where, as Mao (following Engels) puts it, 'politics will have changed its meaning' (Gramsci, 1948: 257f; but cf. ibid., 244 and 208). This is only another way of pointing out the need for the most coercive proletarian dictatorship if proletarian democracy (and with it a new culture and new planning) is to be possible.

There is one curious antinomy between Mao and Gramsci that should perhaps be mentioned before we conclude this section. Gramsci's work is being treated as if it could be summarised by the slogan 'Seek hegemony!' whereas, as is well known, Mao frequently urged 'Never seek hegemony!'. The phrase is quoted by Chou En-lai in the political report to the Tenth Congress of the CPC in 1973 and opposing 'hegemonism' features in the 1973 Constitution of the Party (Ch. 1). Clearly, the objects to which these strategies were directed were quite different – for Gramsci is discussing how an ascendant class should prepare itself for revolution and generally demonstrate its superiority to the class (and system) which constrains it. Mao is discussing (within the framework of his theory of

For Mao

Three Worlds which we have criticised previously, *SCMT*: Chapters 5 and 6) the domination of the two social formations he considers equal 'superpowers', the USA and the USSR, but especially the latter. The same point is captured in the 1975 Constitution of the Peoples Republic of China, when the 'Preamble' states 'China will never be a superpower'. Nevertheless, despite the different objects, some features of our general critique of Third Worldism apply, *mutatis mutandis*, to hegemony as used by Gramsci and as taken-and-used by his followers. We are thinking here of the manner in which both uses of the term diminish the class specificity of the agencies and relations to which they refer. Both mark, in our view, a retreat from historical materialism to a kind of abstracted political analysis – global in the case of Mao, national in the case of Gramsci – in which it becomes possible to chart and categorise quite antagonistic realities (as the heterogeneous collectivity known as 'the Second World' in the Three Worlds analysis, and as many of Gramsci's asides about intellectuals or Jacobinism).

If we have been harsh in our presentation and criticism of Gramsci it is because there are times when it is not only correct but necessary to swim against the tide and make something of a splash whilst so doing. We do so also because we cannot fail to notice that the fight over the possession of Gramsci's soul (the competing declarations of the meaning of his texts) is patterned in a similar way to many other alignments. In sum, we think that the 'Gramsci' that has been erected from those 33 notebooks, 500 or so letters, and series of published journalism is a counterpoint to another figure rarely mentioned as a theorist – indeed we can imagine the scandal that a book *for* him would cause – Joseph Stalin. It seems to us, as perhaps also to Althusser, in so far as we can unravel his recent pronouncements, that the critique of Stalin is part of a wider battle for the class content of historical materialism. This battle over the meaning of Marx has a number of staging posts since the death of Stalin, but the tendency to depoliticisation is very strong. The coincidence of a particular 'Gramsci' and the suppression of the 'dictatorship of the proletariat' from the manifestoes of Communist Party after Communist Party seems more than mere coincidence. It is part of the worldwide battle to defeat that socialist revolution which was begun sixty years ago (and which has succeeded in taking more and more social space from the capitalist world market).

But in posing this alternative (and here 'Gramsci' does stand for all those alternative heroes and heroines of the moment, so

On Practice: Four Studies

passionately embraced and so resolutely discarded in the harlequinades of intellectual Leftism) we are also defending Antonio Gramsci, the Communist militant who lived from 1891 to 1937, and re-presenting his writings. Indeed his genius lay in opening doors which for most of his contemporaries did not even exist as doors; they saw only the invariant 'laws of world economy', the marvels of 'American efficiency', or the deep slumber of 'working class apathy'. In speaking *for Gramsci* – as also *for Mao* – we are reminding practical materialists that historical materialism is a method of analysis and action which can be added to and extended by patiently recording the achievements of working women and men in demonstrating the pliant qualities of reality. We speak *for Gramsci* because it is necessary to speak for 'dictatorship' and for the Party, and to add to him the work of many other militants which reveal the societal relations of production which evade his prison writings. In this we speak – as with all our work – against those who intellectualise marxism (and offer an abstracted historical materialism) by stressing cultural politics (the masses are ignorant or fooled or empty vessels . . .), 'hegemony' (and unprincipled fronts with all progressive forces, plus slavish adherence to the cultural norms of the bourgeoisie), and the 'collective intellectual' (by which they actively and ostensibly define not their unity with, but their distance from, the working class). Gramsci deserves better than that.

Part Three
On Contradiction

In his *Capital*, Marx first analyses the simplest, ordinary and fundamental, most common and everyday *relation* of bourgeois (commodity) society, a relation encountered billions of times, viz. the exchange of commodities. In this very simple phenomenon (in this 'cell' of bourgeois society) analysis reveals *all* the contradictions (or germs of *all* the contradictions) of modern society. (Lenin: 'On the question of dialectics' (1916b: 360–1))

. . . classes do exist in socialist countries and . . . class struggle undoubtedly exists . . . We must acknowledge that classes will continue to exist for a long time. We must also acknowledge the existence of a struggle of class against class, and admit the possibility of the restoration of reactionary classes. (Mao, 1962C: 189)

Opposition and struggle between ideas of different kinds constantly occur within the Party; this is a reflection within the Party of contradictions between classes and between the new and the old in society. If there were no contradictions in the Party and no ideological struggles to resolve them, the Party's life would come to an end. (Mao, 1937J: 317; cf. 1957A: 359f)

In the building of a socialist society, everybody needs remoulding – the exploiters and also the working people. Who says it isn't necessary for the working class? Of course, the remoulding of the exploiters is essentially different from that of the working people, and the two must not be confused. The working class remoulds the whole of society in class struggle against nature, and in the process it remoulds itself. It must ceaselessly learn in the course of work, gradually overcome its shortcomings and never stop doing so. (Mao 1957B: 402)

1 INTRODUCTORY REMARKS

It is the purpose of this third Part of our book to try and indicate the significance of the contribution made to historical materialism by the theories and practice of Mao Tse-tung and of the Communist Party of China.

The title we have chosen for this discussion is deliberate. It would be no service to historical materialism to suggest in any way that Mao's marxism developed easily and evenly. As the quotations which prefaced our first Part indicated, it is the uneven, contradictory, hesitant and constantly struggling *movement* (to transform the agents and the circumstances of change) which is a crucial element in Mao's own self-definition. He wanted to be known as a teacher, not because he had handed out so many tablets of stone (rules that have only to be applied to transform the world) but because he had stressed how hard it is to be good at learning, how there are general methodological principles but very few prescriptive recipes for success. Given the events which have taken place since Mao's death it is more than ever necessary to emphasise this.

But we mean more by our title than an indication of the unevenness of (all) development. We are pointing to the incomplete and only partially secured revolutionising of fundamental (i.e. defining) social relations within China. Mao frequently from the late 1950s speaks of the problem of securing successors to the revolution; that being one (and only one) way of preventing China from 'changing colour'. By the latter Mao meant nothing less than not simply the advent of capitalism within China, but the installation of a Fascist regime· such as he believed had been established within the USSR by 1964. To be sure, he usually linked these prognoses to the inherent instability and short-term potential of such capitalist restorations or Fascist installations; he speaks in several places of the generation after next overthrowing these new tyrants. But, and this is our point, he felt socialist construction in China to be so frail that it was conceivable that, within a few years, capitalism could be restored.

We have indicated here and there in our own analysis within this book and previously *(SCMT)* that one avenue down which those who seek capitalist restoration could easily 'drive' is that which is founded upon the base of foreign policy and foreign trade. The 'drive' of this new bourgeoisie would not be simple – dock-workers,

116 *For Mao*

for example, have refused to unload certain kinds of 'foreign things'. We must not pose against a 'once upon a time' total and secure 'Maoism', an equally total and instantaneous capitalist restoration, as do many analysts of the USSR (not least the CPC and their Friends). Our point is only that this avenue exists.

But there are other avenues internal to the class struggle within the Party and over production in China. Here the unsecured nature of Mao's (and the CPC's) transformation of what we have sketched elsewhere as the 'social problematic of Bolshevism' (*SCMT*: Chapters 2 and 3) becomes crucial. Just as Stalin, Trotsky *and* Brezhnev can claim *truthfully* that they are justified by the very words and actions of Lenin in doing their quite different activities, so it is possible for a number of different lines forward to be drawn from Mao's own writing. This only emphasises once again that it is not texts which are the major tests of historical materialism, but the accumulated historical experience of practices.

2 SOCIALIST CONSTRUCTION IN CHINA

Later we shall seek to indicate the implications of Mao's marxism (and the accomplishments of the CPC) for the International Communist Movement and for the theory and practice of socialist construction within capitalist social formations. Here we begin by examining the historical experience of China. Keith Buchanan's title should be cited again – the last fifty years have indeed seen *The Transformation of the Chinese Earth*. But, as always, it is how that transformation was achieved which is the more remarkable. To solve the basic human problem of self-sufficiency in food – having enough to eat (and here contrasts between both China, India *and* the USSR are apposite)[1] – is possible in a number of ways. We believe that the solutions demonstrated by the historical experience of the Chinese people display methods (and a strategy) which are universally relevant.

Food, clothing, medicine, and housing are now relatively secured for the working people of China. Moreover working people there (Hinton, 1972b: 193; Sweezy, 1975: 10) are not treated as pure labour power and subjected to the violence of things. But the transformation of necessity involving the struggle to change people – to fit them, as Marx indicated, to found society anew – is very broad, protracted, and uneven. That there is still a very great

On Contradiction 117

deal to be done is clear if such central examples as education or the emancipation of women are examined.

In both these areas of class struggle, Mao argues his general strategic method: the full emancipation of the subordinated must be accomplished by themselves, it cannot be 'donated' by the Party. The latter's task is to hold back those who already have power in the given situation. The Party must 'disrupt' and 'contain' what is, above all, hegemonic or definitional power. This reliance upon mass criticism and open struggle (once class enemies have been effectively neutralised at the least) must include

> the making of mistakes. No experience can be considered complete unless it includes the making of mistakes. (1957L: 490–1)

In the same year, Mao noted

> According to a survey made in Peking, most college students are children of landlords, rich peasants, the bourgeoisie and well-to-do middle peasants, while students from working-class and poor and lower-middle peasant families account for less than 20 per cent . . . This situation should change, but it will take time. (1957A: 353)

Three methods can be used to revolutionise education: (1) to proletarianise knowledge, to arm workers not simply with facts but with a view on 'where correct ideas come from'; (2) to open the doors of schools and colleges widely, to ensure that many more workers and poor and middle-peasant families can send their children to colleges; and (3) to make all students engage in 'going down' (to rural areas) and engaging in practical (and political) education with peasants and workers.[2] That is to say, if you really wish to socialise educational relations you must challenge directly assumptions about knowledge and pedagogy. Mao does this himself on several occasions – from 'Oppose book worship' (1930B) through to his 'Remarks on education' (1964F) – and the theme is, of course, generalised in the Great Proletarian Cultural Revolution.

But the struggle is extremely arduous whilst the Three Great Differences – especially the existence of those who mainly labour with their heads, and a majority who mainly labour with their bodies *and* a commanding or directing role for the former – exist.

118   *For Mao*

Hence, again, Mao's insistence upon facilitating and encouraging the widest possible *public* discussion (not least to bring the real Right into the open) coupled with the most rigorous proletarian dictatorship against external and internal capitalists and bourgeoisie. Only if both are practised (the victories in the former decreasing the necessity, scope, and cost of the latter) can transformation take place.

One particular event in 1974 illustrates the difficulties of socialist construction. Pai Chi-hsien graduated from Hopei Teachers University in 1968 and went to a production brigade of the Yentsun People's Commune, Ysanghsien County 'to be re-educated by the poor and lower-middle peasants'. She became a teacher and married an 'ordinary peasant'. For this she was criticised by her father, and many other people. Pai wrote to *Hopei Daily* and her letter was reprinted on the front page of the *People's Daily* 7 February 1974 (extracted *Peking Review* (8), 1974; cf. Pai Chi-hsien, 1974, also). Pai argues that her marriage revealed that a deep struggle was needed since many 'look down on peasants' and think them 'dirty'. Pai's father had been apprenticed in a factory at the age of 12 and her mother had been sold into slavery; Pai was the first ever in her family to graduate. Pai ended her letter thus:

> I think the rotten ideas of looking down on peasants and farm labour that have been handed down over thousands of years should be criticized. This is of great importance in narrowing the differences between workers and peasants, between town and countryside and between manual and mental work, in opposing and preventing revisionism and in building a new socialist countryside. (*Peking Review* (8), 1974, p. 21)

In a later article, Pai concluded:

> The new society taking shape in the midst of struggle involves a clean break not only with the old system of ownership but also with old traditional ideas. (Pai, 1974: 14)

As Elizabeth Croll has shown,[3] after the GLF the neat correlation between women's participation in social production and their automatic full social emancipation was questioned. What was involved, she argues, was 'the removal of a whole history of cultural oppression' (1976: 41). Croll analyses and reprints a *Red Flag* article

On Contradiction

of 1973 (Davin's (1976: Appendix 3) reprinting of a *People's Daily* editorial of March 8 1973 is complementary) which demonstrates the depth of male supremacist practices and indicates some tactics to tackle these. Both Croll (1976) and Davin argue, in the latter's words, that as long as the CPC recognises that the struggles of women are far from complete 'progress will surely continue, for inequality and discrimination can hardly become rigidly institutionalised so long as critical consciousness of them exists' (1976: 197). It is relevant to indicate here the importance of the *general* attack on the division of labour within both the People's Communes and the new worker-peasant villages such as those at Taching.[4]

The problems relating to educational and sexual relations highlight the continuing need for the widest struggle in cultural and political relations. This is equally true regarding matters of technique, particularly problems of overall co-ordinated planning. An article by Tsai Cheng (in *People's Daily*, 12 January 1974)[5] shows, however, that it is possible to generalise the experience of the Border Region years. Tsai notes that 'the questions of how to accumulate funds for construction and on what forces to rely in building socialism have been points of struggle between two lines since the beginning'. Rather than concentrating upon procurement before production, two policies have been adopted (for the two different forms of socialist ownership in China); both place production first. First,

> greater accumulation by China's state-owned enterprises depends mainly in increasing production and practising economy and on the revolutionary enthusiasm and hard work of the masses.

Second, in the sphere of agricultural production, the agricultural tax has fallen to six per cent of farm output (yield to the State has increased because production has risen so greatly) and prices of products needed by the production brigades have all fallen, whilst the State grants many items to the Communes free of charge. There are no internal or external public debts;[6] the loans from the USSR being repaid ahead of time, and internal bonds encashed.

Tsai Cheng's argument can be generalised to the whole problem of transforming the State. We argued above that Mao saw the dangers during the Border Region years of the State (and we stress here that this includes the Army) costing too much, of it being

120

For Mao

productively burdensome. He saw, in addition, that the solution to the problem was to encourage the maximum self-reliance by State and Army units and to minimise administrative apparatuses. By the 1950s – as part of his indication of the dangers of dogmatically following the Soviet path – Mao noted:

> Streamline our organizations. The state is an instrument of class struggle. A class is not to be equated with the state which is formed by a number of people (a small number) from the class in the dominant position. Office work does need some people, but the fewer the better. At present the state apparatus is bloated, with many departments and with many people sitting idle in their offices . . . The above applies equally to the Party, the government and the army. (1957A: 378; cf. 1957K: 460)

The echo of Lenin here (cf. Lenin, 1923d) may be deliberate. Much of the GPCR was aimed at such a streamlining – and its complementary proletarianisation by the participation in productive labour of all cadres and State officials – and it had very directly measurable effects according to Chou En-lai in an interview with Snow (1971).

The interviews with Chou En-lai are a neglected source (as we mentioned previously) in so far as they demonstrate many consequences of a *practical* nature which tend to be obscured by most studies of the GPCR or earlier stages of socialist construction. Within town and country, commune and factory, the GPCR was marked by a surge forward for socialism. This was particularly true in the 1970s as the GPCR *continued*; this can be detected from a close reading of issues of *Peking Review* or *China Reconstructs*. Chou considered, in an interview with Hinton in 1971,[7] that three kinds of bourgeois forces existed in China: (1) Old exploiters still around; (2) Newly generated bourgeois class forces; (3) Ideological influence and corrosion (pp. 48–9). Chou En-lai's remarks are also important because they remind us that total affirmation is as metaphysical as total negation; that is to say, that some methods of work are so thoroughly bourgeois that they negate even the most heroic socialist content. His discussions concerning both the 'cult of Mao' (which Mao opposed) and the slogan 'All public, no self' (p. 50f) are extremely illuminating in this respect. Like Mao he argues against mechanical copying, pointing out that exemplary transformations demonstrate the application of theory to their particular

On Contradiction

conditions: 'You can travel 10,000 *li* looking for a magic method but you will never find it' (p. 60).

Chou's analysis of the GPCR has already been mentioned (quoted in Collier and Collier, 1973: 148f). He confirms that the 1962 Tenth Plenum call, 'Never forget class struggle . . .' was aimed at Liu and his followers, just as the earlier documents on agrarian transformation had been. He counterposes Liu's theory of productive forces (which he argues 'violates Marxism' (p. 62)) to the need to revolutionise all the relations of production, including 'the way people think and the rules they live under, their institutions and their culture' (ibid.). Significantly Liu and other Rightists often counter-attacked by enlarging the scope of Party directives thus ensuring that, since almost everyone would be 'guilty', the campaign would fail. This is similar to the 'mechanical' obedience attempted by some technicians and cadres at the time of the GLF. It is also clearly related to the petit-bourgeois fanaticism that often characterises the apparent opposite of Liuist opportunism and reformism: adventurist 'hitting out in all directions' and dogmatism.[8] Significantly both can only exist where there is some degree of domination exercised by cadres, technicians, and officials – where, in sum, people still have instincts of obedience, or what Mao calls 'the slave mentality'. Thus any socialist transformation cannot be the work of Party disciplinary committees, massive purges and so on. Any disciplining within the Party must be matched by its 'external disciplining' by attempting to diminish any false extension of the Party's power which should only *aid* (rather than *act* for or against) the majority of the people.

We have argued previously (*SCMT*, Chapters 5 and 6) that one major territory upon which old and new bourgeois can survive, and which they can use to make the most of remaining feelings of obedience and slavishness amongst the people, is the area of foreign policy including foreign trade. Through the monopoly agencies that control such trade (and the highly restricted mechanisms for making and declaring foreign policy) it is extremely easy to act in bourgeois and capitalist ways. The questions of what is best ('rational' and 'efficient') can be more easily answered in capitalist terms in what are *in fact* a series of *exchange relations* with the capitalist world market and bourgeois diplomacy. This is a fundamental problem which Chinese experience exposes but does not solve – although, clearly, methods of rotating personnel, involving workers (including dockers and transport workers) in decisions as to what to

122 *For Mao*

import and what to export, and so on, could be applied more generally.

This exposure – in the terrain apparently furthest from the struggle to transform nature and people within a socialist formation – leads back directly to its 'internal location': the State (and, to some extent, the Party). Clearly the Party, State and Army must be partly separated from the people – a specialised set of agencies – in order to defend them from external enemies. But that space (facilitating a correctly dictatorial preparedness *vis à vis* the world market) is also of great significance internally since it does separate State and Party (above all the Centre) *from* the people. Moreover, as Mao has always argued, and we have stressed this throughout, the specialised dictatorial powers of the working people must be available to them to hold back the implicit power (founded on assumptions of superiority/inferiority and habits of deference) of the old bourgeoisie.

Given this contradiction (which cannot be wished away by rhetorical flourish) a practical question then arises. How much real power has the Centre *over* the localities? This in turn relates to *how* any existing transformation *has been accomplished* – donated or achieved, passively or actively, what has been held as unchangeable and what changed? Where socialism has been accomplished through increasingly collective, more conscious, more egalitarian struggles it is more secure from simple commands from above. This, quite simply, is the crucial question for the next few decades in China (as it is also in the USSR and every socialist formation). If it is possible for any clique to seize power, cause China to change colour, *and sustain their rule* over some period of time then the establishment of socialism is a million times more difficult than even Mao (who speaks of several centuries being needed) imagined.

That said, and it is as well to be cautious and sober in these matters, we would still argue that the great body of knowledge available within historical materialism has been irreversibly propelled forward by events within China and by Mao's marxism. What such a terrible lesson would demonstrate would be the extent and depth of capitalist penetration (through competitive trade above all other weapons in its armoury) and the strength of its 'market forces' (to which, we are constantly told, we owe all that we are!). We do not believe that full capitalist restoration by external means, even with internal assistance, is probable; it has *not* taken place in the USSR as any simple inspection of the condition of

On Contradiction 123

working people's lives will demonstrate.

What the future holds is continuing struggle between two classes over two lines and two roads: a zigzag path of uneven but combined development toward more secure socialism – although with quite possibly extended setbacks and reverses, not least the possibility of a total holocaust such as nuclear war.

This can be prised out of the statistical accounts of China's transformation. It really resides in the internal accounts we have so often evoked or in the sensitive perception of visitors. It is there in the confident depiction of the Shanghai dockers in David Selbourne's brilliant *An Eye to China* (1975) and *their* last defiant slogan as he leaves:

INCREASES IN PRODUCTIVE FORCES, ON SUCH A SCALE, ARE BASED NOT ON RAISED INTENSITY OF LABOUR, BUT ON THE SEIZURE OF STATE-POWER, AND THE MASS TRANSFORMATION OF ALL RELATIONS IN PRODUCTION! (Selbourne, 1975: 211–12)[9]

3 THE INTERNATIONAL COMMUNIST MOVEMENT

As is well known there has been a more or less open polemic between the CPC and the CPSU since the death of Stalin.[10] We also know now that there were major disagreements between the two Communist Parties from the foundation of the CPC in 1921; more generally, and quite expectedly, the Comintern itself was the site of continuing and bitter class struggles.[11] Contrary to the majority of interpretations we do not see these as matters of personality, nor yet as abstracted power-struggles; both in the earlier period (particularly after the attempted Bolshevisation of the world socialist revolution) and in the later, the dispute turns upon the major themes presented in our book: What is production? How is it to be increased in a socialist way?

Mao's theories and practices of socialist construction implicitly challenge almost the complete canon of Bolshevik strategy, although – and this is far from a simple linguistic matter – he stays frequently in the same problematic in his writings. Since, however, that Bolshevism represents a magnificent extension of Marx's few brief suggestions regarding socialist construction, we can see that this (partial) transformation of Bolshevism, as theory and practice

124   *For Mao*

of social formations in transition, is a major resource for any socialist construction. This is not to declare China 'better' than the USSR, but points to how socialist construction was accomplished in the former, not least by learning the lessons of the latter.

If we were to summarise Mao's contribution to a theory of socialist construction we should have to emphasise, *inter alia*, (1) the stress upon the ubiquity of contradiction and therefore the range of class struggle within socialist formations; (2) the longevity of these struggles (several centuries); (3) the constant attention that has to be paid to how changes are achieved; and (4) the novel conceptualisation and practices of 'doing a good job of production' we illuminated in Part Two above.

Behind this, we have tried to compare the experiences of working women and men within socialist formations, rather than solely the activity of leaders and Parties. Strategic questions should include: Are achievements experienced as accomplished by working people themselves, or are they obeying orders and accepting gifts from 'outside'? Are the agencies of production solely production units – separated as 'enterprises' – or are they the site of coherent political and cultural struggles also? Do things (production techniques, for example) command people, or people command things? Which is dominant, the general line or a Plan – the latter's existence being no indicator of socialist construction as Bettelheim has argued for a decade?[12] We have tried to show how we might begin to answer these questions when examining and comparing different formations in this book and previously (*SCMT*).

In sum, socialist construction in China demonstrates the implications of a recognition of a mode of production as an ensemble of a social relations (the particular *set* of which endow the whole mode with its meanings as Marx demonstrates in the case of capitalism). Thus, as we have argued previously, capitalism should not be reduced to a form of property and a system of ownership. Where this reduction is attempted it neutralises (i.e. suggests as usable) a whole cluster of what are in fact *capitalist* techniques, theories, and more general assumptions. Moreover, such a reduction grounds a theory and practice which castigates as 'disruptive' or 'going against natural laws' any attempt to challenge and transform these capitalist techniques, theories and assumptions. Following Lenin's remarks on Marx's analysis of the commodity, we would emphasise how Marx throughout his writing stresses that capital 'is not a thing' *but a social relation*. Not to attempt a complete revolutionising of all

On Contradiction

relations, techniques and assumptions of capitalism (with which, to repeat, Marx and Lenin agreed, people are *stamped and marked* through and through) affords a territory for the still-existing capitalist world market relations to establish their partial control within any socialist formation.

Within the USSR (and this is an ever-present possibility in China) certain techniques (e.g. Taylorism), theories (e.g. the laws of world economy), and assumptions (e.g. regarding the capacities of different sorts of human being) were taken as resources to be used for socialist construction. This does not mean that working class women and men in the USSR are units of labour power (nor that surplus value making governs commodity production in the USSR). It means, crucially, that socialist construction has been slowed, deformed and crippled. It means, simply, that the Soviet people are less than they might be; that they have less because they are less. That they have accomplished much in comparison with the working class still exploited and oppressed by capitalism is a precise measure of the success and socialist nature of the Great October Socialist Revolution.

In comparing the two sets of historical experience we must draw attention to orientations toward production as crucial. In China, the major struggle has been to establish what 'doing a good job of production means'. This has not meant, for example, 'Bring in the harvest!', 'Procurement before production!', 'Accumulation before raising living standards!', 'Specialist capital goods before daily necessities!'. It has meant – or aimed at – a general attempt to increase production in such a way that living standards are raised, daily necessities are produced, and that the resulting increase in general well-being is *recognised* as the result of collective social activity. Instead of the pacification which can result from an imposed plan, there has been the engagement and involvement following from the general line. A common contrast made is between the Soviet *kolkhozi* (collectives) in the USSR and the People's Communes in China.[13]

Much of what we have been arguing can also be detected by examining the criticism of the CPC and of Mao provided from within the USSR, especially that given in the texts of what was once called 'Soviet sinology'[14] or now 'marxist sinology'.[15] What we find in this literature is an analysis which is remarkably similar to Kautsky's declarations of the 'impossibility' of socialist construction in 'backward' Russia using 'unmarxist Bolshevism'. The CPC

126 *For Mao*

(reduced often to simply the 'Mao gang') is said to be relying on 'petit-bourgeois' peasants, the productive forces are weak (and *thus* the working class is small), and utopianism has taken the place of materialism. More narrowly, the 'Maoist "model"' is said to be 'barrack-room communism' which does not allow for a better life for the working people, especially in the cultural sphere. In brief, China is perceived and categorised with the help of Bolshevism from which, as we have stressed, it is found to 'deviate'.

What is significant about the polemic in another dimension is illustrative of the limited break made by both Bolshevism and the 'Thought of Mao Tse-tung' from an analysis that does not penetrate beyond phenomena. Both the CPSU and the CPC are happy to cite phenomenal evidence against each other – including making use of bourgeois social science. This is most marked in the case of Mao and the CPC – anyone who could consider the USSR 'a fascist state of the Hitler type' has ceased (however briefly) to be a marxist. Abstracted 'national' power politics has taken the place of any form of historical materialism. This is significant for the whole polemic since the CPSU are able to demonstrate, accurately (the CPC have made no attempt to conceal this), how much service the CPC categorisation of the USSR as *Fascist*, more dangerous (more imperialist) than the USA, militaristic and so on, performs for the most consistently anti-socialist (anti-proletarian) writers, agencies, Parties within the capitalist countries. When the CPC hails the strengthening of Nato, the EEC, and Margaret Thatcher's speeches as 'bulwarks' against the USSR, they are not serving the people.

But this anti-Sovietism (behind which is as much a contempt for Soviet workers as the CPSU reveal toward the Chinese workers when they speak of how the 'Mao gang' has seized power) must not be used to destroy the accurate and internationally significant criticism of dogmatic marxism (which cripples socialist construction in advance) which the achievements of People's China provide. This is not only important in comparison with the experience of the USSR, but in contrast to many marxist criticisms of China (not least those of Trotskyists) who, knowingly or not, reproduce the Bolshevik criticisms of China made by the CPSU!

Fortunately there are some comparative sketches which usefully try to analyse the differences.[16] It has, after all, to be remembered that learning implies not simply pupils, but instructive examples. The fact that the Great October Socialist Revolution occurred

On Contradiction 127

when it did – and that the Comintern was there to shelter and aid the new Communist Parties – cannot be thought away. Neither must it be used, as do some marxists in their replication of the crudest bourgeois Kremlinology, to excuse all non-Soviet socialists and Parties from their many errors. What careful comparative accounts also bring out is the significant material – historical differences in the two socialist formations. But they also reveal, with great clarity – and this has been a major contribution of Jack Gray's work – that events in China have shown that if major *material* successes are to be made, the utmost attention must be paid to cultural and political questions. It is because Mao remains a practical materialist, as we argued in Part Two above, that he has so frequently emphasised the cultural and political, demonstrating – even if only implicitly, in policies rather than verbal percepts – his transcendence of any forces/relations dichtomics and base/superstructure metaphors. The detailed comparisons also indicate the uneven, contradictory, dialectical unity in the campaigns for socialist construction in China containing both gradual step-by-step *and* sudden going-all-out movements. The general contrast is drawn with the 'from above' qualities of much Soviet construction.

We have remarked above that Mao 'disobeyed' and 'argued with' Stalin from the late 1920s onwards. He has also written a number of texts specifically analysing Stalin's theory and practice. Apart from his contributions to various of the polemic documents concerning Stalin, Mao was responsible for the two long editorials in the *People's Daily* on 5 April and 29 December 1956.[17] From the start, Mao welcomes the self-criticism undertaken by the CPSU, admitting that Stalin made mistakes (which were and are to be expected, they were not exceptional) and using those mistakes as lessons for future policy. Mao also argues that on a number of far-from-insignificant issues Stalin 'fell victim to subjectivism and onesidedness, and divorced himself from objective reality and from the masses' (1956C: 9). But, it is equally important, argues Mao, to comprehend Stalin as a phenomenon of the International Communist Movement and, specifically, to see the cult of the individual as a reflection in people's minds of a social phenomenon. Above all Mao opposes one-dimensional explanations:

> Some naive ideas seem to suggest that contradictions no longer exist in socialist society. To deny the existence of contradictions is to deny dialectics. (p. 10).

128 *For Mao*

Mao opposes to Stalin's methods of leadership, the mass-line. As he had done in the 1930s, Mao also outlines two ways of studying and learning from the USSR – 'the Marxist way and the doctrinaire way' (p. 15). In the second part of the 1956 text, Tito's wrong method (but beyond it the wrong method of Khrushchev also) of criticising Stalin is itself criticised, along with the imperialist adventure in Hungary. Two different types of contradictions (the substance of the more famous text of 1957) are also outlined – those between ourselves and the enemy, and those amongst ourselves. Each requires appropriate methods of 'handling'; Stalin erred in confusing both types and in handling those amongst the Soviet Party and people in an entirely wrong way. But this text also accurately portrays the manner in which attacks on the 'doctrinaire' Stalin ('deStalinization') will be used to facilitate the utmost revisionism, leading eventually to major splits within the international Communist movement. But this abdication of marxism is practised, not least in his analysis of the USSR, by Mao himself.

In 1959, at the end of his own self-criticism at Lushan, Mao mentions two speeches on Stalin's *Economic Problems of Socialism in the USSR* (1952a) and adds:

> But these were only speeches. Now we must study it in depth, otherwise we cannot develop and consolidate our cause. (1959K: 146)

In the *Wansui* texts are Mao's *Remarks* on Stalin's text (November 1958) and his *Annotations* (1959).[18] Mao finds many of Stalin's analyses 'totally erroneous'. He thinks 'Stalin walks on one leg' – ignoring politics and the masses, and putting so much emphasis on heavy industry that he neglects light industry. Much of this critique is present in Mao's theory and practice in the Border Region years (analysed in section 1 of Part Two above) and clarified in his speech on 'Ten great relationships' in 1956. Mao recognises in Stalin's texts much that is 'excellent'; for example, Stalin's sketch (1952a: 68f) of the 'preliminary conditions' for the transition to Communism. But Mao argues that Stalin did not find the form for this and points to how the People's Communes provide the basis for the transition to a fully socialist formation in so far as they provide the means for three transitions: first, from collective property to property of the whole people; second, in their onslaught upon the 'three great differences';

On Contradiction 129

and, third, in making possible a fully unleashed class struggle.

In his *Annotations*, Mao takes issue with Stalin's mechanical determinism – particularly noteworthy is Mao's annotation against Stalin's claim that people really are powerless to influence astronomical, geological and other similar processes. Mao thinks this reasoning false since human capacity to know and transform nature is *without limit*.[19] Mao also argues that Stalin uses his mechanical determinism to thereby 'sanctify' and protect from criticism actions of State and Party. Both mechanical determinism in general, and its employment to protect Party and State policies, deny the fundamental argument of Mao (and of Marx) that the emancipation of working women and men must be their own accomplishment. Freedom cannot be donated.

Nevertheless Mao (as Chou En-lai and others within the CC/ CPC) recognises that Stalin did much to protect the material basis of socialism within the USSR and beyond, not least in his recognition of the international significance of keeping the USSR safe. They also recognise, however, that in the manner of his 'protection' Stalin did long-term damage to the *solidity* of socialism within the USSR, paving the way for the theses that suggest the end of class struggle within the Soviet Union which had now become 'the State of the Whole People'.

4 IMPLICATIONS FOR SOCIALIST CONSTRUCTION

We have argued here (and elsewhere)that historical materialism comprises both marxist theory and the historical experience of socialist construction. This shows that what we believe Marx to mean cannot be prescriptive as to the future (this implies the possibility of different readings of Marx). It also indicates that historical experience will extend and illuminate marxist theory.

A number of commentators have tried to draw the general implications of Mao's theory and practice for our general understanding of production. In so doing they transform our understanding not only of socialism but of capitalism and, *ipso facto*, return us to a new reading of Marx or Lenin, a new understanding of what had been thought of as closed questions. Our own understanding of Bolshevism has been aided by the contributions of the Chinese people to world revolution. Bettelheim catches the overall significance when he writes:

130   *For Mao*

In the combination productive forces/production relations, the latter play the dominant role by imposing the conditions under which the productive forces are reproduced. Conversely, the development of the productive forces never directly determines the transformation of the production relations, this transformation is always the focus of intervention by the contending classes – that is, of class struggle. (1973: 91–2)[20]

Both Bettelheim and P. Anderson (1974a: 204) have correctly taken this insight into the 'orthodox' marxist comprehension of the transition from feudalism to capitalism and *thus* – although this is as yet insufficiently realised – point to the *conditions* of capitalist reproduction. In Bettelheim's words

> history shows that changes in the material conditions of labour (the productive forces) are realized after changes in the social conditions of production (in the relations of production).
> . . .
> machine industry is developed within capitalist relations of production.
> . . .
> capitalist relations of production took shape before machine industry; the latter develops under the domination of capitalist relations of production, to form the specifically 'capitalist "mode of production" '. (1970a: 86, 87)

Hence our insistence that socialist[21] construction begins long before any convenient benchmark called 'The Revolution' (which is not to deny the concrete significance of the final expropriation of the bourgeoisie from state power). But what else does historical experience demonstrate?[22] First, methods of Party work before (and State formation after) that revolutionary seizure have to be such as to unleash the *existing* powers (including knowledge) of the existing working class women and men under capitalism. At the moment they produce wealth by producing specific commodities in particular ways. To do this they are encouraged/constrained to reproduce themselves, as a class. As Marx stressed:

> The maintenance and reproduction of the working class is, and must ever be, a necessary condition for the reproduction of capital . . . From a social point of view, therefore, the working

On Contradiction

class, even when not directly engaged in the labour-process, is just as much an appendage of capital as the ordinary instruments of labour. (1867a: 572, 573).

It is entirely to our point that Marx relates this to the constant skilling, de-skilling and reskilling of the working class *and*, moreover, that capitalists are forever reassuring 'the public' (i.e. creating public opinion) that machinery and capital are more important and creative than labour. Apart from supporting Mao's protracted argument (drawn out in several of Bettelheim's writings) that no production technique is 'neutral', Marx also argues that the 'spirit' and methods of capitalist agriculture are antithetical to a proper system of agrarian production (1865a: 616f).

But at the same time it creates the material conditions for a higher synthesis in the future, viz., the union of agriculture and industry on the basis of the more perfected forms they have each acquired during their temporary separation. (1867a: 505).

This 'creation of the material conditions' has to be related to that struggle between 'collective' and 'private' appropriation which Marx recognised to be present in the village commune (*obshchina*) in Tsarist Russia (Marx, 1877; 1881a, b). Moreover, just as Marx saw the bourgeois State sustaining private capital against socialist relations in *that* context, we have to remark again that the socialist potential within the working class *under capitalism* cannot be fully unleashed (indeed, in particular, it cannot be fully 'thought') until the bourgeois State has been *displaced*.

Another way of examining the implications of Mao's theory and practice is to consider his views on the Party during the protracted war to establish socialism in China. He fought, from the start – to the point where he was driven into 'opposition' – two deviations which he characterised as bourgeois opportunism (all unity and no struggle, reflecting a lack of strategic contempt for the whole capitalist system) and petit-bourgeois adventurism or fanaticism (all struggle and no unity, reflecting a lack of seriousness regarding the tactics toward each and every particular facet of capitalism). But he also offers – through the mass-line and his general political epistemology – an alternative to the model violently abstracted (and then reified) from such works as Lenin's *What is to be done?* Mao

132   *For Mao*

recognises the fundamental duality of those who appear the weakest and the most subordinated – yes, they are in part what they appear to be, and this is no delusion, it correctly reveals the profile of power relations. But, Mao also went beyond 'seeing in poverty nothing but poverty' and saw two important qualities of the working people which Party intellectuals ignore at their peril. First, the direct producers do in fact create the wealth of the social formation. Second, they and they alone are not only the 'material' forces without which it is impossible to pull down the old structures of power, they are also the 'spiritual' (and we should add 'technical') forces with which to construct a different kind of power, culture, and production.

Their duality, in short, represents a different set of social relations within which things and people would be endowed with a different meaning. Things, quite literally, would be different. If it is, as Bettelheim and others have noted, social relations that endow the methods and tools of production with meaning, it should be clear that no particular trust can be put in any socialist revolution which claims to be using existing *capitalist* things (and techniques) to construct socialism. If things (objective reality, circumstances) are being used it must be thought that it is people that must be changed. This is true, but the only changing that is fully revolutionary is that accomplished by people themselves in their own efforts to change the circumstances that have oppressed, exploited and limited them. Different kinds of texts by Mao – from the 1920s to the 1970s – signify this in importantly different ways. First, Mao argues that social relations (especially what we might call the 'status-profile' regarding ideas and techniques) have to be transformed through new forms of social organisation. Second, this will be deformed, if not diverted, by a wrong cadre policy; where, in brief, the Party reinforces existing assumptions and habits regarding the 'natural' superiority of intellectuals and experts. Third, in the overall co-ordination of production the 'system of amplification' has to be reversed: it is the Centre that has to be *bombarded* with reports, data, and returning 'planners', who have been to the localities and conducted investigations.

But Mao does not thereby imply that working women and men already have 'ready-made' socialist panaceas and blueprints which they long to implement but fear the local capitalist, policeman or similar representative of bourgeois authority. Just as the Party cannot use (capitalist) things to cajole and coerce working people

On Contradiction

into socialism, so, equally, there are no 'neutral' sets of ideas (concerning 'rationality' or 'efficiency') which can be brought to working people from outside. There are different texts – but again stretching through his writings – which point to the difficulty of transforming people. Nevertheless, Mao has always argued that 'All wisdom comes from the masses . . . it is intellectuals who are most ignorant' (1957K: 468). He has also urged the widest criticism (indeed he has not infrequently used *enlarged* Plenums and work conferences to overwhelm those working for the capitalist road):

> Why be afraid of our own people when we are not afraid of the imperialists? He is no true communist who fears the common people and believes the masses are not open to reason and must be coerced rather than convinced. (1957I: 477; cf. 1956C; 1957B)

How, then, does Mao argue that it is right to rely on the people and yet remark (as firmly as Marx or Lenin) how capitalism, feudalism and imperialism 'stamp' and 'mark' those who live within their relations? Partly, democratic centralism practised through the mass-line is crucial; partly, however, Mao is fundamentally a materialist. He recognised, as against the then orthodoxy (and, of course, thousands of years of 'the Obvious'), that the Peasant Associations of Hunan in the 1920s had been driven to make – or at least begin – a fundamentally socialist revolution. For the poor and many middle peasants (just as much as for the individual worker in a factory) can only survive through co-operation, through pooling their collective labour and sharing their joint product. Within factories the collective nature of production is *lived* (and hopelessly disrupted under capitalism). What Mao has shown here – and Jack Gray has demonstrated empirically the reality with regard to agrarian transformation (Gray, 1970; 1972a, b) – is the importance of the Party (1) to hold back and 'neutralise' the long-standing power of the Old Guard (landlords, capitalists, rich peasants, managerial and technical workers); (2) to systematise and generalise the ideas and innovations made by working people. The investigative texts – starting with those in Hunan – above all those of the *Socialist Upsurge* commentaries – have 'shattered many illusions and erroneous views' (1955H: 216; cf. 1955F, G, J, K).

It is commonly argued that socialism is prefigured at the point of production in capitalist societies. This is true, but dangerously

134 For Mao

partial. First, it reduces 'production' to the workplace (and ignores the totality of social relations which sustain and make possible those 'workplace arrangements'). Second, it ignores the individuation and sectionalism that results from such phenomenal forms of the social and technical division of labour as wage and payment systems, skill differentiation and the enduring significance (within the place of work) of those extra-economic realities (sex, skin-colour, religion, and nationality) which cannot be thought away. A similar duality exists, of course, within the defensive organisations of the working class such as the trades unions. Socialism is prefigured in the total instability of the whole ensemble of capitalist social relations. In myriad ways working class women and men live alternatives to the very social forms they are compelled to inhabit. This is their dual nature, this explains the sudden explosions of action and language. Each worker (and all the working class are workers) bears some image (however frail) of an alternative to the present. This knowledge of the fundamentally limited nature of human life (for all) within capitalism does not have to be brought from 'outside' (thus reinforcing the profile of normal bourgeois relations!) but has to be celebrated and broadcast, and shown to be fundamentally correct. This is what a 'mass-line' strategy amounted to within China – a clear distinction (above all in the methods of work) between the Communist Party and *les autres*: Them, the bosses and the officials (of all kinds), who are not Us. The first myth to be destroyed is the assumption that working women and men do not have contempt – of the deepest and most strategic kind – for the 'world as it is', although, to be sure, many people will feel that this is 'their' personal problem (resulting from their 'being different'). The majority not only realise that they could be more than they are, they sense how this might be possible through some kind of collective action. Indeed, many could begin to specify (to those who are willing to learn rather than preach or command) exactly how and where changes could begin. Capitalism beheads the working class, aiming ultimately at a form of automaton – naked labour-power. Socialist construction begins by giving the working class its head.

5 POSTSCRIPT, 1977

It is now over a year since Mao Tse-tung died. We have deliberately chosen to provide a *presentational* account of Mao's work. This is in

On Contradiction 135

marked contrast to existing alternatives and this book differs from SCMT where we frequently took issue with prevailing interpretations of Bolshevism. We have differed in this book because of the general ignorance of Mao's work as a theorist. Indeed extended attention is mainly found in institutions *defined* (and this is very much to the point) by their geographical, cultural or linguistic specialisation. For some years to come the main task will remain that of presenting the historical experience of China (and Albania,[23] for that too is often neglected) for discussion.

But it would be wrong to conclude a text which will appear in 1979 without some reference to events that have taken place since September 1976. These events have made the general strategy we have drawn from Mao's work all the clearer. We can now contrast the general line for socialist construction we have sketched here and in *SCMT*, not only against prior alternatives – notably that of Bolshevism – but against subsequent reassertions, whether the attempt, through the Jackson Amendment, to draw Soviet labour into capitalist production, or recent changes that have been *attempted* in China.

In what follows we shall not be providing a history of the group now known as the 'Gang of Four',[24] nor an account of events and changes since September 1976. Instead we wish to illustrate the implications of what has taken place for our own analysis, through examining some key texts. What they direct attention to is the consequences of the *implicit* nature of Mao's critique of Bolshevism for socialist construction and the possibility of using Mao's teaching in such a way that its content is obscured or even negated. We think that charge can be just as much directed against Chiang Ching, Chang Chun-chiao, Yao Wen-yuan and Wang Hung-wen, as against Teng Hsiao-ping.

It is worth beginning by stressing the continuities from the mid-1960s. What is now spoken of as 'Chairman Mao's theory of the differentiation of the three worlds'[25] is still seen as the basis for China's foreign policy. This leads, as it always has done, to HSINHUA agency reporting UPI and AP press releases about hostility to Leonid Brezhnev when the General Secretary of the CPSU visits a capitalist country (in contrast, no doubt, to the CPC's warm welcome for Margaret Thatcher in Peking) or concerning Soviet reconnaissance aircraft observing US destroyers.[26] But such an analysis – which sees the Soviet Union as a super-power analogous to, but far more imperialist and militarist than, the

136   *For Mao*

United States of America – also facilitates a crucial 'blindness' in what is seen as 'wrong' with Soviet policy. Thus, a recent HSINHUA[27] carries a report on how the weakness of the USSR is revealed in its 'steeply increasing . . . trade with the west (including Japan) and [its] seeking enormous credits to finance the import of sophisticated equipment . . ..' Such a description could well be applied to one facet of 'Teng-ism'.

This last is more than the nonetheless general point that both sides in the CPSU/CPC polemic continue to remain at the level of phenomenal evidence. We have already indicated our belief that external relations (foreign trade as much as diplomacy) provides a set of 'spaces' within which those who seek to sustain capitalist trading relations and bourgeois-nationalist diplomacy have the greatest security. This, as we shall outline below, was indeed one area of contrast between the views of the two differing tendencies in the CPC. Events since late 1976 have shown a consistent pattern: territory obtained in these 'spaces' has been used to turn back or disrupt a number of the defining strands of socialist construction as we have presented it above.

Moving smartly to a foreign trade policy that concentrates upon *modernisation* (in contrast to socialist construction) has meant, by November 1977, the use of explicit managerialism and material incentives as a matter of policy,[28] and – the most fundamental of the reversals thus far – what is blandly called a 'new college enrolment system' which in fact favours bourgeois forms of education and thus the reproduction of the Three Great Differences.[29] Much of this has been accompanied by the reinterpretation of texts from Mao's writings and accomplished through the attack on the 'Gang of Four' whose methods had the cumulative effect of 'draining the pond to catch the fish'. But, again, we should make it clear that Mao's words were and are there to be used in support of a technicisation and, in our terms, Bolshevisation of socialism in China. Similarly, although Chou En-lai is credited with issuing the call for 'four modernizations' – of science, defence, agriculture and industry – we should note that the term occurs at the close to the 'Foreword' to that 'Maoist' text *Quotations from Chairman Mao Tse-tung*. There – and the text is dated 16 December 1966 – Lin Piao urges

> strive to build our country into a great socialist state with modern agriculture, modern industry, modern science and culture and modern defence!

On Contradiction

137

There have been a number of key additional phrases linked to the campaign for 'socialist modernization' which have deep roots within the CPC's theory and practice. These include, 'Grasp the key link and *run the country well*', and the recasting of the General Line as

> upholding the principle of grasping revolution and promoting production and *fulfilling production tasks* with greater faster better and more economical results. (*People's Daily*, 1 April 1977; our emphasis)[30]

The same day's *Peking Review* ((14), 1977) contains several major texts illustrative of the same tendency – especially Chung Chin's notes on Mao's 'Ten great relationships' which makes maximal use of the linguistic terms and conceptual separations carried on from Bolshevism in Mao's writing. The same issue contains an article on the 'Gang of Four' by Wang Che in favour of 'rational rules and regulations' (it is cruelly ironic that this issue publishes Mao's 'Note on the "Charter of Anshan Iron and Steel Company"'!). The text by Wang Che makes use of Lenin's praise of Taylorism – a text which we have argued (*SCMT*: Chapter 2 and 3) is central to the Bolshevik social problematic. Wang Che argues that opposition to rules and regulations is anarchism.

Another plank in the reversal of the General Line associated with Mao has been a steady attack on *opposition* to the 'theory of productive forces'[31] and an insistence that certain forms of mechanisation *have to* precede co-operation, that – in some sectors – heavy industry *must* be put first.[32] It is quite wrong to see this as even and unanimous – we know very little, as yet, about the consequences for the life experiences of workers and peasants within China. Moreover, in such major texts as the State Planning Commission's 'Great guiding principle for socialist construction',[33] it is still possible to find (in vocabulary and implications for practice) a clear adherence to the socialist construction we discussed in Part Two of our book. But the general tendency is clearly evident across the range of policies which cumulatively *are* socialist construction – not least, of course, in views on agriculture.[34]

All of these policies have their roots in a set of remarkably coherent documents authored wholly or in part by Teng Hsiao-ping: 'On the General Programme for All Work of the Whole Party and the Whole Country' (hereafter: *General Programme*), 'Some

138   *For Mao*

problems in accelerating development' (hereafter: *Twenty Points*)
and 'The Outline Report on Science and Technology' (hereafter:
Outline Report). The full texts of these are given in the semi-official
account by Chi Hsin (1977: Appendices, 203f). We have at least one
instance of a substantial critique (of the *General Programme*) by the
'Gang of Four' in *Red Flag* (7, 1976) and *People's Daily*, 23 August
1976.[35] Not only do we consider the documents important, they are
clearly thought of as in some sense 'public knowledge' and a number
of articles have been published defending the texts against the
criticism of the 'Gang of Four' (and others?)[36]

Having read the texts by Teng (dating, it seems, from mid- to
late-1975), the critique given of them by the 'Gang of Four' (dating
from mid- to late-1976), and the 'defences' given recently (mid- to
late-1977) it seems clear to us that Teng's texts are a fundamental
revision of the General Line for socialist construction argued for by
Mao *and also* articulate the theoretical core of the set of practices
that have been applied since early 1977. They are in many ways
Bolshevik texts which, often using the same vocabulary, call to mind
the texts against which Mao had to argue in his long struggle from
1949 to the mid-1950s and from the so-called 'failure' of the GLF
onwards. They are also texts of an offensive character – they clearly
orient themselves to criticising and defeating positions we can now
identify with the 'Gang of Four'.

The 'Gang of Four' called these three texts 'three poisonous
weeds' and saw them as likely to lead to a restoration of capitalism.
We would agree with this judgement so long as it is understood, as
we have argued at length in *SCMT*, that this restoration is a far from
simple procedure. This programme of restoration is clearest of all in
the *Twenty Points* – especially when it is read with its 'defence'
(*Peking Review* (42), 1977) which makes maximal use of Bolshevik
formulations. Some of the *Twenty Points* are: enterprise manage-
ments to ensure profits are put first; the adoption of advanced
technology (including, crucially, the centralisation of scientific and
technological research) through increased importation of foreign
technologies; and the strengthening of discipline. In a talk Teng
gave on 18 August 1975 (Chi Hsin, 1977: 273f) he clearly sees
'modernization' and 'development' as flowing from factories and
towns outwards and agriculture reduced to a source of food for the
cities. He also suggests using the international and social division of
labour and argues (again) for 'the necessity of a strict system of rules
and regulations'.

On Contradiction 139

The *Outline Report* argues for increasing the separation of scientific and technological research and for the separation of technicians and scientists as different from 'ordinary workers', relegating the mass movement (for the true socialisation of scientific knowledge and technical ability) to that of *popularising* science. This is, of course, very much what has taken place with the new educational policy. It is also clearly articulated in the critique of the 'Gang of Four' made by the Academy of Sciences of China, which defends elitism in scientific and technological research and education and argues against scientists and technologists having to 'go down' and learn from and study with collective production workers. It also reveals that this separation (as one feature of the 'three great differences') had been one of the major elements attacked in the continuing GPCR through the 1970s.

There are many other areas which we could use to illustrate these general points – in the area of cultural production, for example, the revival of the hagiographic opera *The East is Red*, on the one hand, and the importation of bourgeois melodrama films, on the other,[37] are pertinent, as is the increase in package tours.[38] These and other matters can be discovered in press accounts from China and outside.

What has taken place in the last year or so is the shift in the line from a socialist construction strategy which saw class struggle (and the simultaneous changing of circumstances and selves) as the key force for increasing production, to a line which emphasises two related kinds of force. Simultaneous with the rise of the power of expertise we have seen an increasing tendency to argue that machines are more important than people. Taken together these are two key constituents of Bolshevism which also argued that the Soviet State was powerful enough to make use of bourgeois methods, experts and to engage in extensive foreign trade. We do not intend by these remarks to suggest that we are seeing some straightforward Bolshevisation of the People's Republic. Apart from any other limitations on this, the capitalist world in 1977 is not that of 1917, and, most important, there is a dominant socialist Bolshevik power in existence which continues to offer revolutionary aid and assistance to the proletariat.

The significance of recent events in China for socialist construction *within China* is still undecided. Our own analysis would suggest that there is still an extensive struggle between two classes over two lines and two roads being fought out. That struggle will continue until socialism is secured throughout the world and it will

140 *For Mao*

involve major setbacks. In a much more limited sense, we have tried in this brief 'Postscript' to indicate the implications of recent events for *our* analysis of socialist construction, as drawn from the work of Mao and the practice of the CPC over the last fifty years. We think that events and statements since Mao's death – and it is as well to remark here that 1976 also saw the death of Kang Sheng, Chu Teh, and Chou En-lai – have done much to illumine precisely what is of international significance in Mao's marxism and to refute absolutely all those who saw in his work a set of local and largely pragmatic aphorisms. This is not a welcome illustration of Mao's strength, but no negative lessons are ever really welcome.

We have argued previously (*SCMT*: Chapters 5 and 6) that 'Friends of China' are often no true friends of socialist construction. Those who have continued to repeat the latest official line from China, including major reinterpretations of previous history which are only now gathering strength,[39] are performing a major disservice to Mao. Now, far more than when we started to write, it is necessary to argue clearly and consistently *for Mao*.[40]

Notes

PART ONE: MAO AS A MARXIST

1. This Part draws on: Snow, 1937/1961; 1970; 1973; Ch'en, 1965, Schram, 1967a; and Han Suyin 1972; 1976. There have, of course, been thousands of texts on this or that aspect of CPC theory and practice which draw upon Mao's work in a more or less useful manner. Certain of this work has been outstanding, for example: the detailed studies of Jan Myrdal and Jack Gray or the wider ranging work of Macciocchi. Our debt to the studies of Charles Bettelheim, already mentioned in *SCMT*, is acknowledged again here. For one assessment of recent texts by Mao, see Stavis, 1976. We shall deal with Soviet and Trotskyist assessments of Mao in Part Three of our book.

2. Our citation method involves consulting the Bibliography, for fuller details of works cited. The text used – here Marx's *Eighteenth Brumaire* – is identified by date and page(s) after the author's name.

3. Rossanda's text was first published in *Il Manifesto*, July–Aug. 1970, then translated in *Temps modernes*, Dec. 1970/Jan. 1971, thence to *Socialist Register*, 1971. Compare three texts (1971, 1974 and 1976) but note some significant criticisms in Bettelheim (1971b). Rossanda, in general, reifies 'Stalinism' ignoring what Bettelheim *now* sees as the 'Bolshevik ideological formation' (1977: 15f).

4. Since Althusser goes on to speak of 'a silent critique' and because it has been claimed that the critique mentioned by Althusser 'remained so implicit as not to have come to the attention of the Chinese Communist Party [sic], which is under the illusion that it is loyal to Stalin's memory' (Callinicos, 1976: 93); it is as well *now*, in advance of detailed examination in Part Three, to refer the reader to Chapter 4 of *SCMT* and to published texts available in English and French translation for many years which *are* critical of Stalin. First the explicit texts: Mao, 1956C (provenance from Snow, 1961: 521, 1970: 331; Mao, 1956D) translated in 1959 and many of the texts of the CPSU/CPC polemic, notably: *On the question of Stalin* (translated in 1963). Implicit texts are legion: Mao, 1943F (parts of this were available in English in the 1940s – see Gelder, 1946) and Mao, 1936D, can be properly seen as antecedents of his more famous 1950s texts, e.g. 1955F, 1956D, and, above all, 1957B. More recently we have had available explicit texts: 1956F: 87, 1958H: 96–103, 1958M, 1964T and many other *Wansui* texts. Prime amongst all these, however, must be Mao's *Fifteen theses on socialist construction* (1964R) available in English since 1964. Every single one of these texts was available to Callinicos when he made the above statement (which is a theme returned to in his book, e.g. 1976: 94, 108, 125). Relatedly, Rossanda does not – in contrast to Bettelheim (1977:

141

142   *Notes to pages 7–15*

15f) – see CPC theory and practice as a *critique of Bolshevism*. This is true also of the otherwise significant collection of texts: *The Politics of Revolutionary China*, issued by the British and Irish Communist Organisation in 1977. We applaud their critique of the cult of Lenin, their recognition of the importance (i.e. benefit) of Stalin to the International Communist Movement and urge close study of their texts. Their Bolshevism, however, remains unreconstructed because it remains unrecognised.

5. On 'forcible abstraction' see Sayer, 1975a, b; 1977b. We refer here to Mao 1937H, J, often considered to be part of a larger work *On Dialectical Materialism* (1937B). On this see: (i) the discussion in Wittfogel, 1963; Holubnychni, 1964; Doolin and Golas 1964; Rue, 1967; Schram, 1967b; (ii) the texts with Wittfogel (1963: 270–7) and in Schram, 1969: 180–90; (iii) Althusser, 1963; Nicolaus, 1973; 13f; Norman, 1976; Sayers, 1976.
   We suggest the best course here (as so often) is to read all four philosophical texts of Mao (those in the *Four Essays*) 1937H, J; 1957B; 1963A.

6. Note especially, in his philosophical works, how Lenin sees the 'leaps' in matter/consciousness as central and compare the recent discovery of critical exponents common to all matter *qua* matter (e.g. Wilson's work in *Physical Review Letters*, 37, 1976). On Lenin's philosophy: see Pannekoek, 1938; Althusser, 1968; 1969; 1975; Lowy, 1976.
   The recent debate about both 'Dialectics of Nature' and materialism is marred by a failure to comprehend the social message of the former, and the core of the latter, as *practical theory* not abstracted formulae or invariant empirical process ('read off' as dogma). See Hodges, 1965; Timpanaro, 1966; Soper, 1976; Hoffman, 1977; Gunn, 1977; Weiss, 1977. Earlier work by Hodges (1962, 1963, 1964) and that of Sève (e.g. 1968) is relevant to some facets of his debate.

7. Lenin continues: 'He who speaks about politics, democracy and freedom, about equality, about socialism *without posing* these questions, without giving them priority, who does not fight against hushing them up, concealing and blunting them, is the worst enemy of the working people . . . the rabid opponent of the workers and peasants, a lackey of the landowner, the tsars and the capitalists'. He also demonstrates the political definition and class content of this 'freedom' in his repeated calls, to the People's Commissariat of Justice, for *show trials* (Lenin: *On the Soviet State Apparatus*, p. 344; *Collected Works*, Vol. 45: 368), for the closure of newspapers and the deportation of writers and professors (ibid., 555) and – in an instruction to Stalin – for the punishment of anti-Soviet doctors (ibid., 559).

8. We are thinking here of the following assembled texts: *Selected essays on the study of philosophy by workers, peasants and soldiers* (P, FLP, 1971); *Serving the people with dialectics* (P, FLP, 1972) or *Philosophy is no mystery: peasants put their study to work* (P, FLP, 1972). But the same significance may be read from studies of Tachai brigade or Chiliying commune (see Wen and Liang, 1977; Chu and Tien, 1974, respectively). The absolute strategic significance of these questions is set out in the CPC/CC Party School's Revolutionary Mass Criticism Writing Group's *Three major struggles on China's philosophical front (1949–1964)* (P, FLP, 1973). For two different assessments of 'philosophy in China', contrast Sayers, 1975 and Ree, 1976.

9. (Lenin, 1916b: 30). In his 1895 notes on *The Holy Family*, Lenin also argued that (i) 'Marx here advances from Hegelian philosophy to socialism: the

Notes to pages 16–26   143

transition is clearly observable . . .' (ibid., p. 24); (ii) here 'Marx's view – already almost fully developed – concerning the revolutionary role of the proleteriat' is displayed (ibid., p. 26); and (iii) the critique of Proudhon 'shows how Marx approached the basic idea of his entire "system" . . . namely the concept of the social relations of production' (ibid., 30).

10. We refer to that materialist who still awaits critical attention: Wittgenstein. In his 'Grundrisse', *The Blue and Brown books*, for his 'Capital', *The Philosophical Investigations*, Wittgenstein, like Marx, warns us against a number of bewitchments; pervasively he warns of false abstraction and 'our craving for generality'. This is

> The tendency to look for something in common to all the entities which we commonly subsume under a general term – we are inclined to think there must be something in common to all games, say, . . . The idea of a general concept being a common property of all its particular instances connects up with other primitive, too simple, ideas of the structure of language. It is comparable to the idea that *properties* are *ingredients* of the things which have the properties; e.g. that beauty is an ingredient of all beautiful things as alcohol is of beer and wine, and that we therefore could have pure beauty unadulterated by anything that is beautiful. (1969a: 17; cf. 1969b, *passim*)

He later calls this 'craving', 'contempt for the particular' a term Mao would readily appreciate.

11. Lenin argued that 'with Marx the dialectics of bourgeois society is only a particular case of dialectics' ('On the question of dialectics', 1916b: 361), which centred upon the identity of opposites and that 'the individual is the universal' 'Every individual is (in one way or another) a universal. Every universal is (a fragment, or an aspect, or the essence of) an individual' (ibid.).

12. Mao captures both points brilliantly in 'On Practice' where he writes: 'Marxist philosophy . . . has two outstanding characteristics. One is its class nature . . . The other is its practicality . . .' (1937H: 297). Theory generalises the historical experience of the class struggle – in production, in political and cultural relations and in scientific experiment and artistic creation – its validity cannot be generalized to all classes, it remains *unacceptable* to the bourgeoisie.

13. See Mao, 1944B, C; 1949J, K; 1953E, F, J; 1955F–K; 1958H; 1959–N; 1962B; 1964T; 1966S, T; 1969A; 1971A, plus all the texts in *On Literature and Art* (cf. Li Chien, 1973, who emphasises the crucial political importance of the early texts) and Chou En-lai's speech on Liu Shao-chi (quoted in Collier and Collier, 1973: 148f) and his 'Political report' to the 10th Congress of the CPC see J. Harrison, 1972; Houn, 1973; Whyte, 1973; Oksenberg, 1973a, 1974; and Schram, 1973b. For varying Trotskyist analyses of Mao's political theory, contrast Lee, 1972; Cliff, 1957 (cf. Harrington, 1958); 1968 and *International Socialism* (78), 1975; plus G. Benton in INPRECOR (46) and (50), 1976. The document they frequently cite – *Whither China?* – is partly translated in Gittings, 1973: Text 32.

14. This 'getting close' is, of course, a facet of the contradictory relation between Centre and locality addressed in much of Mao's work (e.g. 1956C, D; 1957B). Mao's most dramatic wagers on 'the locality' occur during the High Tide era

144   *Notes to pages 27–32*

and during the GPCR. But even during his supposed 'defeat' (cf. Mao, 1959K: 143f) he wrote to production brigade leaders:

> You should ignore them ['instructions issued by the higher levels'], and pay attention only to the realistic possibilities. (1959P: 7)

> Compared with the high key sung by everybody at the moment, what I have said is certainly at a low key. My aim is truly to mobilize our enthusiasm in order to increase production. If the reality lies at a higher key and loftier goals are to be attained, I shall be grateful for that and feel extremely honoured. (Ibid., 9)

15. To 'go down' means to engage in collective productive labour. A similar analysis can be made for Mao's views on the Army's internal relations and on Army–People relations. See his two letters to Lin Piao (1930A, 1966H), Mao's *Selected military writings* and Mao 1950E, F, G; 1951C; 1953A; 1958F, M; 1959O; 1964M; 1967C. Cf. Gittings, 1967: especially Ch. 9. See also Smedley, 1938, 1956; *New Left Review* (65) 1971 contains a full version of Mao, 1930A, set in context by Bill Jenner.

16. Quoted in the Political Report, 9th Congress CPC 1969. The Great Proletarian Cultural Revolution continues – as do two-line struggles – so any final estimation would be premature. Apart from Section 3 of Part Two of our book, see many of the essays in Schram, 1973c (especially that by Jack Gray), Bettelheim, 1973, and Han Suyin, 1976, as preliminary accounts of the GPCR. A most valuable *Chronology* was issued by the Press Group of the Society for Anglo-Chinese Understanding, whose library is a useful resource for GPCR pamphlets. There is much to be gained from studying the reports from particular villages, for example Myrdal, 1963, 1970; Jack Chen, 1973 (cf. his 1975); Hinton, 1966, 1970a – based on his fieldwork of 1947–50 – cf. his 1969 and 1970b comments. Macciocchi's book (1971) is important for its contents and the reaction it aroused.

17. Cf. Miliband, 1977: 62f, an instance of special pleading? Apart from George Thomson (1974; cf. his 1947) there has been almost no study of Mao's cultural writings. We think his collection *On Literature and Art* (P, FLP, 1st edn, 1960; 3rd edn, 1967) should be compared with the collections of Marx and Engels (M, Progress, 1976) and of Lenin (M, Progress, 1967) of the same title. Mao's own poems (and calligraphy) also deserve study. See, for example, his two 1965 poems 'Chingkangshan revisited' and 'Two birds: a dialogue' (published *Shikan*, January 1976; translated *Peking Review* (1) 2 Jan 1976: 5–6). See the related editorials 'Nothing is hard in this world if you dare to scale the heights' (ibid., pp. 8–10) and the commentary by Yuan Shui-po (1976).

There is insufficient space here to trace through the many debates about *different* cultural forms – the opera, or painting, or Mao's own commentaries upon Lu Hsun. In each case the general contours conform to the pattern we have indicated in our text: avoiding the slavish reproduction of 'art' (whose greatness was defined within the social relations of capitalism, imperialism, or feudalism); eschewing 'blind faith' in things foreign; attempting to challenge the division of audience and performer so central to bourgeois culture; and fighting the dead hand of dogma and formulae.

Notes to pages 36–43 145

18. This text has been available in English since 1946, when Gelder, a reporter for the London *News Chronicle*, included it in his book *The Chinese Communists*. The best detailed study of the Border Region remains that of Snow (1941).

19. Three interviews with Chou En-lai are highly relevant here. The first two, with N. Maxwell, were published in *Sunday Times* 5 and 19 December 1971; the third, with F. Greene, ibid., 30 April 1972. These (and others, see Snow, 1971, 1973) enable some interesting insights into the GPCR to be made. Note, first, however: 'For any country to attain independence the first thing is to achieve self-sufficiency in agriculture – to have enough to eat, which is the first requisite' (*Sunday Times*, 19 December 1971: 8). Apart from the work of Jack Gray, see the two texts on how China solved its food problem in *Peking Review*, (45), 1973, and *China Reconstructs*, 24(1), 1975. As the editorial in *People's Daily* (24 February 1976) explains, 'It is by implementing Chairman Mao's great teaching "Never forget classes and class struggle" that China has reaped rich harvests 14 years running'. Chou En-lai extends this when he argues: 'Classes must be abolished. A scientific socialist guiding thought is needed to attain this goal. Once this thought is grasped by the masses, spiritual force will turn into material force; and they will transform the objective world, and at the same time, their own subjective world' (*Sunday Times*, 30 April 1972). On Chou En-lai, see Davison and Selden (1977) for an outline biography. The same source has four very useful extended interviews with Chou En-lai conducted largely by William Hinton. We return to them in Part Three below.

20. Plus several relevant texts in the fifth volume of Mao's *Selected Works*.

21. In this text (1956D: 304) Mao acknowledges that he wrote the editorials we know as *On the Historical Experience . . .* (1956C; available in English since 1959) which were critical of Stalin and 'deStalinization'.

22. In 1962 Mao noted 'I have paid rather more attention to problems relating to the system, to the productive relationships. As for the productive forces, I know very little' (1962B: 176). At Lushan, he admitted 'I am a complete outsider when it comes to economic construction, and I understand nothing about industrial planning' (1959K: 142).

23. The Red Flag Canal was built through the Taihang Mountains of Honan province in the ten years from 1960 onwards by the Linshien people. It entailed cutting across 1,250 rocky peaks, drilling 134 tunnels and building 150 aqueducts. The best account is given in two issues of *Peking Review* (48–49), 1972. Cf. 'A Commune along the Red Flag Canal', *China Reconstructs*, 23(8), 1974, and Han Suyin, 1976: 129. The best generalisation of this is available in Keith Buchanan's admirable *The Transformation of the Chinese Earth* (1970).

24. On the provenance of this text, see the editorial notes.

25. Lenin's speech, to the Plenum of the Moscow Soviet, was published in *Pravda*, 21 November 1922. We have detailed (in *SCMT*: Chapters 2 and 3) Lenin's long struggle to transform the 'old machinery' he refers to in this speech.

26. These remarks were published in *Pravda*, 30 May 1923.

27. See Mao, 1959K: 134 and editorial note 8 to that text.

28. *SCMT*: Ch. 6; Corrigan, 1974, 1976b; Corrigan and Sayer, 1975.

29. See Sayer, 1977b; *SCMT*: Ch. 1.

30. This is admirably explicated by Draper, 1971 (a section of his multi-volume work, 1977). Cf. Rossanda, 1970: 72f.

146   *Notes to pages 44–46*

31. Mao told Edgar Snow that he wished to be remembered mainly as a teacher (Snow, 1973: 169).
32. The Three Great Differences (first sketched by Marx and Engels, 1846a: Part One) are between mental and manual labour; between town and country; and, between large-scale (industrial) and small-scale (agrarian) production. Of the three pairs, the first dominates the second; of them all the first is definitive. They are not, however, dichotomies but contradictions; a point which Mao has stressed at some length.

PART TWO: ON PRACTICE: FOUR STUDIES

I THE BORDER REGION YEARS

1. Snow 1937/1961; Smedley, 1938, 1956; Belden, 1949; and Hinton, 1966, 1970a. Cf. Gelder, 1946; Stein, 1945. Much of the work of J. Myrdal and J. Gray, in their different ways, draws contrasts with this earlier period.
2. For general background sketches on the period before 1935 contrast Mao's work (1926A, 1927A, 1928A, 1933B, 1935A, 1938F, and especially 1939M *and* 1944B, C) with Moore, 1966: Ch. 4; Wolf, 1969: Ch. 3; and Chesneaux, 1973: Chapters 1–6. More detailed studies of 'modernisers' are Cohen, 1973; Price, 1974; and Treadgold, 1973: Vol. 2 (the two latter emphasise non-marxist Russian influence). On the debate over China's social history, see Schwartz, 1954; Krymov, 1971 (an excellent review of the literature) and Treadgold, 1973: Vol. 2, Ch. 6. For general biographical information, apart from material already cited, see Han Suyin, 1972; Schram, 1967a: Chapters 6–7; Rue, 1966; Hofheinz, 1969; Harrison, 1972; and Houn, 1973. Yakhontoff (1934; cf. Mao, 1933A; 1934B, C) studies the pre-1934 Soviets; Ho Chi-minh (1928; cf. Mao, 1927A) surveys work with peasants; Meisner (1967) and Bianco (1971) trace the construction of the Communist Party. Treadgold (1973: 163) quotes a letter from Kuo Mojo in 1924 which conveys something of how marxism was felt as liberating: 'We have been born in a most meaningful age, the age of a great revolution in human cultural history! I have become a thorough-going believer in Marxism. For this age in which we live Marxism provides the only solution. Matter is the mother of spirit'.
3. The Long March started in October 1934 from the Kiangsi Soviet ending up in northern Shensi. The journey took 368 days, 235 of them in day marches and 18 in night marches; apart from some 56 days in the grasslands of Szechwan, there were only 44 rest days giving an average march distance of 24 miles a day. In January 1935, at Tsunyi, Mao was made Chairman of the Standing Committee of the Politburo of the Central Committee of the Communist Party of China (a post he held until his death in 1976); and his line was strengthened (after the Chang Kuotao incident of June 1935 onwards) at the Politburo meeting of December 1935 at Wayapao. (Houn, 1973: 45f; Uhalley, 1975: 48f, gives slightly different figures, e.g. 370 days instead of 368.) Apart from the standard sources cited already, especially Snow 1937/1961 (there are differing photographs in these two editions; all are important, for example the books on sale (including Marx's *Capital*) or being read (*ABC of Communism*); a banner –

Notes to pages 46–52

in Spanish – expressing solidarity with Spanish republicans; wall newspapers; workers' clubrooms, and slogans . . .) and Smedley, 1938, 1956; see Liu Pocheng, 1959; Wilson, 1971; Chen Chang-feng, 1972; H. Snow, 1973 and *Peking Review* (43), 1975.

4. Uhalley (1975: 56, after Compton, 1952: xxviii) gives a figure of 'perhaps 20,000' for CPC membership in 1936. By 1945 the Army was about one million strong (with a militia of over two million). The Party in 1945 had about 1.2m members. There were by then about 100m people in the territory of Socialist China (cf. Chesneaux, 1973: 139f; Mao, 1945C: 252).

5. Wolf (1969: 102) gives a map to demonstrate other social distinctions. Cf. his discussion (ibid., 149f) and that of Chesneaux (1973: Ch. 7).

6. For further discussion of Mao's thesis of making a socialist army truly popular, see our fourth essay, 'Gramsci and Mao'.

7. For the 1928 version (and 1929 revisions) see *Selected Works*, III: 156 (1947G: n. 1). HSINHUA News Agency issued a very useful 44-page supplement on the fiftieth anniversary of the People's Liberation Army, 8 August 1977. A standard source on the Army is Gittings (1967).

8. But note the 'Chinese People's basic programme for fighting Japan' of 1934 (*Selected Works*, I: 176; 1935A: n. 15).

9. Mao argued in 1947: 'Confiscate monopoly-capital, headed by Chiang Kai-shek, T. V. Soong, H. H. Kung and Chen Lifu and turn it over to the new-democratic State . . . During their twenty-year rule the four big families . . . have piled up enormous fortunes valued at ten to twenty thousand million U.S. dollars' (1947H: 167). This group owned 80 per cent of the fixed assets of China's industry in 1949 ('Public ownership of the means of production in China', *Peking Review* (51), 1972). Recently a meeting of experts has decided that the main 'obstacles to development' in pre-1949 China (outside the Border Region areas) were 'the nation's governmental and social structure' and 'surplus funds . . . expended largely on consumption by the well-to-do' (Perkins, 1974). Cf. Belden, 1949: Ch. 60 and the illuminating interview with T. V. Soong (ibid., 217f).

10. Apart from the biographies (especially Schram, 1967a: Ch. 8), cf. Compton, 1952; Selden, 1969, 1970, 1971; Meisner, 1970; Chesneaux, 1973: Ch. 7; Uhalley, 1975: Ch. 4.

11. Snow (1937: 225f; 1961: 221f) and Wolf (1969: 149f). Part Six of Snow's classic (1937/1961) is still remarkably accurate in its grasp of essentials.

12. Given this solid attention to 'having enough to eat' it is surprising to find that Schram's chapter on these years (1967a: Ch. 8) is almost devoid of any reference to production. Where production is invoked it is only to support curious images of Mao which abound in the literature: Bianco praises Mao's 'common sense'; Meisner, his 'voluntarism' and Selden his 'ethical theory', his vision of 'Promethean man'. Nevertheless, the two latter writers (along with Chesneaux, 1973: 127f) do succeed in giving a critique of the once fashionable thesis that the CPC succeeds by 'a combination of nationalist appeals and moderate land policies'. Very precisely to *make* the KMT choose between capitulationism and 'patriotic war' was to expose them. As to the 'moderate' land policies, we doubt that Chalmers Johnson would have thought this had he been a landlord in the Border Region!

13. The preceding sentence reads: 'Clearly the tendency of the Soviet co-operative

148   *Notes to pages 53–57*

movement was Socialistic' (1937: 232); it has been *excised* from the 1961 edition.

14. There is a contemporary discussion of the co-operatives in Bishop R. O. Hall: *China's fight for freedom* (Odhams Press, n.d. [circa 1942]), see especially p. 43.

15. For explicit rejection of this view see Mao (1964T: 216) and the second and third essays of Part Two.

16. John Gurley has provided an exploration of 'The formation of Mao's economic strategy, 1927–1949' (1975a, it is supplemented by his 1975b for the years after 1949) which gives further illustrative quotation from Mao. But, as his title indicates, Gurley abstracts (forcibly) 'the economic' in such a way that he can argue 'Mao's strategy called for an attack on the economic base after political power had been assured' (1975a: 112). This 'theory of political forces' ignores that it is precisely a strategy for production which guarantees *socialist* political power and makes possible the continuing, complex class struggles (amongst them different 'cultural revolutions') to extend and safeguard the wellbeing of the people. There is a tendency (evidenced in Gurley, as also in Schurmann (1963), for instance) to abstract 'models' which become exactly what Mao himself was trying to overcome. This is not to deny the illustrative value of Gurley's work (or the very pertinent chart comparing two strategies of 'development' in Schurmann, 1963: 66); but it is to point up that there is not some overarching human destiny ('development') for which there may be 'variations' that are more 'efficient' in different historical contexts. No more does the new strategy of the World Bank from the mid-1960s (with its Keynesian emphasis upon certain democratic changes, some participation and a 'better' income distribution) mean that they are converted to 'Maoism'. If we 'think away' the specific social forces and politics of socialist construction, then we can pretend that Mao was a 'good moderniser'. In fact he was a superlative marxist. It is all the more necessary to emphasise this in the current climate of marxism *and* the present two-line struggle within the CPC. There is a growing tendency to precisely *forget* class struggle.

17. Mavrakis 'Stalin and Trotsky on the Chinese Revolution' (1973: Ch. 6) is very useful. There are some thorough sketches of Comintern policy given in Carr's *History* (1953: 484–540, up to 1922; 1964: Ch. 40 (130 pages) up to 1926; and Par III of his *Foundations of a Planned Economy* (Macmillan, forthcoming)). Cf. *SCMT*: Chapters 4 and 5 plus the references there. Watson (1972) and Magdoff (1975) provide useful comparative sketches to which we shall turn, along with recent Soviet sinology (some examples of which are provided by Schram, 1973b), in Part Three.

In 1949, after the successful crossing of the Yangtze, Mao wrote a poem which concluded:

If heaven had feelings, heaven too would grow old,
The true way that governs the world of men is that of radical change.
(quoted in Schram, 1967a: 244)

Kuo Mojo (in a *Red Flag* commentary when the poem was first published in 1964) related the poem to Mao's disagreement with Stalin who wanted to have his own 'Two-Chinas policy' (cf. Schram, 1967a: 245). Recently Professor Christopher Thorne (BBC Radio 3, 5 August 1977) revealed that Stalin was

Notes to pages 58–63   149

'given' rights over large areas of China's territory at Yalta – neither Chiang Kai-shek nor Mao were informed!

18. This is the second comment on the Open Letter of the CC/CPSU, by the CC/CPC, of 13 September 1963 (P, FLP, 1963). It has been available in English since that date.

19. 'In the Shensi-Kansu-Ninghsia Border Region cultivated land increased from 9 million *mou* in 1936 to 12½ million in 1942.' (Chesneaux, 1973: 132). A *mou* is roughly one-sixth of an acre.

20. It is worth stressing here *how* implicit were many of Mao's own criticisms of (and distance from) orthodox Bolshevism. It is clear that he did not fully comprehend some of his later insights into that experience at the time, otherwise it is unlikely that he would have taken 'second seat' after 1949; although, to be sure, he soon counter-attacked from the early 1950s onwards. At various points he dates his own recognition of the dangers of 'copying' the USSR from 1955–1958.

The implicitness of Mao's critique may also mean that it was (and remained?) partial. Thus the vocabulary of 'base' and 'superstructure'; the notions of 'forces' and 'relations' (used quite mechanically) are not overcome just by being reversed (as Bettelheim has noted in criticism of Rossanda), or by stressing their interactive qualities.

Nevertheless, the emphasis upon (i) social practice, (ii) being good at learning, (iii) voluntary participation for mutual benefit, (and the later placing of agriculture as the foundation; and never forgetting class struggle) stand as a real advance in historical materialism and offer the means to think through a critique of Bolshevism that is not deterministic ('backward Russia') or voluntaristic (Lenin being good, Stalin bad, and Trotsky somewhere in between). We ourselves were able to use Mao's theory and practice as a means of establishing how Bolshevism was produced and sustained. The theory of the Border Region years, far from being guerrilla stuff (as Mao's opponents constantly suggest), also gives us some equipment to think out our own situation and to remain good at learning.

2 THE MASS-LINE AT WORK: THE HIGH TIDE OF SOCIALISM IN THE CHINESE COUNTRYSIDE

Note. Otherwise unattributed page references here are to Mao, 1955J.

1. Korbash, 1974, is perhaps the most systematic Soviet critique of 'Maoism' available in English.

2. Gray's 1969a, 1971 and 1973b are general discussions. The latter contrasts 'Maoist' with what we would identify as Bolshevik development strategies. His 1970 and 1972a discuss the High Tide years considered here; his 1972b, the Great Leap which immediately followed.

3. *International Socialism*, 92, 1976 – the Socialist Workers' Party obituary issue on Mao – typifies this.

4. On Bolshevik views of 'backwardness' see *SCMT*, Ch. 2, 39f; on its role in Trotskyist analyses of socialist formations, ibid., Chapters 3 and 6.

5. *SCMT*, Ch. 3, details occasions on which Lenin and in particular Stalin came

150 *Notes to pages 64–67*

close to realising the extent to which co-operation could itself be a major productive force. Mechanisation before co-operation nonetheless remained the dominant imperative of Soviet agrarian policy.

6. The spiral we schematise here is best exemplified in the *High Tide* by the 'pauper's co-op' (1955J: 67–81), which Gray (1970) also discusses. See also the articles on Chienho Advanced APC (1955J: 285–91), the Pingshun County plan (342–60), and Pingpao APC (389–401).

7. It is the convention in some quarters to view the official propaganda of socialist governments as lies. In this connection it is therefore worth emphasising first, that the *High Tide* was compiled not for Western consumption, but in the context of a fierce inner-Party struggle, and second, that the APCs described were available for inspection by both 'Maoists' and their opponents internally. Gray's judgement on the *High Tide*, with which we would generally concur, is as follows:

> Clearly this is not a balanced source. The aim of the compilers was to prove that rapid co-operativization was possible, and in particular that there was a widespread popular demand for it. The compilers do not try to prove this, however, by selecting examples only of smooth cooperativization or of perfect cooperatives; rather, they were concerned to prove that all the problems of the process of founding and of consolidating cooperatives had been solved somewhere and could therefore be solved elsewhere. It is of the essence of this approach that the problem must be described and analysed. Being a collection of articles and reports of a local nature, the collection does not provide a consistent systematic comparison of cooperatives. It is consistent only in its use of a single criterion of choice, the successful solution of a general problem in a particular instance. It gives a wide range of information about every aspect of the cooperative movement. . . . Clearly this material cannot serve as a basis for generalisation about the actual practice of the process of collectivisation . . . The *High Tide*, however, is not merely the ephemeral propaganda of a particular moment in the history of collectivisation. It is a body of political and social theory, couched in terms of examples of actual development, with comments interspersed. (1970: 90–1).

Gray goes on to talk of the 'degree of frankness characteristic of these volumes' (ibid.,) 91.)

8. On new-liberated areas, see 44–59, 187–97; on backward areas, 150–8, 266–73; on mountainous areas, 67–81, 82–92, 342–60; on national minority areas, 93–114, 178–86; on co-operation and natural disasters, 253–65, 292–301, 313–27; on poverty and fund-raising, 67–81, 128–35, 228–34; on overcoming illiteracy and shortages of skilled personnel, 211–18, 415–24, 425–32, 433–42; on stages of growth and peasant consciousness, 342–61, 362–77, 378–88, 449–59, 477–88; on the problem of surplus labour, 285–92, 389–401. We discuss and document Party policy and methods of work below.

9. As several articles make clear, illiteracy was a massive practical problem for the infant APCs (425–32, 433–42). It also occasions a comment from Mao which in many ways sums up the message of the entire *High Tide* and with it Mao's break with Bolshevism:

Notes to pages 67–77   151

Lenin said: 'A nation of illiterates cannot build communism". Although there are many illiterates in our country today, we cannot wait until illiteracy is eliminated before commencing to build socialism. This has created an acute contradiction . . . This is a serious problem which must be solved in the course of bringing cooperation to agriculture; in fact it is only during this stage that a solution can be found. After the peasants from coops, they demand to be taught to read and write. For them it is a matter of economic necessity. Once they form coops, they have collective strength. The situation changes completely. They can organise their own literacy courses. (425)

10. An important contrast with the USSR, this is consonant with Mao's warnings against pressuring middle peasants, which we document below.
11. Relations between middle and poor peasants are a major theme of the *High Tide*, several articles being devoted specifically to this issue (67–81, 136–49, 219–27, 228–34, 235–52; see also 254–5, 321–2, 366–73); Mao himself devotes several extended comments to it (136–9, 219–20, 228–9, 235–9), urging the *practical* importance of adhering to principles of voluntary participation and mutual benefit throughout.
12. Trotsky, 1909b: 73. *SCMT*, Ch. 3, fn. 31 lists other similarly abusive descriptions of agrarian producers in Trotsky's writings.
13. See his 1968, 1969, 1970.
14. See the quotations given in *SCMT*, pp. 161–2.
15. Excepting of course the dictatorship of the proletariat, central to which is sustained *attack* on the division of labour. Marx exemplifies with regard to the Paris Commune – see his 1871b: 171–2. Engels offers a more extended statement in his 1894a: 311–25.
16. See *SCMT*, Ch. 5, fn. 18.

3 BOMBARD THE HEADQUARTERS: THE GREAT PROLETARIAN CULTURAL REVOLUTION

1. Some of the better accounts can be found in Brugger, 1977; Han Suyin, 1976; Jack Chen, 1975; Collier and Collier, 1973; Daubier, 1974; Hinton, 1972b; Karol, 1975.
2. Mao, 1962A. All quotations are from Mao unless otherwise indicated.
3. Quoted by Han Suyin (1976: 331) from an unpublished text, *Some Opinions* written in 1970 and directed against Lin Piao and Chen Po-ta, rejecting the proposal that Mao should become a 'head of state'.
4. This latter comment was also uttered in a dialogue with Lin Piao, questioning the cult of the individual being built around Mao. See also 1964Q: 242, where Mao tells his nephew ' . . . You must not allow everything to be settled by the word of one man'.
5. This is taken from the version in Ch'en, 1970: 29. See also the *'Sixty points on working methods'* (1958F), especially no. 33 (Ch'en, 1970: 70).
6. The committee to organise a socialist cultural revolution was in fact first formed in mid-1964 (Han Suyin, 1976: 232). The main drive of the cultural revolution seems to have been ignited at a work conference in September/

152 *Notes to pages 77–81*

October 1965 at which Mao in allegorical fashion criticised Wu Han and by implication those behind him. In October 1966 (1966T) Mao indicated that his full suspicions of others solidified at the time of the 'Twenty-three articles' (January 1965), and refers to having raised the question of what the localities should do in the event of revisionism emerging at the centre in the September/October 1965 conference.

7. See Han Suyin (1976: 253) quoting from the *People's Daily* on 18 October 1965.

8. See, for example, 1976H: 466, where Mao observes 'I am a fellow who has been expelled by others five times, and then invited back. Thus the leader of the masses is not self-appointed. He attains his stature in mass struggle'.

9. Quoted by Ch'en' 1970: 149 from *People's Daily* editorial.

10. See CPC (1965) especially *On Khrushchev's Phoney Communism and its Historical Lessons for the World*, Document IX, July 14, 1964.

11. See also especially 1962C. Mao regarded any extension of New Democracy – i.e. encouragement of markets, entrepreneurs free to operate under Party surveillance, and preoccupation with modernity, technology and stability–as the consolidation of capitalism (see 1964T: 216). He seems, too, to regard conservative policies in the period between the Great Leap and the GPCR as an attempt at just such an extension (Liu Shao-chi advocated it in the 1950s also).

12. In Mao's view philosophy is emergent from experience, and cannot be learnt indirectly. Thus 'philosophy must be discussed in the course of practical work' (1963G: 319) and 'it is only when there is class struggle that there can be philosophy' (1964T: 212). See also 1965H.

13. This applies also to more recent campaigns against Teng Hsiao-Ping, and latterly against the 'Gang of Four', where serious criticism is prone to be lost amidst petty and absurd accusations of 'sabotage'.

14. See, for instance, 1958H (talk of 10 March); 1958K; 1962A; 1962B.

15. See, for instance, 1962B; 1962C; 1963G; 1964M; 1964S; 1966D; 1966M; 1966P; 1966Q; 1966S; 1967E; 1967F; 1967H; 1969C; and instructions quoted by Ch'en (1970) of 23 February 67 (p. 136), 12 June 67 (p. 141), 8 August 67 (p. 143), 31 December 68 (p. 157), and 'Four instructions' at a Standing Committee Meeting of the Politburo in 1967 (p. 150).

16. Quoted by Ch'en (1970: 138) from 'The Revolution in Szechuan' adopted by the CC/CPC (*The Ten Red Articles*), 7 May 67.

17. See Mepham (1972), Geras (1972) and the ongoing debate in *Radical Philosophy* for discussion. Our own contributions include Corrigan and Sayer (1975), Sayer (1975a, 1975b) and Ramsay (1976).

18. This is further noteworthy since it occurs in Mao's December 1965 speech at Hangchow, a major moment in the inception of the GPCR.

19. Mao's concept of democracy is, in fact, just the opposite of that contained in the recent manifestoes of the Communist Parties of Italy and France. The latter not only seek to inter the dictatorship of the proletariat, but thereby also to use the bourgeois state machine, i.e. to perpetuate capitalist relations.

20. Cf. the following, from 2 September 1967: 'Throughout the socialist stage, there exist classes and class struggle . . . the instruments of our dictatorship must not be weakened, on the contrary, they should be strengthened (Ch'en, 1970: 145).

21. See also Ch'en's quote from 10 June 1968 (1970: 154)

Notes to pages 82–84

153

The old Social Democrats . . . and modern revisionists in the past dozen years or so . . . have formed a group of anti-communist, anti-people, and counter-revolutionary elements against whom we are waging a life-and-death struggle. There is no equality between us and them . . . it is a relationship of one class oppressing another . . .

22. Cf. 1966I: 107.
23. 'We shouldn't read too many books. We should read Marxist books, but not too many of them either' (1964F: 210). Other attacks on bookishness are to be found throughout his statements at this time – see, for example, 1965B; 1966A; 1966F; 1968A. On the other hand see also 1964A: 434 on the positive role of the theorist.
24. See also, *inter alia*, Mao's talks with his nephew, Mao Yuan-hsin (in Schram II) especially 1966Q. Mao Yuan-hsin has been purged since his uncle's death, accused of being a supporter of the 'Gang of Four'. In many ways this seems symbolic of the attempted diversion of the GPCR.
25. Cf. Han Suyin, 1976: 272.
26. The text of Mao's *tatzebao* runs:

China's first Marxist–Leninist big-character poster and Commentator's article on it in People's Daily are indeed superbly written! Comrades, please read them again. But in the last fifty days or so some leading comrades from the central down to the local levels have acted in a diametrically opposite way. Adopting the reactionary stand of the bourgeoisie, they have enforced a bourgeois dictatorship and struck down the surging movement of the great cultural revolution of the proletariat. They have stood facts on their head and juggled black and white, encircled and suppressed revolutionaries, stifled opinions differing from their own, imposed a white terror, and felt very pleased with themselves. They have puffed up the arrogance of the bourgeoisie and deflated the morale of the proletariat. How poisonous! Viewed in connection with the Right deviation in 1962 and the wrong tendency of 1964 which was 'Left' in form but Right in essence, shouldn't this make one wide awake?

Meanwhile, on 1 August Mao had written a letter to the Red Guards (1966M) in which he affirmed that it was correct to 'rebel against reactionaries'. This extended the general 'right to rebel' pronounced by Mao in 1939 (1939P), to include rebellion should the Communist Party itself become corrupted. It should be noted, however, that even at this stage he also commented: 'at the same time we ask you to pay attention to uniting with all who can be united with'.

27. See Jack Chen. 1975: 171ff. Cf. also Wheelwright and McFarlane, 1970.
28. For this reason we are inclined to prefer the terms 'political material incentive' and 'economic material incentive' to the more usual dichotomy of 'material' and 'moral' incentive. The reason for this is that the latter distinction is equivalent in many ways to the standard misconception of the struggle in China as being between pragmatists and idealists. It implies that 'Maoist incentives' are somehow non-material. In fact as we have seen the conflict is rather a matter of conflicting practical policies. The conservatives support

154 *Notes to pages 84–87*

greater control from above, and economistic, individual-oriented material incentives, whilst the Left sought to make gains collective. With collectivisation in agriculture, for instance, Mao's aim has emerged clearly as one of creating the conditions for people to discover that socialist co-operative work practices leave them all better off than individualism. Hence, the real distinction is between economistic (capitalist) and socialist political *forms* of material incentive.

The productive yield of such policies is well-documented for one period in the previous essay to this. For accounts of the advances following on the GPCR see, for instance, Wheelwright and McFarlane, 1970; Macciocchi, 1971; Bettelheim, 1973; Hinton, 1973; and many others.

29. See 1962A: 259, 288–9.
30. This also forms the basis of Mao's criticims of the Soviet text on political economy, cf. 1962A: 279.
31. See, for example, 1958F: 64 or 1962A: *passim* for Mao's arguments on this.
32. Mao later modified this phrase and elaborated on it – see 1964A: 430–1.
33. No. 14 of 'The 16 Articles' (1966P) begins: 'The aim of the Great Proletarian Cultural Revolution is to revolutionize people's ideology and as a consequence to achieve greater, faster, better and more economical results in all fields of work' (Ch'en' 1970: 125–6).
34. Quoted from *People's Daily* 3 August 67, in Ch'en' 1970: 143.
35. See 'Where do correct ideas come from?' (1963A), an important short article that is critical of those cadres who fail to comprehend that 'matter can be transformed into consciousness and consciousness into matter'. Originally this piece was part of a Party statement on rural work, which as with the High Tide comments shows the extent of Mao's theorisation from peasant experience and advances.
36. Teng's recent return and the policies which have accompanied it illustrate the significance of this point well.
37. See Jack Chen, 1973, or compare Myrdal, 1963, with Myrdal, 1970, for an idea of the impact in rural conditions. See also Corrigan, 1974, or the work of Jack Gray.
38. These were originally intended as temporary organisations it seems. They have survived, however, the restoration of the status of Party Committees and the reintroduction of the trade unions in 1973, becoming an established symbol of the GPCR and a replacement for the old management system. There are reports that some are seeking to dismantle them (John Gittings, *The Guardian*, 19 November 1977).
39. Thus Mao is inclined to repudiate those who view things as chaotic – see, for example, 1966N, 1966R.
40. Exceptions include Brugger, 1977, and the postscript of Bettleheim, 1973, though both of these discussions contain arguments with which we would take issue. Bettleheim, for instance, first makes the mistake of placing struggles outside the people and the CPC, and so represents the ultra-Left as largely a bourgeois faction *simpliciter*. Secondly, he seems to regard a line as identifiable throughout as ultra-Left, whereas apart from what is said below we would argue that the objectives, e.g. of criticising inequalities or any surviving form of bureaucratisation, are commendable. It is the idea that erasure can be achieved in one step, entailing methods of revolution that in fact generate

Notes to pages 88–93 155

disappointment and despair, to which a correct Left line must be opposed.

41. Quoted in Ch'en' 1970: 150.
42. Mao's views on this are clear. Those from wealthy backgrounds may be more likely statistically to take a bourgeois line, but one should not label people by birth. 'It is . . . important to distinguish between class background and one's own performance, with emphasis on the latter . . . if we consider only the background then even Marx, Engels, Lenin and Stalin would be unacceptable' (1964A). Indeed 'were our own family backgrounds all that good?' Mao adds later (1966S: 268).
43. As with, for example, Maitan (1976), Padoul (1975), Benton (1975, 1977), Halliday (1977).
44. See the discussion in Han Suyin, 1976. In 1967E Mao elaborates on his own reasons for opposing the Paris Commune model, arguing that in form it was vulnerable to bourgeois takeover, whilst the name itself does not change political content which is what really counts. For a more detailed discussion of this and other issues arising out of the experience of Shanghai in the GPCR see Nee, 1975.
45. See Brugger, 1976. For further discussion of industrial democracy in China see Andors, 1977; Ramsay, 1977b.
46. Quoted in Ch'en' 1970: 99. It is by reference to this that Mao ties up the question of 'expertise' and so the Red-expert issue. 'They [technicians and engineers] are not that expert. They won't unite with the masses or participate in labour' (1964Y: 423).
47. As in, for example, 1957A: 378; 1957B; 1966F.
48. See *inter alia*, Bettleheim (1973), Wheelwright and McFarlane (1970), Robinson (1975), Berger (1975). See also 1964L and 1966F: 380.
49. 'Our power – who gives it to us? The working class give it to us and the masses of the labouring people who comprise over ninety per cent of the population give it to us', 16 October 68, quoted by Ch'en, 1970: 156.
50. Mao makes a similar point in his discussion of the Paris Commune 'model'; cf. 1967E: 453–4.
51. 18 May 1967, quoted by Ch'en, 1970: 139.

4 GRAMSCI AND MAO

1. Apart from his published writings, only now being translated into English, Gramsci left two bodies of writing at his death: 2,848 manuscript pages in 32 (or 33 according to his English editors, Gramsci, 1948: xi) notebooks – the equivalent of about 4,000 typewritten sheets (Fiori, 1965: 294) - and many letters: there are 428 prison letters in the official full edition, of which about 300 have been translated into English. The most important are Hamish Henderson's translations which could find no English publisher between 1950 and 1974. Guidance to the writings of Gramsci is provided through the work of Davidson, G. Williams, and several others cited in the next note.
2. Cozens (1977) provides a list of writings (by and about) in English for the twenty years following 1957. Fiori (1965) seems the best 'life' in English, although the intellectual biographies of G. Williams (1974a, b, c; 1975) and Davidson (1974, 1977) are particularly useful. Other general studies include Cammett (1967; cf. Genovese, 1967); Merrington (1968, the best short

156 *Notes to pages 94–103*

introduction); Pozzolini (1968), Kiernan (1972, 1974), Piccone (1976), Boggs (1976) and Clark (1976). Studies of Gramsci's politics, apart from the above, include Martinelli (1968), Todd (1974) and Hobsbawm (1977); for his relations with Communism, apart from those cited, see White (1974a, b) and Maisels (1974); and, with Fascism, Showstack (1974). The two major studies of Gramsci's 'hegemony' are G. Williams (1960; cf. his later writings for his partial repudiation of this text) and Anderson (1977; pp. 15f trace the history of the term); cf. Simon (1977).

3. Piccone concludes this article: 'Given the closure of the Marxist perspective elsewhere, if Marxism is to become a meaningful political force in the West, it will have to follow a Gramscian path' (1976: 506). The force of the 'if' here (its querulous timbre) is indicated in the total rejection of historical materialism announced by Piccone in the polemic amongst the editors given in *Telos* (31, 1977, especially pp. 178, 183, 195).

4. Note Davidson's (1974: 142) endorsement of this. Maria Macciocchi's work (1971: Ch. 19) draws upon unpublished work by Althusser. Her book occasioned 'l'affaire Macciocchi' in France, generating an excellent text by Bettelheim (1972) which should be more generally known. It is also perhaps noteworthy that among the few marxist–leninist parties to accurately grasp the lessons of the GPCR was a major formation in Italy; one of us was privileged to be present at the *Unione* January 1970 meeting. Note also *Il Manifesto* and the work of Rossanda.

5. This text remained unpublished in English until 1974. Its immediate relevance to the issues we are discussing was recognised by Maisels (1974).

6. For two other contrasting accounts on this theme, cf. Rossanda 1974 and Gouldner 1975.

7. See G. Williams (1974a, b, c; 1975), Davidson (1974; 1977), Piccone (1976) and Anderson (1977).

8. This must be understood as criticism of Gramsci's own support for Amadeo Bordiga. At the Second Congress of the PCI, Bordiga's Rome theses were advanced and accepted, these had a sectarian core and also made insufficient distinction between Fascism and bourgeois democracy. The Rome theses were not fully overthrown until Gramsci's Lyons theses of 1926. Bordiga's views on Fascism – in 1922 he saw it as part of 'bourgeois policy' (quoted in Carr, 1964: 83) and in 1923 he saw it as only a 'change in governing personnel' (quoted in Carr, 1964: 84) – were not, of course, unique to him as Carr shows in his accounts of Comintern discussions. Cf. Gramsci (1948: Part II; 1977a: Texts 68 and 72), Cammett (1966, 1967), Showstack (1974), Poulantzas (1970), Rosenberg (1976) and references there.

9. For the Fourth Comintern Congress of 1922 see Fiori (1965: Ch. 16). The Third Comintern Congress of 1921 took the slogan 'To the Masses', sharpened by the 21 December 1921 Comintern Executive's 24 theses and slogan 'The Workers United Front', upheld by the Fourth Comintern Congress and loosened (the critique of social democracy had already begun) at the Fifth Comintern Congress of 1924. The latter (as the enlarged Plenum of the Comintern Executive that followed) took the twin themes of Bolshevisation and stabilisation which we briefly examined in our previous book, *SCMT*.

10. Given this, Mussolini could claim, 'In opposition to the social communists we want the land to belong not to the State but to the cultivator' (February 1921).

Notes to pages 105–116 157

As the Fascist Lazillo noted in 1924, 'There does not exist one fascism . . . whereas in the cities and industrial zones it appears as a romantic movement . . . in the agrarian zones it is the party of the big and little landowners'. The actual history of the class struggle in the Italian countryside, which demonstrates the fundamental (and somewhat coherently Bolshevik) weakness of the PCI, is brilliantly sketched by Snowden (1972; he gives both the quotations with which this note begins). For more general background see Salvemini (1936), Lambardini (1968), Carocci (1972), plus material cited in note 8 above.

11. Compare, as examples, the *Notebooks* (1948: 118f, 180f, 229f) and such published articles as we have (1977a: Texts 40 and 57).

12. For Mao's writings see his 1928A: 70; 1928B: 8of; 1929B; 1935A: 159f; 1936D; 1938B, C, D, F – the last four texts extend for over 150 pages. For the history see the work of Snow or Belden and (for Chu Teh) that of Agnes Smedley.

13. Compare here the discussions in Anderson (1977), Simon (1977) and Bates (1975). Todd (1974) and Macciocchi (1971: Ch. 19) offer explicit comparisons between Gramsci and Mao.

14. The 'antinomy' here is that Anderson's whole argument leads to just those positions in Gramsci he considers so worrying! He argues that it is the State apparatuses that secure the rule of capital (1977: 42f, 70, 77). This formulation itself is fatally incorrect since it is capital – labour relations (Marx's *pump*) that secure the rule of capital, the State organises it. That is why Marx begins and ends with production relations. Anderson conflates, additionally, role performance and role commitment within the working classes under capitalism when he claims that they do not know 'the real limits of bourgeois democracy' and that it will take intellectuals to toll the bell to signal when the 'hour of reckoning' is at hand (1977: 77). In every socialist revolution of which we have any account, however sketchy, we find many instances when this was exactly reversed – the intellectuals, figuratively or actually, having to be shaken free from their libraries, lecture rooms, or beds, by the alarm-bells of the working class on the move. Vanguardism, whether 'hegemonic' or not, can easily turn into a brake upon the abilities of the production collectivities to liberate *themselves* by transforming just those circumstances (and just those selves) which intellectuals (by definition clustered on one side of the founding division of labour which sustains exploitation and oppression) declared could not be changed, or, if at all, only slowly and under expert guidance. Hence Mao's cadre policy discussed above in Part One.

15. We do realise that our points here require full elaboration – this can be obtained, in part, from *SCMT*, and, in part, from reading Sayer's *Marx's Method* and Corrigan's *State Formation* together.

PART THREE: ON CONTRADICTION

1. In the case of India it is solving the problem that matters (Jacoviello, 1973; Bhattacharya, 1974); in the case of the USSR it is the methods that differ (*SCMT*; Salisbury, 1973; Magdoff, 1975). On China's food production see 'How China solved its food problem', *Peking Review* (45), 1973; *China*

158 *Notes to pages 117–123*

Reconstructs, 24(1), 1975, and 'China achieves grain self-sufficiency', *HSINHUA*, Special issue 5, January 1974.

2. It is not possible to trace educational struggles here. cf. 'Chronology of the two road struggle in the educational front in the last seventeen years', *Education Research*, 6 May 1967, translated *Chinese education*, 1 (1), 1968; Price, 1970; Alley (1973: Ch. 13); Gardner and Idema, 1973; Gardner, 1977; P. Mauger *et al.*, 1974. Particular struggles are detailed in Nee (1969), Hinton (1972a), and the materials by/about Tsinghua University in *Peking Review* (8), 1973, and (22), 1974 plus *Strive to build a socialist university of science and engineering* (P, FLP, 1972). The more diffused, but nonetheless central, educational revolution can be traced in the village studies, e.g. by Jan Myrdal.

3. On the women's movement in China, see the readings in Croll (1974) and the articles in *New Women in the New China* (P, FLP, 1972), plus the monographs by Davin (1976), Croll (1978) and articles in China's press every International Working Women's Day (March 8).

4. This is brought out with clarity in 'Worker-peasant Villages', *China Reconstructs*, 26 (9), 1977. Again the village studies are important. Excellent analysis of both agrarian and industrial production can be found in papers of Tse Ka-kui (1977a, b).

5. Translated in *HSINHUA Weekly* (258), January 17 1974, and *Peking Review* (17), 1974. Our quotations are from HSINHUA.

6. But note the discussion in the *Sunday Times Business News*, 21 August 1977: 'Vance and Ping poised for US – China breakthrough'; and compare Alec Nove, 'Russia still burdened by a huge trade deficit with the West', *The Times Business News*, 31 August 1977. The latter shows China's imports from the USSR nearly doubled (by rouble value) comparing 1976 to 1975. Cf.n.28.

7. In *Conversations with Americans* (Los Angeles, USCPFA; L, SACU, 1977) page references in our text are from this source. Cf. Note 20 to Part One above.

8. On Lin Piao, see Mao (1971A) and Yao Wen-yuan (1975). Chi Hsin (1977) and J. Gray (1976b) give accounts of the 'Gang of Four'. We are not convinced that they were reactionaries, although they do demonstrate how Right-wing methods of work (commandism and coercion, for example) do tend 'to drain the pond to catch the fish', i.e. negate socialist content. But their removal has cleared the way for a coherent policy which reverses many verdicts of not only the GPCR, but also the GLF, and negates the lessons of the Border Region years. It is entirely to the point of our work as a whole that this is revisionism (correctly perceived as such by Charles Bettelheim in his letter of resignation from l'Association des Amities Franco-chinoises of 11 May 1977, published in *Le Monde* and extracted in the *Guardian* and *Socialist Challenge* in early July 1977; note also the relevant editorial of the Albanian Party newspaper *Zeri i Popullit*, 7 July 1977, later published as *The Theory and Practice of the Revolution*, Tirana, '8 Nentori'; L, CPBML, 1977). This 'making use of' certain formulations within the work of Mao and others demonstrates in turn, the incompleteness of Mao's break from Bolshevism, just as Lenin (see *SCMT*: Chapters 2 and 3) incompletely transformed the 'Marxism of the Second International'. Cf.n.40.

9. Contrast and compare 'Study political economy and run the docks well' *Peking Review* (17), 1974.

10. Major texts involved here are: *Whence the differences?* Bath, New Era, n.d.

Notes to pages 123–127

(documents up to 9 March 1963); *A proposal concerning the General Line of the International Communist Movement*, Bath, New Era, n.d. (Various texts including the 26 January 1960 'Statement' and the 'Five proposals' of 10 September 1960.) Nine 'Comments' were issued separately in 1963 and 1964 by the Foreign languages Press in Peking; these were collected in 1965 as *The Polemic on the General Line* . . . from the same publisher and reprinted London, Red Star Press, n.d. Subsequent documents include *The historical experience of the war against fascism*, and, *Carry the struggle against Khrushchov revisionism through to the end*. Cf. Zagoria (1962), Mehnert (1963) and Sulzberger (1974). Many of the Soviet texts are available in the above CPC publications, plus (recently) the speeches of L. Brezhnev and the supplements to *Socialism: Theory and Practice*, which has also carried extracts from the work of Wang Ming and Vladimirov, part of the new historiography of China discussed by Schram (1973b: 10f) and the more frankly polemical work of Korbash or Altaisky.

11. One of the more remarkable features of the Wansui documents is the many criticisms of Stalin found in them. See *SCMT*: Chapters 2 and 3; Mao 1956C, F: 87; 1958 : 102f; 1962B: 172; 1964T: 217f, and the two documents of the *Polemic* collection *On the question of Stalin*, and, *On Khrushchov's Phoney Communism*. (cf. Mavrakis, 1973). The International is discussed admirably in the work of E. H. Carr (1953, up to 1922; 1964, up to 1926 and from 1926 to 1929 in his *Foundations of Planned Economy*, Part III, forthcoming). A different perspective is available in Claudin (1970).

12. It is important to indicate the significance of the work of Bettelheim here. (1966, 1967, 1969, 1970a, 1970b, 1971a, 1971b, 1972, 1973, 1974, 1977). We have indicated our critical differences from Bettelheim in *SCMT*: Ch 6, Corrigan (1976b) and Ramsay (1977a). Cf Mavrakis (1973) and Linhart (1976).

13. Mao noted in 1959 'As for the people's communes, the whole world opposed them; the Soviet Union opposed them' (1959K: 145). Apart from *SCMT*, where the contrast permeates the whole book, see Salisbury (1973: 88f) and G. Thomson (1973: 122f). More generally the work of Bettelheim and Macciocchi (1971, especially Chapters 5–9) is relevant here.

14. Apart from the material mentioned under Note 10 above (of which the supplements to *Socialism: Theory and Practice* are very instructive) see the very important translation by Kirby (1975) of the Russian text (circulated in an edition of only one thousand copies) *Problems of Soviet Sinology . . . Papers delivered at the All-Union Scientific Conference of Sinologists, November 1971* (Moscow, 1973). The bibliography to this text has 547 items.

15. Apart from the material mentioned under Note 10 above, see the new journal *Far Eastern Affairs*, (especially the editorial, 'Some topical questions in Marxist sinology' (1), 1976), produced by the USSR. Academy of Sciences.

16. Apart from Macciocchi (1971), see Watson (1972), Magdoff (1975) Nolan (1975), and references there.

17. Translated into English as *On the Historical Experience of the Dictatorship of the Proletariat* (P, FLP, 1959). Mao noted at Chengtu, 'When Stalin was criticized in 1956, we were on the one hand happy, but on the other hand apprehensive. It was completely necessary to remove the lid, to break down blind faith, to release the pressure and to emancipate thought. But we did not agree with demolishing him at one blow' (1958H: 101 cf. 1956D: 304; 1956S: 341).

160   *Notes to pages 128–135*

18. See also Mao (1957A: 376), comments on Stalin's reply to Savina and Vensher, and his 1961/62 comments on the Political Economy textbook of the Soviet union, both in *Wansui*. The latter text and the two we use are also available as *Mao or Stalin* (Edinburgh, Proletarian Publishing, 1977) and in a French translation: *Mao Tsé-toung et la construction du socialisme* (Paris, Seuil, 1975). Monthly Review Press are to issue their own English translation shortly.

19. In 1955, Mao noted 'there is no such thing as an invincible "magic weapon". Hosts of "magic weapons" have in fact been defeated. We believe that so long as we rely on the people there is no "magic weapon" in this world' (1955B: 168). The following year he argued against sectarianism for internationalism: 'Right now I won't go into matters outside our planet, for the travel routes beyond the earth have not yet been opened. If human beings should be discovered on Mars or Venus, we would then discuss the matter of uniting with them and forming a united front' (1956G: 316).

20. See the work of Bettelheim, Mavrakis, Linhart and others. For previous attempts to generalise the implications of socialist construction in China for class politics in capitalist formations, note the work of Rossanda, Macciocchi, and Althusser (1976). The recent (self-critical) work of Hindess and Hirst (1977) should also be contrasted with Bettelheim's (and Althusser's) recent work.

21. We have not repeated here the extended argument in our other work, especially *SCMT*: Ch. 6, which attempts to generalise a strategy of socialist contruction drawing upon negative and positive lessons. A fully developed account would of course, have to examine the long history of class struggle within England and examine the relations between the wider (and longer) socialist tradition and that of marxism. But there are many problems with the existing historiography of class struggle since that which is marxist is not infrequently Bolshevik (not least, recent attempts to suggest that the CPGB was formed 'prematurely' in advance of the productive forces!). The best resources we have are available for the period up *until* the 1830s – above all the work of Christopher Hill and Edward Thompson.

22. As a complement to Magdoff (1975), Sweezy (1975) contrasts China with capitalism in an extremely informative way, thus complementing, in turn, our attempt to draw lessons for socialist construction under capitalism. There are many visitors' reports to China which we have not mentioned – Macciocchi's is only amongst the most famous – not because we deny their significance. We would only add that they should always be integrated with *as much* reading of materials from within China, including such long-stay visitors as Snow, Belden and, Smedley (for the early years), and Hinton, Jan Myrdal, Jack Chen and Rewi Alley (for the later). More casual visitors' reports are often useful – not least for the surprise indicated by economists (for example) that the laws of (bourgeois) political economy do not govern the whole world!

23. Far too often we can read, even in 'Left' newspapers and journals, talk of the likelihood of 1975 seeing the 'first Communist Party in Government' of that we have recently seen the most 'socialist land reform' *in Europe*. Albania is simply dismissed without a mention, along with the Peoples' Democracies, let alone Finland. The political power of bourgeois definitions of geographical space (condensed in the theory and practice of *Eurocommunism*) is much in evidence.

Notes to pages 135–138 161

24. Apart from material mentioned in Note 8 above see issues of both *China Now* and the China Policy Study Group's *Broadsheet* for 1977 to follow their debate on the 'Gang of Four'. The fullest analysis in English is by Chi Hsin (1977) – a pseudonym for a group of CPC aligned journalists in Hong Kong. Cf.n.40.
25. The history of this concept (as with many others) is being rewritten to make it a discovery of the 1970s. See the long article by the editorial department of *Peoples Daily* in *HSINHUA Weekly* special supplement 1 November 1977 and *Peking Review* (45), 1977, pp.10–41. Apart from the *89 references* there, this and subsequent issues of *PR* contain explanatory notes. As we noted above, the 'three worlds theory' has been criticised by the Albanian Party of Labour and the Communist Party of Britain (Marxist – Leninist). Our own critique is given in *SCMT*: Chapters 5 and 6.
26. *HSINHUA Weekly* (453), 1977, item 101828. Cf. ibid. (439), item 0704403, and (442), item 072238.
27. *HSINHUA Weekly* (460), 1977, item 120432; ibid. (449), item 092019 Cf. 'Foreign Trade', *Peking Review* (9), 1977.
28. 'China opens its doors to technology from West', *Times*, 13 September 1977; 'China will accept foreign deposits', *Guardian*, 14 October 1977; 'Chinese industry urged to show profit . . .', *Times*, 29 August 1977; Y. Preston, 'Displacing Maoist ideals', *Financial Times*, 25 November 1977. Cf. issues of *China's Foreign Trade* (P, Guozi Shudian); *Red Flag*, editorial, September 1977; 'China' (supplement), *Times*, 12 October 1977; *HSINHUA Weekly* (457), 1977, item 111012.
29. 'New college enrolment system', *Peking Review* (46), 1977, and 'A great debate on the educational front', *Red Flag* (12), 1977; *Peking Review* (51), 1977. This – especially the latter – shows that the policies now implemented are those attempted by Teng in 1975. Basically from December 1977, 'Entrance examinations will be restored and admittance based on their results', this 'new way of enrolment will enable students to complete their school and college studies without a break'. The main social basis of the dominant line in China appears to be intellectuals and technicians, although there are many evident struggles within these strata, notably in the State Planning Commission and within various media of communication.
30. Translated *HSINHUA Weekly* (426), 1977, item 040146.
31. See, for example, 'Why did the "Gang of Four" wield the big stick of the "theory of productive forces"', *Peking Review* (26), 1977, and issues of China Policy Study Group's *Broadsheet* through 1977.
32. See especially two major articles in *Peking Review* (11) and (12), 1977.
33. *HSINHUA Weekly* (448), 1977, item 091150, pp. 15–27, has the full text. There are other similar texts, for example those interpreting Mao's *Selected Works*, Volume Five, which are against the general dominant tendency.
34. See 'Mechanization: fundamental way out for agriculture' *Peking Review* (9), 1977, and the editorial in *People's Daily*, 11 December 1977, translated *HSINHUA Weekly* (461), 1977, item 121174. All the reports of the Second National Learn-From-Tachai Conference are relevant here.
35. Translated in *Peking Review* (35), 1976, and *HSINHUA Weekly*, (39), 1976, item 082303. According to Agence France Presse (*Times*, 18 September 1976) the HSINHUA translation leaves out many sentences concerning Teng. These are given in the *Times*.

162 *Notes to pages 138–140*

36. On the 'General Programme', *Peking Review* (33) and (34), 1977; on the 'Twenty Points', ibid. (44), 1977; and, equally important as a general manifesto of the intellectuals challenged by the GPCR, the article by the Theoretical Group of the Academy of Sciences of China, *People's Daily*, 30 June 1977, translated *HSINHUA Weekly* (439), 1977, item 070216. The latter text quotes significantly from the *Grundrisse* (Nicolaus ed.), to imply that for Marx 'science' was supra-historical and thus politically 'neutral'. In fact the text (1858a: 699) shows that for Marx the use of science is always itself defined by the given mode of production whose set of relations illuminate and use science in a certain way – capitalism takes science and uses it to intensify the exploitation of people and nature for profit. Socialist construction must socialise and democratise science.
37. *Times*, Diary, 14 September 1977.
38. 'Package Tours to China attract good response' *Times*, 1 October 1977.
39. For example, Hsueh Mu-chiao's multi-part article on 'The two-road struggle in the economic field [n.b.] during the transition period', *Peking Review* (49 onwards), 1977.
40. *Addendum*: Charles Bettelheim has now added to his letter of resignation by producing an extended analysis of Post-Mao China which complements our brief sketch here. Cf. *Monthly Review*, 30 (1–2), July–August 1978.

Bibliography

This bibliography is arranged as follows:

PART ONE A Marx/Marx and Engels
     B Engels
     C Lenin
     D Trotsky
     E Stalin
     F Mao

PART TWO All other sources, preceded by a brief indication of useful empirical sources.

In Part One we have followed – with the important exception of Mao's writings – the arrangement and coding used in *SCMT* to which readers should refer for a very full listing of the classical writers other than Mao. For the convenience of readers we have kept to the codes used for individual texts in *SCMT* (192f) even though we have used far fewer texts in *For Mao*. Since the date and suffix code is purely for internal purposes this will not alter the ease with which the system can be used.

In Part Two we list works alphabetically by author or title (where the work is anonymous) with subdivision by date and suffix where required. Dates are always dates of publication unless specified otherwise.

Throughout we abbreviate London as L, Moscow as M, New York as NY, and Peking as P. All other abbreviations as in journal titles should be self-explanatory. In *SCMT* we provided some addresses of publishers and bookshops where marxist materials may be obtained.

164   *For Mao*

PART ONE

A *MARX/MARX AND ENGELS*

COLLECTIONS

I   Karl Marx (KM) and Frederick Engels (FE) *Collected Works*.
     M, Progress, NY, International, L, Lawrence and Wishart,
     1975 onwards. To comprise 50 volumes. Cited as MECW, 1,
     etc.

II General Collections

KM/FE   *Selected Works in Three Volumes*. M, Progress,
         1969–70. Cited as: MESW, I, II, III.
KM/FE   *Selected Works in One Volume*. M, Progress, 1968.
         Cited as: MESW.

III Anthologies

KM   *The Revolutions of 1848*; *Surveys from Exile*; *The First
         International and after*. Pelican Marx Library,
         Political Writings Vols 1–3. Ed. D. Fernbach, L,
         Penguin, 1973, 1973, 1974. Cited as: MPW, 1, 2,
         3.
KM/FE   *On the Paris Commune*. M, Progress, 1971. Cited as:
         PC.
KM/FE   *Writings on the Paris Commune*. Ed. H. Draper, NY,
         Monthly Review Press, 1971. Cited as: WPC.
KM   *Texts on Method*. Ed. T. Carver, Oxford, Black-
         well, 1974. Cited as: TM.

TEXTS

1844   *The Holy Family* (with FE). MECW, 4, 5–211.
1845   'Theses on Feuerbach.' Two variants exist, Marx's own,
        and that edited by Engels. Both are given in MECW, 5,
        and appended to Ryazanskaya ed. of 1846a.
1846a   *The German Ideology* (with FE). MECW, 5. Ed. S.
        Ryazanskaya, M, Progress, 1968.

Bibliography

1847b *Wage Labour and Capital.* M, Progress, 1970. MESW, I, 142–74, MESW, 64–94.

1848a *Manifesto of the Communist Party* (with FE). M, Progress, 1973; P, FLP; L, Penguin (under title *The Communist Manifesto*), 1967. MESW, I, 98–137, MESW, 31–63, MPW, 1, 62–98.

1848b 'Speech on the question of free trade.' MECW, 6.

1852b *The Eighteenth Brumaire of Louis Bonaparte.* MESW, I, 394–487, MESW, 97–180, MPW, 2, 143–249.

1858a *Grundrisse.* Full edition, ed. M. Nicolaus, L, Penguin, 1973.

1863a, b, c *Theories of Surplus Value* [*Capital, IV*]. Parts I–III. M, Progress, 1963, 1968, 1971.

1865a *Capital, III.* Ed. F. Engels, M, Progress, 1971.

1867a *Capital, I.* Ed. F. Engels, tr. S. Moore/E. Aveling from 3rd German ed., L, Lawrence & Wishart, 1967. Different trans., L, Penguin, 1976 (from KM/FE *Werke* Vol. 23, incorporating changes in German and French editions).

1871a *The Civil War in France.* P, FLP, 1970. MESW, II, 202–44, MESW, 273–313, PC, 48–102, WPC, 35–101, MPW, 3, 187–235.

1871b First draft of 1871a. With P ed. of 1871a. PC, 102–81, WPC, 103–78.

1871c Second draft of 1871a. With P ed. of 1871a. PC, 182–224, WPC, 179–213.

1871d Notebook on the Paris Commune [Press excerpts and notes for 1871a]. Ed. H. Draper, Berkeley, Independent Socialist Pr., 1971.

1872a 'Preface' to 2nd German ed. of 1848a (with FE). With M, P, and Penguin eds of 1848a. MESW, I, 98–9, MESW, 31–2.

1875 *Critique of the Gotha Programme.* P, FLP, 1972. MESW, III, 13–30, MESW, 315–35, MPW, 3, 339–59.

1877 Letter to Editorial Board of *Otechestvenniye Zapiski*. In KM/FE *Selected correspondence.* M, FLPH, 1956; M, Progress, 1965; Rev. ed., M, Progress, 1975.

1878 *Capital, II.* Ed. F. Engels, M, Progress, 1967.

1880 'Marginal notes on Adolph Wagner *Lehrbuch Der Politischen Oekonomie.*' *Theoretical Practice*, 5, 1972. Alt. trans: TM.

166 *For Mao*

1881a Letter to V. Zasulich, 8 Mar. *Text*: KM/FE *Selected correspondence*, all eds. *First Draft*: MESW, III, 152–61.
1881b 'Preface' to Russian ed. of 1848a (with FE). With M, P, and Penguin eds of 1848a. MESW, I, 100–1.

B *ENGELS*

COLLECTIONS

All KM/FE Collections listed above.

TEXTS

1891c 'Introduction' to *The Civil War in France*. With KM, 1871a, P, M, PC and WPC eds.
1894a *Anti-Duhring: Herr Eugen Duhring's Revolution in Science*. NY, International, 1972; M, Progress.

C *LENIN*

COLLECTIONS

I *Collected works*, M, Progress, 1960 onwards. 45 vols. Cited as LCW, 1, 2. *Note*. In some reprints of LCW vols, pagination is different.
II **General Collections**

Selected Works in Three Volumes. M, Progress, 1970–71. Cited as: LSW, 1, 2, 3.
Selected Works in One Volume. M, Progress, 1968. Cited as: LSW.

TEXTS

1908c *Materialism and Empiriocriticism*. LCW, 14. Also from P, FLP.
1916b *Philosophical Notebooks*. LCW, 38.
1917a *Marxism on the State* [Preparatory materials for 1917b]. M, Progress, 1972.
1917b *The State and Revolution*. LCW, 25, LSW, 2, 283–376, LSW, 264–351.
1917c 'Lecture on the 1905 Revolution.' LCW, 23, LSW, 1, 779–94.
1917e 'Peasants and workers.' LCW, 25.

Bibliography 167

1919 'Soviet power and the status of women.' LCW, 30.

1920b 'Left-wing' Communism – An Infantile Disorder. LCW, 31, LSW, 3, 345–430, LSW, 516–91.

1920c 'Tasks of the youth leagues.' LCW, 31, LSW, 3, 470–83, LSW, 607–20.

1920d 'The trade unions, the present situation, and the mistakes of Comrade Trotsky.' LCW, 32.

1921a 'Once again on the trade unions, the current situation, and the mistakes of Trotsky and Bukharin.' LCW, 32, LSW, 3, 523–54.

1922d 'Speech at a Plenary session of the Moscow Soviet.' LCW, 33, LSW, 3, 729–38, LSW, 674–80.

1922f 'On the significance of militant materialism.' LCW, 33, LSW, 660–7.

1923a 'Pages from a diary.' LCW, 33, LSW, 3, 755–9, LSW, 685–9.

1923b 'On co-operation.' LCW, 33, LSW, 3, 760–6, LSW, 690–5.

1923c 'Our Revolution.' LCW, 33, LSW, 3, 767–70, LSW, 696–9.

1923d 'Better fewer, but better.' LCW, 33, LSW, 3, 776–88, LSW, 700–12.

D TROTSKY

SELECTIONS

The Age of Permanent Revolution: A Trotsky Anthology. Ed. I. Deutscher, NY, Dell, 1964.
The Basic Writings of Trotsky. Ed. I. Howe. L, Heinemann, 1964. Cited as: *TBW*

TEXTS

1906 *Results and Prospects.* With his 1930a, L, New Park, 1962.
1909b *1905.* L, Penguin, 1973. Extract, *TBW*.
1930a *The Permanent Revolution.* With his 1906.

E STALIN

COLLECTIONS

I *Collected works*, M, FLPH, 1952 onwards, Reprinted, L, Red Star Pr., 1975 onwards. 15 vols. Cited as: SCW, 1, 2.

168 *For Mao*

II **Other Collections**

Leninism. L, Lawrence & Wishart, 1942. Cited as: *L*.
On the Opposition. P, FLP, 1974. Cited as: SO.

TEXTS

1924a   *The Foundations of Leninism. L*, 1–85. SCW, 6. Sep. ed., P,
FLP, 1965.
1926   'On the problems of Leninsim.' *L*, 118–74. As 'Concerning questions of Leninism', SO, 268–346, SCW, 8.
1931b   'Some questions concerning the history of Bolshevism.' *L*,
388–400, SCW, 13.
1938   *Dialectical and Historical Materialism*. [From: *History of the
Communist Party of the Soviet Union (Bolshevik): Short Course*,
M, FLPH, 1939. Reprinted L, Red Star Pr., 1972.] *L*,
591–618.
1952a   *Economic Problems of Socialism in the USSR*. P, FLP, 1972.

F *MAO TSE-TUNG*

Note. For a chronological bibliography of Mao's writings (1917–
68) see Ch'en (1970: 163f); where an item is cited there we give
Ch'en's number code in our last column below.

COLLECTIONS

I **General Collections**

(*a*) Authorised by CC/CPC
Selected works. 5 vols. P, FLP, 1965 (Vol. 4, 1961; Vol. 5, 1977).
[*Note*: (1) Pagination changes as between different printings; (2)
it is often worth while comparing, e.g. SR and SW translations.]
Cited as: SW,1, 2, etc.
Selected Readings. P, FLP, 1971. Cited as: SR.

(*b*) Unauthorised
The Political Thought of Mao Tse-tung. Ed. S. R. Schram. L,
Penguin, 1969. Cited as: S,I.
Mao Tse-tung Unrehearsed: Talks and Letters, 1956–71. Ed. S. R.
Schram, L, Penguin, 1974. Cited as: S,II.
Mao Papers. Ed. J. Ch'en, Oxford Univ. Pr., 1970. Cited as:
Ch'en.

Bibliography

[Wansui:] *Miscellany of Mao Tse-tung Thought*. 2 vols, Virginia, Joint Publications Research Service, 1974. JPRS 61269-1,-2. Cited as: WS.

II **Anthologies/Selections**

(*a*) Authorised by CC/CPC
Five Articles. P, FLP, 1968. Cited as: *FA*.
Five Documents on Literature and Art. P, FLP, 1967. Cited as: *FDLA*.
Four Essays on Philosophy. P, FLP, 1966. Cited as: *FE*.
On Literature and Art. P, FLP, 1967. Cited as: *LA*.
Poems. P, FLP, 1976.
Quotations from Chairman Mao Tse-tung. P, FLP, 1967. Cited as: *Q*.
Selected Military Writings. P, FLP, 1968. Cited as: *SMW*.

(*b*) Unauthorised
Mao Tsé-tung et la construction du socialisme. Ed. Hu Chi-hsi, Paris, Seuil, 1975. Cited as: *Hu Chi-hsi*.

TEXTS

Note. *X* after a title indicates extracts. Many titles are available as single pamphlets.

1917A	'A study of physical education.'	*X*: S,I	2
1917B	Letter to Hakuro Toten.	Ch'en	
1919A	'The great union of the popular masses.'	*X*: S,I	7
1919B	[Miss Chao's suicide.]	*X*: S,I	15–20
1920A	Letter to Ts'ai Ho-seng.	*X*: S,I	26
1921A	Idem.	*X*: S,I	26
1923A	[The role of merchants in the national revolution.]	*X*: S,I	31
1923B	'The Chinese government and the foreigners.'	*X*: S,I	3
1926A	'An analysis of the various classes of the Chinese peasantry . . .'	*X*: S,I	49
1926B	'Analysis of the classes in Chinese society.'	SW,1, SR, S,I	50
1927A	'Report on an investigation of the peasant movement in Human.'	SW,1, SR. *X*: *LA*, S,I	55
1928A	'Why is it that Red political power can exist in China?'	SW,1, *SMW*. *X*: S,I	61

170   *For Mao*

1928B	'The struggle in the Chingkang mountains.' SW,1, *SMW*. *X*: S,I	62
1929A	'On the second anniversary of An Wu-ch'ing's martyrdom.' Ch'en	67
1929B	'On correcting mistaken ideas in the Party.' SW,1, *SMW*, *FA*. *X*: S,I	71
1930A	'A single spark can start a prairie fire.' [Letter to Lin Piao.] SW,1, *SMW*	72
1930B	'Oppose book worship.' SR	73
1931A	'A letter from the . . . Red Army . . .' S,I	
1931B	Decree concerning marriage. S,I	
1932A	Telegram [on the League]. S,I	
1933A	'Pay attention to economic work.' SW,1	94(?)
1933B	'How to differentiate the classes in the rural areas.' SW,1	
1934A	Proclamation on the northward march . . .. *X*: S,I	115
1934B	'Our economic policy.' SW,1	102
1934C	'Be concerned with the wellbeing of the masses . . . .' SW,1, SR	104
1935A	'On tactics against Japanese Imperialism.' SW,1. *X*: S,I	119
1936A	Letter to Lin Piao. Ch'en	120
1936B	'Appeal to the Ko Lao Hui.' *X*: S,I	121
1936C	[Interview with Edgar Snow.] In Snow, 1937/ 1961, Part IV. *X*: S,I	
1936D	'Problems of strategy in China's revolutionary war.' SW,1, *SMW*. *X*: SR, S,I	122
1936E	'A statement on Chiang Kai-shek's statement.' SW,1	125
1937A	'On Lu Hsun.' Ch'en	
1937B	[Lectures on dialectical materialism.] *X*: S,I	202
1937C	Letter to Hsu T'eh-li. Ch'en	126
1937D	'The tasks of the CPC in the period of resistance to Japan.' SW,1	129(?)
1937E	'Win the masses in their millions . . . .' SW,1. *X*: S,I	130
1937F	Letter to the Spanish people. *X*: S,I	131
1937G	Letter to Comrade E. Browder. *X*: S,I	132
1937H	'On practice.' SW,1, SR, *FE*. *X*: S,I	133

Bibliography 171

1937I	'Policies, measures and perspectives for resisting the Japanese invasion.'	SW,2	135
1937J	'On contradiction.' SW,1, SR, *FE. X: LA*, S,I		136
1937K	'For the mobilization of all the nation's forces . . ..'	SW,2	137
1937L	'Combat liberalism.' SW,2, SR, *FA*		138
1937M	'Urgent tasks . . ..'	SW,2	139
1937N	Speech	Ch'en	140
1937O	Inscription	Ch'en	141
1937P	Interview with . . . James Bertram.	SW,2	142
1937Q	'The situation and tasks . . . after the fall of Shanghai . . ..'	SW,2	143
1938A	'We must not fear the enemy.'	*X*: S,I	
1938B	'Problems of strategy in guerrilla war against Japan.' [From *On Guerilla Warfare.*] SW,2, *SMW. X*: S,I		151
1938C	'On protracted war.' SW,2, *SMW. X*: S,I		152
1938D	'The role of the CPC in the national war.' [From *On the new stage.*] SW,2, SR. *X: LA*, S,I		155
1938E	'The question of independence and initiative within the United Front.'	SW,2	157
1938F	'Problems of war and strategy.' SW,2, *SMW, X*: S,I		158
1939A	'May 4th movement.'	SW,2	163
1939B	'The orientation of the youth movement.' SW,2, *LA. X*: S,I		164
1939C	'To be attacked by the enemy is not a bad thing but a good thing.'	SR	167
1939D	'Oppose capitulationist activity'.	SW,2	
1939E	'The reactionaries must be punished,'	SW,2	170(?)
1939F	Interview with a *New China Daily* correspondent on the new international situation.	SW,2	171
1939G	Outline of a speech on the Second Imperialist War.	*X*: S,I	173
1939H	Interview with three correspondents.	SW,2	177(?)
1939I	'The identity of interests between the Soviet Union and all mankind.'	SW,2	179
1939J	'Introducing *The Communist*.' SW, 2, SR. X: S, I		175
1939K	'Youth needs experience.'	S,I	176

172		*For Mao*	

1939L	'The current situation and the Party's tasks.'		
		SW,2	178
1939M	'The Chinese revolution and the Communist Party of China.'	SW,2. *X*: S,I	182
1939N	'Recruit large numbers of intellectuals.'		
		SW,2	180
1939O	'Stalin, friend of the Chinese people'.	SW,2	184
1939P	'Stalin is our commander.'	S,I, Ch'en	
1939Q	'In memory of Norman Bethune.'		
		SW,2, SR, *FA*. *X*: S,I	185
1940A	'On New Democracy'.	SW,2. X: S,I	188
1940B	'Overcome the danger of capitulation . . ..'		
		SW,2	189
1940C	'Unite all anti-Japanese forces . . ..'	SW,2	
1940D	'Ten demands on the KMT.'	SW,2	190
1940E	'Introducing *The Chinese Worker*.'	SW,2	192
1940F	'We must stress unity and progress.'	SW,2	194
1940G	'New-Democratic constitutional government.'		
		SW,2	196
1940H	'On the question of political power in the anti-Japanese base areas.'	SW,2	197
1940I	'Current problems of tactics in the anti-Japanese United Front.'	SW,2, SR	198
1940J	'Freely expand the anti-Japanese forces . . ..'		
		SW,2	199
1940K	'Unity to the very end.'	SW,2	200
1940L	'On policy.'	SW,2	201
1941A	Order and statement on the Southern Anhwei Incident.	SW,2	203
1941B	'Preface' to *Rural Surveys*.	SW,3, SR	204
1941C	'Postscript' to 1941B	SW,3	204
1941D	'The situation after the repulse of the second anti-Communist onslaught.'	SW,2	205
1941E	'Conclusions on the repulse . . ..'	SW,2, *SMW*	206
1941F	'Reform our study'.	SW,3, SR, *LA*	207
1941G	'Expose the plot for a Far-Eastern Munich'.		
		SW,3	208
1941H	'On the international United Front against Fascism.'	SW,3	209
1941I	Speech at the Assembly of representatives of the . . . Border Region.	SW,3	215

Bibliography

173

1942A	'Rectify the Party's style of work.'	SW,3, SR. *X*: S,I	
1942B	'Oppose stereotyped Party writing'.	SW,3, SR, *LA. X*: S,I	217
1942C	Talks at the Yenan Forum on literature and Art.	SW,3, SR, *LA. X*:S,I	222
1942D	'A most important policy.'	SW,3	223
1942E	'The turning point in World War II.'	SW,3, *SMW*	224
1942F	'In celebration of the twenty-fifth anniversary of the October Revolution.'	SW,3	225
1942G	'Economic and financial problems in the anti-Japanese war.'	SW,3	227
1943A	Comrade Mao Tse-tung's report on the question of the dissolution of the Communist International.	*X*: S,I	231
1943B	'Some questions concerning methods of leadership.'	SW,3, SR. *X*: S,I	232
1943C	'Some pointed questions for the KMT'.	SW,3	235
1943D	'Spread the campaigns to reduce rent, increase production and "support the government and cherish the people" in the Base Areas.'	SW,3	236
1943E	A comment	SW,3	237
1943F	'Get organized!'	SW,3, SR. *X*: S,I	240
1944A	Letter to the Yenan Peking Opera Theatre	*FDLA*, Ch'en	241
1944B	'Our study and the current situation.'	SW,3. X: SR	242
1944C	[Ibid., Appendix:] Resolution on certain questions in the history of our Party.	SW,3	242
1944D	'Serve the people'.	SW,3, SR, *FA*	249
1944E	'On Chiang Kai-shek's speech . . ..'	SW,3	251(?)
1944F	'The United Front in cultural work.'	SW,3, *LA. X*: S,I	
1945A	'We must learn to do economic work.'	SW,3	266
1945B	'Production is also possible in the guerrilla zones.'	SW,3	267
1945C	'China's two possible destinies.'	SW,3	271
1945D	'On coalition government.'	SW,3. *X*: SR, *SMW*, S,I, *LA.*	275

174	*For Mao*	
1945E	'On production by the Army for its own support . . ..' SW,3 *SMW*	273
1945F	'The foolish old man who removed the mountains.' SW,3, SR, *FA*.	277
1945G	'The Hurley–Chiang duet is a flop.' SW,3	279
1945H	'On the danger of the Hurley policy'. SW,3. *X*: S,I	280
1945I	[F. Hurley, Chiang Kai-shek and the *Readers Digest* are a menace to world peace.] HSINHUA editorial. *X*: S,I	
1945J	'Telegram to Comrade William Z. Foster'. SW,3. *X*: S,I	281
1945K	'The last round with the Japanese invaders.' SW,3	283
1945L	'The situation and our policy after the victory . . ..' SW,4, SR	204(?)
1945M	'Chiang Kai-shek is provoking Civil War.' SW,4	285
1945N	'Two telegrams . . ..' SW,4	286
1945O	'On a statement by Chiang Kai-shek's spokesman.' SW,4	287
1945P	'On peace negotiations with the KMT . . ..' SW,4	288
1945Q	'On the Chunking negotiations.' SW,4	293
1945R	'The truth about the KMT attacks.' SW,4	294
1945S	'Rent reduction and production are two important matters for the defence of the Liberated Areas.' SW,4	295
1945T	'Policy for work in the Liberated Areas for 1946.' SW,4	298
1945U	'Build stable Base Areas in the North East.' SW,4	299
1946A	'Some points in appraisal of the current international situation.' SW,4, SR	304
1946B	'Salute the April 8th martyrs.' Ch'eñ	305
1946C	'Smash Chiang Kai-shek's offensive . . ..' SW,4	313
1946D	Talk with American correspondent Anna Louise Strong. SW,4, SR. *X*: S,I	315
1946E	'Concentrate a superior force to destroy the enemy forces one by one.' SW,4, *SMW*	316

Bibliography 175

1946F	'The truth about US "mediation" . . ..'	SW,4	317
1946G	'A three-month's summary.'	SW,4 *SMW*	318
1946H	'On the temporary abandonment of Yenan.' SW,4		327
1947A	'Greet the new high tide of the Chinese Revolution.'	SW,4	326
1947B	'The defence of the . . . Border Region.' SW,4		327
1947C	'The concept of operations for the North West War theatre.'	SW,4 *SMW*	328
1947D	'The Chiang Kai-shek government is beseiged by the whole people.'	SW,4	329
1947E	'Strategy for the second year of the War of Liberation.'	SW,4, *SMW*	330
1947F	Manifesto of the Chinese People's Liberation Army.	SW,4, *SMW*	331
1947G	'On the reissue of the three main rules of discipline and the eight points for attention . . ..' SW,4, *SMW*		332
1947H	'The present situation and our tasks.' SW,4, *SMW*. X: S,I		333
1948A	'On setting up a system of reports.'	SW,4	335
1948B	'On some important problems of the Party's present policy.'	SW,4. X: SR	336
1948C	'The democratic movement in the Army.' SW,4, *SMW*		337
1948D	'Different tactics for carrying out the Land Law in different areas.'	SW,4	338
1948E	'Correct the "Left" errors in land reform propaganda.'	SW,4	
1948F	'Essential points in land reform in the New Liberated Areas.'	SW,4	340
1948G	'On the policy concerning industry and commerce.'	SW,4	341
1948H	'On the question of the national bourgeoisie and the enlightened gentry.'	SW,4. X: S,I	342
1948I	'On the great victory in the North West . . ..' SW,4, *SMW*		343
1948J	'A circular on the situation.'	SW,4	345
1948K	Speech at a conference of cadres . . ..' SW,4. X: S,I		346

176 *For Mao*

1948L   A talk to the editorial staff on the *Shansi-Suiyuan Daily*.   SW,4, SR, *LA*   347
Telegram to the H.Q. of the Loyang Front.   SW, 4   348

1948N   'Tactical problems of rural work in the New Liberated Areas.'   SW,4   349

1948O   'The work of land reform and of Party consolidation in 1948.'   SW,4   350

1948P   'The concept of operations for the Liaohsi-Shenyang campaign.'[1.]   SW,4, *SMW*   351

1948Q   'On strengthening the Party Committee system.'   SW,4, *SMW*   352

1948R   'The concept . . ..' [As 1948P, 2.] SW,4, *SMW*   351

1948S   'On the September meeting.'   SW,4   353

1948T   'Concept of operations for the Huai-Hai campaign.'   SW,4, *SMW*   354

1948U   'Revolutionary forces of the world, unite, fight against imperialist aggression!'   SW,4. X: S,I   355

1948V   'The momentous change in China's military situation.'   SW,4, *SMW*   356

1948W   'The concept of operations for the Peiping-Tientsin campaign.'   SW,4, *SMW*   357

1948X   'Message urging Tu Yu-ming and others to surrender.'   SW,4   358

1948Y   'Carry the Revolution through to the end.'   SW,4, *SMW*   359

1949A   'On the War Criminals' suing for peace.' SW,4   360

1949B   'Statement on the present situation . . ..'   SW,4   361

1949C   Comment by the spokesman for the CPC . . ..'   SW,4   362

1949D   On ordering the reactionary KMT government to re-arrest Yasuji Okamura . . ..   SW,4   363–4(?)

1949E   'Peace terms must include the punishment of . . . War Criminals . . ..'   SW,4 365(?)

1949F   'Turn the army into a working force.'   SW,4, *SMW*   366

1949G   'Why do the badly-split reactionaries still idly clamour for "total peace"?'   SW,4   367

1949H   'The KMT reactionaries turn from an "appeal for peace" to an appeal for war.'   SW,4   368–9(?)

Bibliography 177

1949I	'On the KMT's different answers to the question of responsibility for the war.'	SW,4	370
1949J	Report to the second Plenum of the 7th CC/CPC.	SW,4. *X*: SR, S,I	371
1949K	'Methods of work of Party Committees.'	SW,4, SR. *X*: S,I	372
1949L	'Whither the Nanking government?'	SW,4	375
1949M	Order to the Army for the country-wide advance.	SW,4, *SMW*	377
1949N	Proclamation of the Chinese People's Liberation Army.	SW,4, *SMW*	378
1949O	'On the outrages by British warships . . ..'	SW,4	379
1949P	'Address to the preparatory committee of the new Political Consultative Conference.'	SW,4	381
1949Q	'On the People's Democratic Dictatorship.'	SW,4, SR. *X*: S,I	382
1949R	'Cast away illusions, prepare for struggle.'	SW,4. *X*: S,I	383
1949S	'Farewell, Leighton Stuart!'	SW,4	384
1949T	'Why it is necessary to discuss the White Paper.'	SW,4	
1949U	'"Friendship" or aggression?'	SW,4	386(?)
1949V	'The bankruptcy of the idealist conception of history.'	SW,4. *X*: S,I	387
1949W	'The Chinese people have stood up.'	SW,5	388(?)
1949X	'Long live the great unity of the Chinese people!'	SW, 5	
1949Y	'Eternal glory to the heroes of the people!'	SW,5	
1949Z	'Always keep to the style of plain living and hard struggle.' (Cf. 1949J: Section 10.)	SW,5	
1949AA	'China supports the Algerian people's struggle for liberation.'	S,I	
1949BB	'India's path is similar to that of China.'	S,I	390
1949CC	Instructions on the Army's participation in production	WS	
1949DD	'Stalin's 70th birthday.'	Ch'en	391
1950A	Request for opinions on the tactics of dealing with rich peasants.	SW,5	
1950B	'Fight for a fundamental turn for the better . . ..'		

178 *For Mao*

	[Report to third Plenum, 7th CC/CPC.]		
		SW,5. X: S,I	396
1950C	'Don't hit out in all directions.'	SW,5	
1950D	'Be a true revolutionary.'	SW,5	398
1950E	'You are models for the whole nation.'	SW,5	
1950F	Order to the Chinese People's Volunteers.		
		X: SW,5	
1950G	'Strike surely, accurately and relentlessly . . . .'		
		SW,5	
1951A	'The Chinese People's Volunteers should cherish every hill, every river, every tree and every blade of grass in Korea.'	SW,5	
1951B	Main points of the resolution adopted at the enlarged meeting of the Politburo CC/CPC.	SW,5	
1951C	Resolutions of the third National Conference on Public Security.	WS	
	'The Party's Mass Line must be followed . . . .'		
	[Instructions added to the above.]	SW,5	
1951D	'Pay serious attention to the discussion of the film "The life of Wu Hsun".' *Abridged text.*		
	SW,5. X: *FDLA, LA,* S,I, Ch'en		401
1951E	'Great victories in three mass movements.'		
		SW,5	402
1951F	On the struggle against the 'Three evils . . . .'		
	[Cf. 1952B.]	SW,5	
1951G	'Take mutual aid and co-operation in agriculture as a major task.'	SW,5	
1952A	New Year's Day message.	SW,5	
1952B	[On the struggle against] the 'Five evils'. [Cf. 1951F above.]	SW,5, WS.	
1952C	'On the policies for our work in Tibet.'	SW,5	
1952D	'The contradiction between the working class and the bourgeoisie is the principal contradiction in China.'	SW,5	
1952E	'Let us unite and clearly distinguish between ourselves and the enemy.'	SW,5	
1952F	'Hail the signal victory of the Chinese People's Volunteers!'	SW,5	
1953A	'Combat bureaucracy, commandism and violations of the law and of discipline.'	SW,5	

Bibliography

1953B	'The greatest friendship.'	X: S,I	409
1953C	'Criticize Han chauvinism.'	SW,5	
1953D	'Solve the problem of the "Five excesses".'	SW,5	
1953E	'Liu Shao-chi and Yang Shang-kun criticized for breach of discipline in issuing documents in the name of the CC without authorization.'	SW,5	
1953F	'Refute Right-deviationist views that depart from the General Line.'	SW,5	
1953G	'The Youth League in its work must take the characteristics of youth into consideration.'	SW,5	410
1953H	'On State capitalism.'	SW,5	
1953I	'The Party's General Line for the transition period.'	SW,5	
1953J	'Combat bourgeois ideas in the Party.' [Three texts at the National Conference on Financial and Economic Work.]	SW,5	
1953K	'The only road for the transformation of capitalist industry and commerce.'	SW,5	
1953L	'Our great victory in the war to resist U.S. Aggression and aid Korea . . ..'	SW,5	
1953M	'Criticism of Liang Shu-ming's reactionary ideas.' Essential Parts.	SW,5	
1953N	'Talk on mutual aid and co-operation in agriculture.'	SW,5	
1953O	[A second Talk. As 1953N.]	SW,5	
1954A	'On the draft constitution of the PRC.'	SW,5	
1954B	Directive on work in traditional Chinese medicine.	WS	
1954C	'The Albanian people has a glorious revolutionary tradition.'	X: S,I	
1954D	'Strive to build a great socialist country.'	SW,5	413
1954E	Letter concerning the study of 'The Dream of the Red Chamber.'	SW,5, FDLA, Ch'en	414
1955A	'The Chinese people cannot be cowed by the atom bomb.'	SW,5	
1955B	Speeches at the National Conference of the CPC.	SW,5	415

180 *For Mao*

1955C 'In refutation of "Uniformity of public opinion".' SW,5

1955D Preface and Editor's notes to *Material on the Counter Revolutionary Hu Feng Clique.* SW,5

1955E Comments [on the second and third groups of materials on the above]. Ch'en 416–7

1955F 'On the question of agricultural co-operation.' [SR title.] SW,5. SR. *X*: S,I 418

1955G 'Rely on Party and League members and poor and lower middle peasants in the co-operative transformation of agriculture.' SW,5

1955H 'The debate on the co-operative transformation of agriculture and the current class struggle.' [Concluding speech at the Enlarged Sixth Plenum, 7th CC/CPC.] SW,5

1955I Talk opposing Right-deviation and conservatism. WS

1955J *Socialist Upsurge in China's countryside.* P, FLP, 1957. Prefaces and Editorial notes are by Mao. *Selections.* SW,5, SR. *X*: S,I 419

1955K 'Request for opinions on the seventeen-article document concerning agriculture.' SW,5

1956A Talk at the conference for intellectuals called by the Centre. *X*: Ch'en 420

1956B 'Speed up the socialist transformation of handicrafts.' SW,5

1956C *On the historical experience of the dictatorship of the proletariat.* P, FLP, 1959. *X*: S,I

1956D 'On the ten great/major relationships.' SW,5, WS, S,II 421

1956E 'U.S. Imperialism is a paper tiger.' SW,5

1956F Talk to music workers. S,II

1956G 'Strengthen Party unity and carry forward Party traditions.' SW,5

1956H 'Some experiences in our Party's history.' SW,5

1956I 'In commemoration of Dr. Sun Yat-sen.' SW,5, Ch'en 424

1956J Speech at the 2nd Plenum 8th CC/CPC. SW,5 425

1956K Instructions at a discussion meeting . . .. WS

Bibliography

1957A	Talks at a conference of secretaries of Provincial, Municipal and Autonomous Region Party Committees.	SW,5, WS	
1957B	'On the correct handling of contradictions among the people.'	SW,5, SR, *FE. X*: S,I, *LA*	427
1957C	Speech at the CPC's National Conference on Propaganda Work.	SW,5, SR, *LA*	428
1957D	'Persevere in plain living and hard struggle, maintain close ties with the masses.'	SW,5	
1957E	Talk at the Hangchow conference of the Shanghai Bureau.	WS	
1957F	'Things are beginning to change.'	SW,5	431
1957G	'The CPC is the core of leadership of the whole Chinese people.'	SW,5	432
1957H	'Muster our forces to repulse the Rightists' wild attacks.'	SW,5	
1957I	'The situation in the summer of 1957.'	SW,5, Ch'en	434
1957J	'*Wen Hui Pao*'s bourgeois orientation should be criticized.'	SW,5, Ch'en	433
1957K	'Beat back the attacks of the bourgeois Rightists.'	SW,5	
1957L	'Be activists in promoting the Revolution.' [Speech at Enlarged 3rd Plenum 8th CC/CPC.]	SW,5	
1957M	'Have firm faith in the majority of the people.'	SW,5	435(?)
1957N	Statement at Moscow Airport.	*X*: Q, S,I	436
1957O	'Outline of views on the question of peaceful transition.' In: CC/CPC, *The origin and development of the differences between the leadership of the CPSU and ourselves*. P, FLP, 1963, Appendix I.		
1957P	'A dialectical approach to inner-party unity.'	SW,5	
1957Q	'All reactionaries are paper tigers.'	SW,5	
1957R	Conversation with Chinese students.	*X*: S,I	439
1958A	Talks at the Nan-Ning Conference.	WS	
1958B	Letter to the Kwangsi Regional Party Committee, on newspapers.	Ch'en	440

182 *For Mao*

1958C	Speech at the Supreme State Conference.	*X*: S,II	441
1958D	'Red and expert.'	Ch'en	442
1958E	'Part-time work and part-time study.'	Ch'en	444
1958F	Sixty points on working methods.	Ch'en	
1958G	'National minorities.'	Ch'en	445
1958H	Talks at the Chengtu Conference.	S,II	
1958I	Speech at the Hangchow Conference.	WS	
1958J	'Introducing a Co-operative.' SR. *X*: S,I		446
1958K	Speeches at the 2nd session, 8th Congress CPC.	WS	447
1958L	Speech at a conference of Heads of Delegations [to the same session].	WS	
1958M	Speech at the Group Leaders Forum	*X*: S,II	448
1958N	'Communes are better.'	*X*: S,I	
1958O	Resolution on the establishment of People's Communes in Rural Areas, of the CC/CPC. In: I. Ascher, *China's Social Policy*, L, Anglo-Chinese Educational Institute, 1972, Appendix.		
1958P	[Interview with a HSINHUA reporter.]*X*: S,I		456
1958Q	Speech at the 1st Chen Chao Conference. WS		
1958R	'On Stalin's *Economic Problems of Socialism in the USSR*.' WS, *Hu Chi-Hsi* A different translation is available as Mao Tse-tung, *A Critique of Soviet economics*, NY, Monthly Review Press, 1977.		
1958S	Talk with directors	WS	
1958T	'On Huan Hsiang's comment on the disintegration of the Western World.'	WS	
1958U	Letter to Chou Shih-chao.	WS	
1958V	Speech at the 6th Plenum 8th CC/CPC.	WS	
1958W	Reply to the article 'Tsinghua University Physics Teaching and Research Group inclines toward the "Left" rather than the "Right" in handling teachers'.	WS	
1959A	Comments on [Stalin's] 'Reply to Comrades A. V. Sanina and V. G. Venzher'.	WS	
1959B	'Examples of dialectics.' [Compilation.]	WS	
1959C	Annotations to Stalin's *Economic Problems* . . .. WS, *Hu-Chi-Hsi*		

Bibliography

	A different translation is available in *A Critique of Soviet Economics*, cited above at 1958R.	
1959D	Speech at a conference of provincial and municipal secretaries.	WS
1959E	Talk at a symposium	WS
1959F	Intra-Party correspondence.	WS
1959G	Comment on T'ao Lu-ch'ien's report	WS
1959H	Talk at 7th Plenum, 8th CC/CPC.	WS
1959I	Sixteen articles concerning work methods.	WS
1959J	Several important instructions.	WS
1959K	Speech at the Lushan Conference.	S,II 464(?)
1959L	'Why do Right-opportunists now launch an offensive?.'	WS
1959M	Comment on Chang Went-t'ien's letter.	WS
1959N	Comment on Peng Te-huai's letter of 9th September.	WS
1959O	Speech at the enlarged session of the Military Affairs Committee and the External Affairs Conference.	S,II 498
1959P	Letter to production brigade leaders.	Ch'en 480
1960A	'Classical works recommended to high ranking cadres.'	WS
1960B	'Principles of educating youth.'	WS
1960C	'Opinion on the free supply system.'	WS
1960D	Chairman Mao's important talks with guests	X: S,I
1960E	Criticism disseminated by the CC/CPC on 'Anshan Municipal Party Committee's report on the developing situation . . .'.	WS
1960F	'On the anti-China question'.	WS
1960G	Comments on Vice-Premier Nieh Jung-chen's report on the technical revolution.	WS
1960H	'Summing up ten years!'	WS
1960I	Dissemination of the CC/CPC's criticism of the Shansi Provincial Party Committee's report on the rural labour force problem.	WS
1961A	Speech at 9th Plenum 8th CC/CPC.	WS
1961B	Preface to '*Oppose book worship*'.	WS
1961C	Letter to the Communist Labour University at Kiangsi.	Ch'en 485
1962A	Reading Notes on the Soviet Union's *Political Economics*.	WS

184   *For Mao*

A different translation is available in *A Critique of Soviet Economics*, cited above at 1958R.

1962B	'On democratic centralism.'	S,II	489
1962C	Speech at 10th Plenum, 8th CC/CPC. ['Never forget class struggle . . .'.]	S,II	490
1963A	'Where do correct ideas come from?' [Part of draft decision CC/CPC on 'certain problems in our present rural work.']	SR, *FE*	495
1963B	Instruction on the Commune Education Movement.	WS	
1963C	Note on the 'Seven well-written documents of Chekiang Province concerning cadres' participation in physical labour'. In 1964R and *Q*		
1963D	Statement supporting the American Negroes' just struggle against imperialist racial discrimination.	*X*: S,I	496
1963E	Instruction [concerning literature and art].	*FDLA*, S,I, Ch'en	499
1963F	The Centre's instruction on learning from each other	Ch'en	500
1963G	Speech at Hangchow	WS	
1964A	Directive on the question of class distinction.	WS	
1964B	'Why the "First ten articles" and the "Sixty articles" can mobilize manpower.'	WS	
1964C	On education – conversation with Nepalese delegation	Ch'en	509
1964D	Statement on . . . Panamanian People's just patriotic struggle.	S,I	501
1964E	Talk on health services.	WS	
1964F	Remarks at the Spring Festival [on education]. *Summaries*.	S,II, Ch'en, WS	503
1964G	Remarks at a briefing.	WS	
1964H	Talk at Hantan Forum on "Four clean-ups" work.	WS	
1964I	Directive on labour reform.	WS	
1964J	Some interjections at a briefing of the State Planning Commission leading group.	WS	
1964K	Interjection at a briefing by four Vice-Premiers.	WS	
1964L	Talk on the Third Five Year Plan.	WS	

Bibliography

1964M	Talk on putting military affairs work into full effect and cultivating successors to the revolution.	WS	
1964N	Conversation with Zanzibar expert M. M. Ali and his wife.	WS	
1964O	Instruction [concerning literature and art].	*FDLA*, Ch'en	505
1964P	Comment on a report by comrade Wang Tung-hsing.	WS	
1964Q	First talk with Mao Yuan-hsin.	S,II	
1964R	[Fifteen theses on socialist construction.] In CC/CPC *On Khrushchov's phoney communism and its historical lessons for the world.* P, FLP, 1964 ('The Ninth Reply').	*X*: S,I	
1964S	Talk on methods of solidarity.	WS	
1964T	Talk on questions of philosophy.	S,II, WS	
1964U	Talk on Sakata's article.	WS	
1964W	Statement supporting the people of the Congo (Leopoldville) against U.S. aggressors.	S,I	508
1964X	'China's Great Leap Forward.'	S,II	
1964Y	Highlights of forum on CC work.	WS	505
1964Z	Interjections at Central Work conference.	WS	
1964AA	Speech at Central Work conference.	WS	
1965A	Directives after hearing reports of Ku Mu and Yu Chiu-li on planning work.	WS	
1965B	Talk on the 'Four clean-ups' movement.	WS	
1965C	Twenty-three articles of rural socialist education.	*X*: S,I	511
1965D	Notes on Comrade Ch'en Cheng-jen's report on his 'squatting point'.	Ch'en	513
1965E	'You fight your way and I'll fight my way' conversation with P.L.O. delegation.	WS	
1965F	Instruction on public health work.	Ch'en, S,II	518
1965G	Notes on the report of an investigation of the Peking Teachers' Training College.	Ch'en	520
1965H	Speech at Hangchow.	S,II	
1966A	Second talk with Mao Yuan-hsin.	S,II	
1966B	'Down with the prince of Hell/Liberate the little devil.' Talk with such comrades as Kang Sheng.	WS	

186 *For Mao*

1966C	Letter of instruction on the question of agricultural mechanization.	WS	
1966D	Third talk with Mao Tuan-hsin.	S,II	
1966E	Talk at an enlarged SC/PB/CC/CPC meeting.	WS	
1966F	Talk	WS	
1966G	'Criticise Peng Chen.'	WS	
1966H	'May 7th instruction' [Letter to Lin Piao].	Ch'en	521
1966I	Circular of the CC/CPC.	Ch'en	522
1966J	Talk to leaders at the Centre.	S,II, Ch'en	523
1966K	Talk at a meeting with regional secretaries and members of the cultural revolution group of the CC/CPC.	S,II, Ch'en (2 versions)	527
1966L	Talk at an enlarged work conference at the Centre.	Ch'en	529
1966M	Letter to the Red Guards of Tsinghua University Middle School.	S,II	525
1966N	Interjection at an enlarged meeting of SC/PB/CC/CPC.	WS	
1966O	*Bombard the Headquarters!* My Big Character Poster.	Ch'en	526
1966P	Resolution on the GPCR, 11th Plenum 8th CC/CPC. ['The sixteen articles'.]	Ch'en	527

In: J. Robinson, *The Cultural Revolution* . . . L, Penguin, 1969, 85–96.

1966Q	Closing speech, 11th Plenum 8th CC/CPC.	S,II, Ch'en	528
1966R	Talk at a work conference at the Centre.	Ch'en	530
1966S	Talk at general report conference. ['Make revolution and reform yourselves.']	S,II	533
1966T	Talk at the central work conference.	S,II, Ch'en	534
1966U	Message of greetings to the Fifth Congress of the Albanian Party of Labour.	S,I	535
1967A	Conversation with Premier Chou on power struggles.	Ch'en	543
1967B	Talk at a meeting of the central cultural revolution group.	S,II, Ch'en	537
1967C	Talk at the enlarged meeting of the Military Commission.	Ch'en	541

Bibliography

1967D	Talk at three meetings with comrades Chang Chun-chiao and Yao Wen-yuan.	S,II
1967E	Directive on the GPCR in Shanghai.	WS
1967F	Speech to the Albanian Military Delegation.	WS
1967G	Directive on external propaganda work.	WS
1967H	Dialogues during inspection of North, Central, South and East China.	WS
1967I	Letter to Liu, Chou and CC cultural revolution Group.	WS
1967J	Telegram to Chairman Nhuyen Huu Tho	S,I 544
1968A	Dialogue with responsible persons of Capital Red Guards Congress.	WS
1968B	The Party is the leading nucleus. [Part of draft Constitution of CPC for 12th Plenum 8th CC/ CPC.]	S,I
1969A	Address at opening session 9th Congress CPC.	S,II
1969B	The Chinese and world revolution.	Ch'en
1969C	Talk at 1st Plenum 9th CC/CPC.	S,II
1971A	Talks with responsible comrades during a provincial tour. *Summary.*	S,II

PART TWO

SOME EMPIRICAL RESOURCES

Note. As we have stressed, our account here is not historical in the conventional sense. To assist those who wish to examine further empirical details, we provide here a brief indication of resources which are useful starting points. Fuller details are available in the subsequent sequence. This list can be supplemented by that provided in *SCMT*, 103f.

Mao's Life and Work

Han Suyin, *The Morning Deluge . . . 1893–1953*, and *Wind in the Tower, . . . 1949–1975*, 1972, 1976.

S. Uhalley, *Mao Tse-tung*, 1975.

D. Wilson (ed.), *Mao Tse-tung in the Scales of History . . . 1977.*

188 *For Mao*

General Studies

E. Snow, *Red Star over China*, 1937/1961.
E. Snow, *Red China Today* (in the US as *The Other Side of the River*), 1962. Rev. edn, 1970.
R. Alley, *Travels in China, 1966–1971*, 1973.

Specific Studies

Modern China series of the Anglo-Chinese Educational Institute, available from the Society for Anglo-Chinese Understanding, 152, Camden High Street, London NW1. *China Now* (SACU's journal), monthly.

Documents

China Readings. 4 vols. L, Penguin, 1967, 1974.
Peking Review (weekly), *China Reconstructs* (monthly), from P, Guozi Shudian.

Compendium

J. Gittings, *A Chinese View of China*, 1973.

SOME THEORETICAL STUDIES

Mao Tse-tung, *Selected readings*, 1971.
G. Thomson (1973), *Capitalism and After*, and (1971), *From Marx to Mao Tse-tung*.
The works of C. Bettelheim and of J. Gray.
We would also draw attention to the theoretical value of the studies by Macciocchi, Hinton, Myrdal and Jack Chen.

TEXTS

Alley, R., 1973. *Travels in China 1969–1971*. P, New World Press.
Altaisky, M., 1970. *What is Maoism?* M, Novosti.
——1974. *What the Maoists are Concealing.* L, Soviet Booklets.
Althusser, L., 1963. 'On the materialist dialectic.' In his 1965.
——1965. *For Marx.* L, Allen Lane, 1969.

Bibliography

189

——1968. 'Lenin and philosophy.' In his 1971.

——1969. 'Lenin before Hegel.' In his 1971.

——1971. *Lenin and Philosophy*, and other essays. L, New Left Books.

——1972a. 'Reply to John Lewis.' In his 1976.

——1972b. 'Note on "The Critique of the Personality Cult".' In his 1976.

——1973. 'Remark on the category "Process without a Subject or Goals".' In his 1976.

——1974. 'Elements of self-criticism'. In his 1976.

——1975. 'Is it simple to be a Marxist in Philosophy' In his 1976.

——1976. *Essays in Self-criticism*. L, New Left Books.

Anderson, P., 1974a. *Passages from Antiquity to Feudalism*. L, New Left Books.

——1974b. *Lineages of the Absolutist State*. L, New Left Books.

——1974c. *Considerations on Western Marxism*. L, New Left Books, 1976.

——1976. Afterword to his 1974c.

——1977. 'The antinomies of Antonio Gramsci.' *New Left Rev.*, 100.

Andors, S., 1977. *China's Industrial Revolution: Politics, Planning and Management, 1949 – the Present*. L, Martin Robertson.

Balibar, E., 1972. 'La rectification du manifeste Communiste.' *La Pensée*, 164.

——1976a. 'The dictatorship of the proletariat.' *Marxism Today*, 21: 5.

——1976b. *The dictatorship of the proletariat*. Paris, Maspero; L, New Left Books, 1977.

Bates, T. R., 1975. 'Gramsci and the theory of hegemony.' *J. History of Ideas*, 36.

Belden, J., 1949. *China Shakes the World*. L, Penguin, 1973.

Benton, G., 1975. 'Introduction to "The Yenan 'Literary Opposition'".' *New Left Rev.*, 92.

——1977. 'The factional struggle in the Chinese Communist Party.' *Critique*, 8.

Berger, R., 1975. 'Economic planning in the People's Republic of China.' *World Development*, 3: 7/8.

Bettelheim, C., 1950. 'Discussion on the problem of choice between alternative investment projects.' *Soviet Studies*.

——1966. 'La construction du socialisme.' *La Pensée*, 125 & 126.

——1967. *The Transition to Socialist Economy*. Hassocks, Harvester, 1975.

——1969. 'Preface' to Fr. edn of, and 'Theoretical comments' on,

A. Emmanuel, *Unequal exchange*, L, New Left Books, 1972.
—1970a. *Economic Calculation and Forms of Property*. L, Routledge, 1976.
—1970b. 'Sur la persistence des rapports marchands dans les "pays socialistes".' *Temps modernes*, 27.
—1971a. His contributions to *On the Transition to Socialism*. With P. Sweezy, NY and L, Monthly Rev. Pr.
—1971b. 'A propos du "marxisme de Mao" lettre de Rossana Rossanda.' In *Il Manifesto*, 1971.
—1972. 'Note de lecture sur l'article: "de la Chine et des racines de la Sinophile occidentale".' *Tel Quel*, 48/49.
—1973. *Cultural Revolution and Industrial Organisation in China*. NY and L, Monthly Rev. Pr., 1974.
—1974. *Class Struggles in the USSR. 1st Period: 1917–1923*. Hassocks, Harvester, 1976.
—1977. *Les Luttes de classes en URSS. 2ème periode: 1923–1930*. Paris, Seuil-Maspero.
Bhattacharya, D., 1974. 'India and China . . .'. *J. Contemp. Asia*, 4: 4.
Bianco, L., 1971. *Origins of the Chinese Revolution, 1915–1949*. Rev. edn, Oxford.
Blackburn, R., (ed.), 1972. *Ideology in Social Science*. L, Fontana.
Boggs, C., 1976. *Gramsci's Marxism*. L, Pluto Pr.
British and Irish Communist Organisation, 1977. *The Politics of Revolutionary China*. Belfast, B & ICO.
Brown, A., and Gray, J., (eds), 1977. *Political Culture and Political Change in Communist States*. L, Macmillan.
Brugger, B., 1976. *Democracy and Organisation in the Chinese Industrial Enterprise, 1948–1953*. Cambridge Univ. Pr.
—1977. *Contemporary China*. L, Croom Helm.
Buchanan, K., 1970. *The Transformation of the Chinese Earth*. L, Bell.
Bukharin, N., 1921. *Historical Materialism: a Systematic Sociology*. Michigan, Ann Arbor, 1969.
Bulkeley, R., 1977. 'On "On Practice".' *Radical Philosophy*, 18.
Callinicos, A., 1976. *Althusser's Marxism*. L, Pluto.
Cammett, J. M., 1966. 'Communist theories of Fascism, 1920–1935'. *Science and Society*, 31, 1967.
—1967. *Antonio Gramsci and the Origins of Italian Communism*. Stanford Univ. Pr.
Carocci, G., 1972. *Italian Fascism*. L, Penguin, 1974.

Bibliography

Carr, E. H., 1953. *The Bolshevik Revolution, 1917–1923. Vol. 3.* L, Penguin, 1966.
——1964. *Socialism in One Country, 1924–1926. Vol. 3.* L, Penguin, 1972.
Ch'en, J., 1965. *Mao and the Chinese Revolution.* Oxford.
——1970. *Mao Papers.* Oxford.
Chen, Jack, 1973. *A Year in Upper Felicity.* L, Harrap.
——1975. *Inside the Cultural Revolution.* L, Sheldon Pr.
Chen Chang-feng, 1972. *On the Long March with Chairman Mao.* 2nd. edn, P, FLP.
Chesneaux, J., 1973. *Peasant Revolts in China, 1840–1949.* L, Thames & Hudson.
Chi Hsin, 1977. *The Case of the 'Gang of Four'.* Hong Kong, Cosmos Books.
Chu Li and Tien Chiehyen, 1974. *Inside a People's Commune.* P, FLP.
Clark, M., 1976. *Antonio Gramsci and the Revolution that Failed.* Yale Univ. Pr., 1977.
Claudin, F., 1970. *The Communist Movement from Comintern to Cominform.* L, Penguin, 1975.
Cliff, T., 1957. *Mao's China,* by Y. Gluckstein. L, Allen & Unwin.
——1968. 'The Sheng-wu-lien faction.' *International Socialism,* 37.
Cohen, P., 1973. *Between Tradition and Modernity . . ..* Harvard, 1974.
Collier, J. and Collier, E., 1973. *China's Socialist Revolution.* L, Stage One.
Communist Party of China, 1963. *A Proposal Concerning the General Line of the International Communist Movement.* P, FLP.
——1964. *Whence the differences?* Bath, New Era, n.d.
——1965. *The Polemic on the General Line . . .* P, F.L.P. Reprinted L, Red Star Pr., n.d.
——1973. *The 10th National Congress of the CPC: Documents.* P. FLP.
——1975. *Documents of the 1st Session of the 4th National People's Congress . . ..* P, FLP.
Compton, B., 1952. *Mao's China: Party Reform Documents 1942–1944.* Seattle, Univ. of Washington Pr.
Corrigan, P. R. D., 1974. 'On the historical experience of the People's Republic of China.' *J. Contemp. Asia,* 4.
——1975a. 'On the politics of production.' *J. Peasant Stud.,* 3.
——1975b. 'Dichotomy is contradiction.' *Sociological Rev.,* 24.
——1976a. *State Formation and Moral Regulation in 19th Century*

192 *For Mao*

Britain: Sociological Investigations. PhD, Durham Univ., 1977.

——1976b. 'On socialist construction.' *J. Contemp. Asia*, 6.

——1977. 'Feudal relics or capitalist monuments.' *Sociology*, 11.

Corrigan, P. R. D., Ramsay, H., and Sayer, D., 1978. *Socialist Construction and Marxist Theory: Bolshevism and its Critique.* L, Macmillan; NY, Monthly Rev. Pr.

Corrigan, P. R. D., and Sayer, D., 1975. 'Moral relations, political economy and class struggle.' *Radical Philosophy*, 12.

Cozens, P., 1977. *Twenty Years of Antonio Gramsci: a Bibliography* . . .. L, Lawrence & Wishart.

Croll, E., (ed.), 1974. *The Women's Movement in China: a Selection of Readings, 1949–1973.* L, Anglo-Chinese Educational Inst.

——1976. 'Social production and female status: women in China.' *Race & Class*, 18: 1.

——1978. *Feminism and Socialism in China.* l, Routledge.

Cutler, A., *et al.*, 1977. *Marx's 'Capital' and Capitalism Today, I.* L, Routledge.

Daubier, J., 1974. *A History of the Chinese Cultural Revolution.* NY, Vintage.

Davidson, A., 1974. 'Gramsci and Lenin 1917–1972.' *Socialist Register* (L, Merlin Pr.).

——1977. *Antonio Gramsci: Towards an Intellectual Biography.* L, Merlin Pr.

Davin, D. 1976. *Woman-work: Women and the Party in Revolutionary China.* Oxford, Clarendon Pr.

Davison, D., and Selden, M., 1977. *Chou En-lai and the Chinese Revolution* . . .. Los Angeles, US China Peoples Friendship Assoc.

Debray, R., 1969. 'Schema for a study of Gramsci.' *New Left Rev.*, 59, 1970.

Deutscher, I., 1949. *Stalin.* Oxford.

——1967. *The Chinese Cultural Revolution.*' Nottingham, Bertrand Russell Peace Foundation.

Doolin, D. J., and Golas, P. J., 1964. ' "On Contradiction" . . .'. *China Qu.*, 19.

Draper, H., 1971. 'The principle of self-emancipation in Marx and Engels.' *Socialist Register* (L, Merlin Pr.).

——1977. *Karl Marx's Theory of Revolution. Part I.* NY and L, Monthly Rev. Pr. (In progress.)

Fanon, F., 1968. *Black Skins, White Masks.* NY, Grove Pr.; L, MacGibbon and Kee.

Bibliography 193

——1969. *The Wretched of the Earth*. L, Penguin.

——1970. *Towards the African Revolution*. L, Penguin.

Fiori, G., 1965. *Antonio Gramsci: Life of a Revolutionary*. L, New Left Books, 1970.

——1975. 'Antonio Gramsci: "This century's most original Marxist thinker".' *The Times*, 21 Nov.

Gardner, J., and Idema, W., 1973. 'China's educational revolution.' In Schram, 1973c.

Gardner, J., 1977. 'Chinese education: a turbulent decade.' *New Society*, 28 Jul.

Gelder, S. (ed.), 1946. *The Chinese Communists*. L, Gollancz (Left Book Club).

Genovese, E., 1967. 'On Antonio Gramsci [Review of Cammett, 1967].' *Studies on the Left*, 7. Reprinted as Ch. 19 in his *In Red and Black* . . .. NY, Vintage, 1971.

Geras, N., 1972. 'Marx and the critique of political economy.' In R. Blackburn, 1972.

Gittings, J., 1967. *The Role of the Chinese Army*. L, Oxford Univ. Pr. and Royal Inst. Inter. Affairs.

——(ed.), 1973. *A Chinese View of China*. L, BBC.

——1977. 'The statesman.' In Wilson, 1977.

Gouldner, A. W., 1975. 'Prologue to a theory of revolutionary intellectuals.' *Telos*, 26.

Gramsci, A., 1947. [*Lettere del carcere*, 218] *Prison Letters*; trans. H. Henderson. *New Edinburgh Rev.*, 1975.

——1948. [*Quaderni del Carcere*] *Selections from the Prison Notebooks*. L, Lawrence & Wishart, 1971.

——1977a. *Selections from Political Writings, 1910–1920*. L, Lawrence & Wishart.

Gray, J., 1965. 'Political aspects of the land reform campaigns in China.' *Soviet Studies*, 16.

——1966. 'Some aspects of Chinese agrarian policies.' In R. Adams (ed.) *Contemporary China*. L, Owen, 1969.

——1969a. 'The economics of Maoism.' In H. Bernstein (ed.), *Development and underdevelopment*. L, Penguin, 1972.

——1969b. *Recapitulation of Factors in the Cultural Revolution*. Hong Kong, Centre for Asian Studies.

——1970. 'The High Tide of Socialism in the Chinese Countryside.' In J. Chen (ed.), *Studies in the social history of China* . . .. Cambridge Univ. Pr.

——1971. 'The Chinese model.' *L'Est*, 2. In A. Nove and D. Nuti

194 *For Mao*

(eds) *Socialist Economics*, L, Penguin, 1972.

——1972a. 'Mao Tse-tung's strategy for the collectivisation of Chinese Agriculture.' In E. de Kadt and G. Williams (eds), *Sociology and Development*, L, Tavistock, 1974.

——1972b. 'Theory of the Great Leap Forward.' Unpublished paper.

——1973a. Contribution to discussion. *The Listener*, 5 Jul.

——1973b. 'The two roads: alternative strategies for social change and economic growth in China.' In Schram, 1973c.

——1973c. *Mao Tse-tung*. Guildford, Lutterworth Pr.

——1974. 'Politics in command.' *Pol. Qu.*, 45: 1.

——1976a. 'Stalin, Mao, and the future of China.' *New Society*, 1 Apr.

——1976b. 'What is the crime of China's "Gang of Four"?.' *New Society*, 4 Nov.

——1977a. 'China: communism and confucianism.' Ch. 7 in Brown and Gray, 1977.

——1977b. 'Conclusions.' Ch. 91, in Brown and Gray, 1977.

Gunn, R., 1977. 'Is nature dialectical?' *Marxism Today*, 21: 2.

Gurley, J., 1975a. 'The foundation of Mao's economic strategy, 1927–1949.' *Monthly Rev.*, 27: 3.

——1975b. 'Rural development in China, 1949–72.' *World Dev.*, 3: 7/8.

Hailsham, *Lord*, 1977. 'When professors disagree.' *The Listener*, 24 Mar.

Halliday, F., 1977. 'Marxist analysis and post-revolutionary China.' *New Left Rev.*, 100.

Han Suyin, 1972. *Morning Deluge: Mao Tse-tung and the Chinese Revolution*. L, Cape.

——1976. *The Wind in the Tower: Mao Tse-tung and the Chinese Revolution, 1949–1975*. L, Cape.

Harrington, M., 1958. 'Despotism's fortress in Asia: is China ruled by a new democracy or a new class?' *New International*, 24: 2–3.

Harrison, J., *The Long March to Power: a History of the Communist Party of China, 1921–1972*. L, Macmillan.

Hindess, B., and Hirst, P. Q., 1977. *Mode of Production and Social Formation*. L, Macmillan.

Hinton, W., 1966. *Fanshen*. NY, Monthly Rev. Pr.; L, Penguin, 1972.

——1969. *China's Continuing Revolution*. L, China Policy Study Group.

Bibliography 195

——1970a. *Iron Oxen: a Documentary of Revolution in Chinese Farming.* NY, Vintage.

——1970b. 'Postscript' to his 1970a.

——1972a. 'Hundred Day War: the Cultural Revolution at Tsinghua University.' *Monthly Rev*, 24: 3.

——1972b. *Turning Point in China: an Essay on the Cultural Revolution.* NY, Monthly Rev. Pr.

——1973. 'Reflections on China.' *Monthly Rev.*, 25.

Ho Chi-minh, 1928. 'The Party's military work among the peasants.' In 'A. Neuberg' [i.e. Comintern Secretariat], *Armed Insurrection.* L, New Left Books, 1970.

Hobsbawm, E. J., 1977. 'Gramsci and political theory.' *Marxism Today*, 21: 7.

Hodges, D. C., 1962. 'Historical materialism and ethics.' *Philosophy and Phenomenological Research*, 23: 1.

——1963. 'Socialists in search of an ethic.' *Studies on the left*, Winter.

——1964. 'Marx's ethics and ethical theory.' *Socialist Register* (L, Merlin Pr.).

——1965. 'Engels' contribution to marxism.' *Socialist Register* (L, Merlin Pr.).

Hoffman, J., 1977. 'The dialectics of nature.' *Marxism Today*, 21: 1.

Hofheinz, R. 1969. 'Ecology of Chinese communist success: rural influence patterns, 1923–1945.' In A. D. Barnett (ed.), *Chinese Communist Politics in Action*, Washington Univ. Pr.

Holubnychni, V., 1964. 'Mao Tse-tung's materialist dialectics.' *China Qu.*, 19.

Horn, J., 1971. 'The mass-line.' *In Health Care in China*, L, Anglo-Chinese Educational Institute, 1976.

Houn, F., 1973. *A Short History of Chinese Communism*, New Jersey, Prentice-Hall.

Jacoviello, A., 1973. 'Contrasting China and India.' *China Now*, 39.

Kaplan, L. (ed.), 1973. *Revolutions: a Comparative Study.* NY, Random House.

Karol, K. S., 1975. *The Second Chinese Revolution.* L, Cape.

Kiernan, V., 1972. 'Gramsci and Marxism.' *Socialist Register* (L, Merlin Pr.).

——1974. 'Gramsci and the other continents.' *New Edinburgh Rev.*

Kirby, E. S., 1975. *Russian Studies of China: Progress and Problems in Soviet Sinology.* Totawa, N. J., Rowman & Littlefield.

Korbash, E., 1974. *The Economic 'Theories' of Maoism.* M, Progress.

Krymov, A., 1971. 'The debate on pre-capitalist relations in China.' Tr. *Soviet Sociology*, Fall 1972.

196   *For Mao*

Lambardini, F., 1968. 'Italian fascism and the economy.' In Woolf, 1968.

Lee Chen-chung, 1972. 'Trotsky's theory of "permanent revolution" and Mao Tse-tung's theory of "continuous revolution".' *Issues & Studies*, 8: 7, 8.

Li Chien, 1973. 'Attach importance to the revolution in the superstructure.' *Peking Rev.*, 34.

Linhart, R., 1976. *Lénine, les paysans, Taylor*. Paris, Seuil.

Liu Po-cheng, 1959. 'Looking back on the Long March.' *August First*, 20; Tr. *Peking Rev.*, 45, 1975.

Lowy, M., 1976. 'From the *Logic* of Hegel to the Finland Station in Petrograd.' *Critique*, 6.

Lu Yu-lan, 1972. *New Women in the New China*. P, FLP.

Lukács, G. 1924. *Lenin*. L, New Left Books, 1970.

——1925. 'Technology and social relations (Critique of Bukharin, 1921).' *New Left Rev.*, 39, 1966; reprinted in his 1968.

——1968. *Political writings, 1919–1929*. L, New Left Books, 1972.

Macciocchi, M., 1971. *Daily Life in Revolutionary China*. NY and L, Monthly Rev. Pr., 1972.

Magdoff, H., 1975. 'China: contrasts with the USSR.' *Monthly Rev.*, 27: 3.

Maisels, C. K., 1974. 'Gramsci between two Internationals.' *New Edinburgh Rev.*

Maitan, L., 1976. *Party, Army and Masses in China*. L, New Left Books.

Manifesto, Il, 1971. *Analyses et thèses de la nouvelle extrême-gauche Italienne . . ..* Paris, Seuil.

Martinelli, A., 1968. 'In defense of the dialectic: Antonio Gramsci's theory of revolution.' *Berkeley J. of Sociology*, 13.

Mauger, P., *et al.*, 1974. *Education in China*. L, Anglo-Chinese Educational Institute.

Mauger, S., 1973. 'The political theory of Mao Tse-tung.' *China Now*, 31–33.

Mavrakis, K., 1973. *On Trotskyism: Problems of Theory and History*. L, Routledge, 1976.

Mehnert, K.; 1963. *Peking and Moscow*. L, Weidenfeld.

Meisner, M., 1967. *Li Ta-chao and the Origins of Chinese Marxism*. Harvard Univ. Pr.

——1970. 'Yenan communism and the rise of the Chinese People's Republic.' In J. Crowley (ed.), *Modern East Asia*, NY, Harcourt.

Bibliography

Mepham, J., 1972. 'The theory of ideology in *Capital.*' *Radical Philosophy*, 2.

Merrington, J., 1968. 'Theory and practice in Gramsci's marxism.' *Socialist Register* (L, Merlin Pr.).

Miliband, R., 1977. *Marxism and Politics*. Oxford Univ. Pr.

Milton, D., 1977. *People's China*. L, Penguin (China Readings, 4).

Moore, B., 1966. *The Social Origins of Democracy and Dictatorship*. L, Penguin, 1969.

Myrdal, J., 1963. *Report from a Chinese Village*. L, Penguin, 1967.

——1970. *China: the Revolution Continues*. L, Penguin, 1973.

Nee, V. 1969. *The Cultural Revolution at Peking University*. NY, Monthly Rev. Pr.

——1975. 'Revolution and bureaucracy; Shanghai in the Cultural Revolution'. In V. Nee and J. Peck (eds), *China's Uninterrupted Revolution: from 1840 to the Present*, NY, Pantheon.

Nicolaievski, B., 1956. 'Toward a history of the Communist League, 1847–1852.' *Int. Rev. Social His.*, series ii, 1.

Nicolaus, M., 1973. 'Foreword' to Marx, 1858a (Penguin edn).

Nolan, P., 1975. 'Collectivisation in China: some comparisons with the USSR.' *J. Peasant Stud.*, 3: 2, 1976.

Norman, R., 1976. 'On dialectic.' *Radical Philosophy*, 14.

Nowell-Smith, G., 1977. 'Gramsci and the national-popular.' *Screen Education*, 22.

Oksenberg, M., 1973a. 'On learning from China.' In his 1973b.

——(ed.) 1973b., *China's Developmental Experience*. NY, Praeger, 1973.

——1974. 'Political changes and their causes in China 1949–1972.' *Political Qu.*, 45: 1.

——1977. 'The political leader.' Ch. 3 In Wilson, 1977.

Padoul, G., 1975. 'China, 1974: problems not models.' *New Left Rev.*, 89.

Pai Chi-hsien, 1974. 'Integration with the poor- and lower-middle peasants.' *Peking Rev.*, 30.

Pannekoek, A., 1938. *Lenin as philosopher* . . . with additional notes by Paul Mattick. L, Merlin Pr., 1975.

Perkins, D., 1974. 'The Chinese economy in historical perspective.' *Items*, 28: 1.

Piccone, P., 1976. 'Gramsci's Marxism.' *Theory & Society*, 3: 4.

Poulantzas, N., 1970. *Fascism and Dictatorship: the 3rd International and the Problem of Fascism*. L, New Left Books, 1974.

Pozzolini, A., 1968. *Antonio Gramsci* . . .. L, Pluto Pr., 1970.

198 *For Mao*

Price, D. C., 1974. *Russia and the Roots of the Chinese Revolution, 1896–1911.* Harvard Univ. Pr.

Price, R. F., 1970. *Education in Communist China.* L, Routledge.

Ramsay, H. E., 1973a. 'Conceptual confusion and contradiction: workers' control and the lone monk with the leaky unbrella.' *Bull. of North Staffs. Labour History Group*, 1974.

——1976. 'Power, ideology and social reality: sociology at the university of the greenwoods.' Paper to EGOS Conference, University of Bradford.

——1977a. 'Review (of Bettelheim, 1970a).' *Sociological Rev.*, 25: 2.

——1977b. 'Magnitogorsk, Zenica, Anshan: State form and workers' control.' Paper to 2nd International Conference on Participation . . ., Paris.

Ree, J., 1976. 'Philosophy in China.' *Radical Philosophy*, 14.

Robinson, J., 1975. *Economic Management in China.* Rev. edn, L, Anglo-Chinese Educational Institute.

Rosenberg, D., 1976. (Review essay on fascism). *Sociological Rev.*, 24.

Rossanda, R., 1970. 'Mao's Marxism.' *Socialist Register* (L, Merlin Pr.), 1971.

——1971. 'La révolution culturelle et la structure sociale de la Chine communiste.' *L'Homme et la Société*, 21.

——1974. 'Revolutionary intellectuals and the Soviet Union.' *Socialist Register* (L, Merlin Pr.).

——1976. (Interview on '1956'). *Politique Hebdo*; *Socialist register* (L, Merlin Pr.).

Rue, J. E., 1966. *Mao Tse-tung in Opposition.* Stanford Univ. Pr.

——1967. 'Is Mao Tse-tung's "Dialectical Materialism" a forgery?' *J. Asian Stud.*, 26: 3.

Salisbury, H., 1973. *To Peking and Beyond.* L., Fontana.

Salvemini, G., 1936. *Under the Axe of Fascism.* L, Gollancz (Left Book Club).

Sayer, D., 1975a. 'Method and Dogma in Historical Materialism.' *Sociological Rev.*, 23: 4.

——1975b. *Some Issues in Historical Materialism.* Ph D, Durham Univ., 1975.

——1977a. 'Precapitalist societies and contemporary Marxist theory.' *Sociology*, 11: 1.

——1977b. *Marx's Method.* Hassocks, Harvester, forthcoming.

Sayers, S., 1975. 'Philosophy in China.' *Radical Philosophy*, 10.

——1976. 'The Marxist dialectic.' *Radical Philosophy*, 14.

——1977. 'Productive forces and relations of production.' *CPSG Broadsheet*, 14: 2.

Bibliography

Schram, S. R., 1967a. *Mao Tse-tung*. L, Penguin.
——1967b. 'Mao Tse-tung as a Marxist dialectician.' *China Qu.*, 29.
——1969. *The Political Thought of Mao Tse-tung*. Rev. edn, L, Penguin.
——1973a. Contribution to 'Mao Tse-tung and Maoist Society.' *The Listener*, 7 Jun.
——1973b. 'The Cultural Revolution in historical perspective.' Introduction to his 1973c.
——(ed.), 1973c. *Authority, Participation and Cultural Change in China*. Cambridge Univ. Pr.
——1977. 'The Marxist.' In Wilson, 1977.
Schurmann, F., 1963. 'Economic policy and political power'. *Annals of the American Academy*, 349.
——and Schell, O. (eds), 1967. *China Readings, I, II, and III*. L, Penguin, 1968. (Vol. IV, cf. Milton, 1977).
Schwartz, B., 1954. 'A Marxist controversy on China.' *Far Eastern Qu.*, 13 Feb.
Selbourne, D., 1975. *An Eye to China*. L, Black Liberator Pr.
Selden, M. 1969. 'The Yenan legacy: the mass-line.' In A.D. Barnett, (ed.), *Chinese Communist Politics in Action*. Washington Univ. Pr.
——1970. 'People's War and the transformation of peasant society.' In M. Friedman and M. Selden (eds), *America's Asia*, NY, Vintage, 1971; reprinted in Kaplan, 1973.
——1971. *The Yenan Way in Revolutionary China*. Harvard Univ. Pr.
Sève, L., 1968. *Marxism and the Theory of Human Personality*. L, Lawrence & Wishart, 1975.
Showstack, A., 1974. 'Gramsci's interpretation of Italian fascism.' *New Edinburgh Rev.*
Simon, R., 1977. 'Gramsci's concept of hegemony.' *Marxism Today*, 21: 3.
Smedley, A., 1938. *China Fights Back*....L, Gollancz (Left Book Club).
——1956. *The Great Road: the Life and Times of Chu Teh*. NY and L, Monthly Rev. Pr.
Snow, E., 1937. *Red Star over China*. L, Gollancz (Left Book Club).
——1941. *Scorched Earth*. *2 vols*, L, Gollancz (Left Book Club).
——1961. *Red Star over China*. Rev. and enl. edn, L, Gollancz, 1968.
——1970. *Red China Today*. Rev. edn, L., Penguin.
——1971. 'The open door' (Interview with Chou En-lai).' *China Now*, 15.

200 For Mao

——1973. *The Long Revolution*. L, Hutchinson.

Snow, H. 1973. *China's Communists*. L, Greenwood Pr.

Snowden, F. M., 1972, 'On the social origins of agrarian fascism in Italy.' *Archives européenes de sociologie*, 13.

Soper, K., 1976. 'On materialisms.' *Radical Philosophy*, 15.

Stavis, B., 1976. 'The new Mao literature.' *Monthly Rev.*, 28: 2.

Stein, G., 1945. *The Challenge of Red China*. L, Pilot Pr.

Sulzberger, C. L., 1974. *The Coldest War: the Russian Game in China*. NY, Harcourt Brace.

Sweezy, P., 1971. His contributions to C. Bettelheim and P. Sweezy, *On the Transition to Socialism*. NY and L, Monthly Rev. Pr.

——1974. 'The nature of Soviet society (Review of Bettelheim, 1974).' *Monthly Rev.*, 26: 6, 8, 1974–1975.

——1975. 'China: contrasts with capitalism.' *Monthly Rev.*, 27: 3.

——1977a. 'Theory and practice of the Mao period.' *Monthly Rev.*, 28; also in *Problems of Communism*, 8 (L, B & ICO).

——1977b. 'Bettelheim on revolution from above: the USSR in the 1920s.' *Monthly Rev.*, 29: 5.

Thompson, E. P., 1963. *Making of the English Working Class*. L, Penguin, 1968.

——1965 'Peculiarities of the English.' *Socialist Register* (L, Merlin Pr.).

——1968. 'Postscript' to Penguin edn, of his 1963.

——1975. *Whigs and Hunters: the origin of the Black Act.*, Allen Lane.

Thomson, G., 1947. *Marxism and poetry*. Reprinted. L, Lawrence & Wishart, 1975.

——1957. 'Gramsci, the first Italian Marxist.' *Marxism Today*, 1.

——1971. *From Marx to Mao Tse-tung: a Study in Revolutionary Dialectics*. L, China Policy Study Group.

——1973. *Capitalism and After: the Rise and Fall of Commodity Production*. L, China Policy Study Group.

——1974. *The Human Esence*. L, China Policy Study Group.

Ticktin, H., 1976. 'The contradictions of Soviet society and Professor Bettelheim.' *Critique*, 6.

Tien Chih-sung, 1976. 'Grasp the principal contradiction in socialist society.' *Peking Rev.*, 17.

Timpanaro, S., 1966. 'Considerations on materialism.' *New Left Rev.*, 85, 1974.

Todd, N., 1974. 'Ideological superstructure in Gramsci and Mao Tse-tung.' *J. Hist. Ideas*, 35.

Bibliography

Tomlinson, J., 1977. 'Hillel Ticktin and Professor Bettelheim: a reply.' *Critique*, 8.

Treadgold, D., 1973. *The West in Russia and China*. 2 vols. Cambridge Univ. Pr.

Tse Ka-kui, 1977a. *Institutional Change and Agricultural Modernization: Aspects of the Chinese Theory and Practice of Socialist Transition*. Hong Kong, Centre of Asian Studies.

—— 1977b. 'Socialist vs. Capitalist division of labour: aspects of the Chinese approach to industrial transformation.' Paper to the 5th Leverhulme Conference, Hong Kong, Dec. 1977.

Uhalley, S., 1975. *Mao Tse-tung: a Critical Biography*. NY, New Viewpoints.

Wang Kuo-fan, 1977. 'Paupers build a new life together.' *China Reconstructs*, 26: 12.

Watson, A. J., 1972. 'Case studies of Chinese institutional development.' Paper to the Conference of the National Association for Soviet and East European Studies, London.

Weiss, D. D., 1977. 'The philosophy of Engels vindicated.' *Monthly Rev.*, 28: 8.

Wen Yin, and Liang Hua, 1977. *Tachai: the Red Banner*. P, FLP.

Wheelwright, E. L., and McFarlane, B., 1970. *The Chinese Road to Socialism*. NY, Monthly Rev. Pr.; L, Penguin, 1973.

White, S., 1974a. 'Gramsci and proletarian power.' *New Edinburgh Rev.*

—— 1974b. 'Gramsci and Soviet historiography.' *New Edinburgh Rev.*

Whiting, A. S., 1977. 'Chinese foreign policy: a workshop report.' *Items*, 31.

Whyte, M. K., 1973. 'Bureaucracy and modernization in China.' *American Sociological Rev.*, 38: 2.

Williams, G., 1960. 'Gramsci's concept of "Egemonia".' *J. Hist. Ideas*, 21: 4.

—— 1974a, b. 'Proletarian forms...'. *New Edinburgh Rev.* (Gramsci issues I and II).

—— 1974c. 'The making and unmaking of Antonio Gramsci.' *New Ediburgh Rev.* (Gramsci, III).

—— 1975 *Proletarian Order*. L, Pluto Pr.

Williams, R., 1975. 'Developments in the sociology of culture.' *Sociology*, 10, 1976.

Wilson, D., 1971. *The Long March, 1935*. L, H. Hamilton; NY, Avon; L, Penguin, 1977.

202 *For Mao*

Wilson, D., 1977. (ed.) *Mao Tse-tung in the Scales of History.* . . . Cambridge Univ. Pr.

Wittfogel, K. A., 1963. 'Some remarks on Mao's handling of concepts and problems of dialectics.' *Studies in Soviet Thought*, 3: 4.

Wittgenstein, L., 1969a. *The Blue and the Brown Books: Preliminary studies for the 'Philosophical Investigations'.* Oxford, Basil Blackwell.

——1969b. *Philosophical Investigations.* 3rd edn, Oxford, Basil Blackwell.

Wolf, E., 1969. *Peasant Wars of the Twentieth Century.* L, Faber, 1971.

Woolf, S. J., (ed.), 1968, *The Nature of Fascism.* L, Weidenfeld.

Yakhontoff, V., 1934. *The Chinese Soviets.* L, Greenwood Pr.

Yao Wen-yuan, 1975. *The Social Base of the Lin Piao anti-Party Clique.* P, FLP.

Yuan Shui-po, 1976. 'Magnificent poems that inspire us in battle.' *Peking Rev.*, 2.

Yung Ping-chen, 1966. *Chinese Political Thought: Mao Tse-tung and Liu Shao-chi.* The Hague, Nijhoff.

Zagoria, D. S., 1962. *The Sino-Soviet Conflict.* Princeton Univ. Pr.

Index

NOTE: Most proper names in the text (but not in the Notes or Bibliographies) have been indexed. Abbreviations used are:

    s meaning *see* another index entry
    sa meaning *see also* another (related) entry
    n (after a number, as $158n$) means the entry refers to a Note, *bib* means the Bibliography

Accumulation: of capital, 39, 119, Part II *passim*, 137-9
Adventurism, 21-2, 28, 40, 56, 107, 121, 131; *sa* Opportunism
Agrarian production, 23, 38, 49-75, 102-4, 117-19, 137, $157n$
Agricultural Producers' Co-operatives (APCs), 23, 64-75
Albania, 135, $158n$, $160-1nn$
Alley, R., 53-4
Althusser, L. 5, 112
Anderson, P., xiii, 94, 105, 108-9, 130
Anshan, 92, 137
Army, *s* People's Liberation Army, State, War

'Backwardness', *s* 'Underdevelopment'
Base/Superstructure distinction, xiv, 15, 28, 110-11, $149n$
Bettelheim, C., ix, xiv, 6, 129-30, 131, $158n$, $162n$, 189-90 *bib*
Bolshevism, xiv, xv, 5, 9, 29, 30, 36, 57, 62-4, 68, 78, 97, 109-10, 116, 123, 125, 129, 136-9
Border Region Years, xvii, 34, 45-61, 90, 119, $146-9nn$
Bourgeoisie, 26, 31, 75-91, 115, 120-1
Brezhnev, L., 116, 135
British and Irish Communist Organisation, xiii
Brzezinski, Z., xii
Buchanan, K., 50, 116

Cadres, 11-12, 14, 24-33, 70-5, Part II *passim*
Capitalism, 15, 35, 62, 72, 112, 115, 121-5, 130-4
Carr, E. H., xi
Chang Chun-chiao, 135
Chiang Ching, 92, 135
Chiang Kai-shek, 47
Ching Chi, 137
Chou En-lai, xviii, 88, 120-1, 129, 136, 140
    interviews with, $145n$
Chu Teh, xviii, 106, 140
Class, classes, class-struggle, 6, 7, 8, 14, 26, 28-32, 44, 66-9, 75-9, 99, 114, 130-2
    positional theory of class, 28-9
    relational theory of class, 28-9
Collectivisation, *s* Co-operation, Co-operatives, Mutual Aid Teams, Peasantry, Peoples Communes
Colletti, L., xii
Comintern, 57-8, 99-102, 104, 109, $156n$
Communes, *s* Paris Commune, Peoples Communes, Co-operation
Communism, 26, 73, 128, Part III *passim*
Communist Party, *sa* Party
Communist Party of China (CPC), xvii, 5, 6, 7, 9, 24-33, 36, 45-61, 76, 107, 111-12, Part II *passim*, 119-22, 123-9, 135, 191 *bib*

204 *Index*

Communist Party of Italy (PCI), 95, 101–2
Communist Party of the Soviet Union (CPSU), 59, 123–9, 135
Confucianism, 47, 93
Consciousness, *s* Epistemology
Contradiction, xiv–xv, 9–10, Part II *passim*
Co-operation, 23, 35, 49, 52–6, 61–75, 133, and *passim*
Co-operatives, Industrial (Indusco), 53–4
Croll, E., xv, 118
Cultural Revolution, 28, 31, 51, 97; *sa* Great Proletarian Cultural Revolution
Culture, cultural relations, 10, 24–33, 55–6, 75–91, 139, 144n

Davin, D., xv, 119
Deutscher, I., xiii
Development/Modernisation, 9, 38–9, 121, 136–40; *sa* Theory of Productive Forces
Diplomacy, *s* Foreign Policy
Division of labour, 44, 117–18, 138; *sa* Epistemology, Redness, Production, Three Great Differences
Dockworkers, 115, 121, 123, 158n
Dogmatism, 11–12, 20–3, 32, 56, 58, 77, 104–5, 121; *sa* Mistakes

Economics, economic work, 2, 35, 119, and *passim*; *sa* Production
Education, *s* Learning
Emancipation of Labour, 32, 67, 134, and *passim*
Emancipation of Women, *s* Women: emancipation of
Engels, F., 2, 7, 8, 9, 13, 15–16, 35, 76, 166 *bib*; *sa* Marx, K.
Epistemology, 6–15, 18–20, 65, 107, 131
Epstein, I., 49
Errors, *s* Mistakes
Essential relations/Phenomenal forms., 51, 66, 75, 79–80, 87
Eurocommunism, xiii, 80, 112, 152n, 161n

Exemplary transformations, 37–8, Part II *passim*
Experience, 1, 20–4, 33, 41, 65, 68, 72, 103, 125
Expertise, 2, 15, 20, 61, 95, 101, 139, 155n

Fanon, F., 69
Fascism, 47–8, 102, 115, 126
Feminism, *s* Women: emancipation of
Feudalism, 35
Fiori, G., 94
First World, 112, 126, 135
Fiscal policy; 49, 52–3, 56–8, 119
Food, *s*. Agrarian production
Foreign policy, 115, 121–9, 136
Foreign trade, 115, 121–2, 136
'Four clean-ups', *s* Socialist Education Movement
Fourth International, *s* Internationals, Fourth
Freedom, 12–13, 80–1, 84, 142n
Friends of China, 5, 75, 116, 140

'Gang of Four', 134–40
General Line, 39, 86, 105, 124, 138; *sa* Class
Gramsci, A., xii, 93–113, 155–7nn
Gray, J., ix, 53, 59, 62, 127, 133, 193–4bib
Great Leap Forward (GLF), xvii, 39, 41, 77, 121, 138
Great October Socialist Revolution, 125–7; *sa* Bolshevism
Great Proletarian Cultural Revolution (GPCR), xiii, xviii, 4, 23, 31, 34, 38, 43–4, 75–93, 94, 117, 120, 151–5 nn

Hegel, G. W. F., 17, 111
Hegemony/Hegemonism, 94, 101, 111–13
High Tide Years, xvii, 38, 61–75, 149–51nn
Hinton, W., 46
Historical experience, *s* Experience
Historical materialism, v, xi, 3, 9, 45, 62, 97, 100, 105, 111, 129
Hobsbawm, E. J., 94

Index

205

Hunan, 10, 96, 133
Hundred Flowers Campaign, 80

Idealism, 1, 9, 15–16, 22, 75, 84, 89, 95, 107
Ideology, 16, 108–9, 120, and *passim*
India, 116, 157n
Indusco, s Co-operatives, industrial
Industrialisation, 59–60, 63, Part II *passim*
Intellectuals, 1, 10, 16–20, 26, 48, 78, 82, 95, 97, 109, 113, 133, 157n, 161–2nn
International Communist Movement, 123–9, 158–9nn
Internationals, Second, 58, 93; Third, 58; Fourth, 126
Italy, 93–113

Japan, invasion of China, 47–61, 106–7

Kang Sheng, xviii, 140
Kant, I., 17
Kautsky, K., v, 58, 125
Khrushchev, N., 78, 128
Kiangsi Soviet, xvii, 46, 146n
Knowledge, s Learning
Kolkhozi, 125
Kuomintang (KMT) 47, 50, 55, 57, 67, 106

Labour, emancipation of, s Emancipation of labour, Women, emancipation of
Labour-power, 3, Part II *passim*, 130–1, 134
Landlords, 56, 67, 133
Language, 18–19
Law, 111
Learning, 10–11, 17, 27, 44, 48–9, 66, 73–5, 83–4, 96, 99–100, 117–18
Lenin, V. I., v, 8, 9, 11, 13, 15, 28–9, 30, 35, 42, 58, 76, 93, 97–8, 100, 114, 131, 156–7 *bib*
Lin Piao, xviii, 75, 79, 93, 136, 158n
Line/Lines, 1, 39, 105, 123; sa Class, General line
Liu Shao-chi, 35, 83, 121
Long March, xvii, 34–5, 45, 46, 146n
ukács, G., xii, 96, 100

Macciocchi, M., 43.

Mao Tse-tung
and: Bolshevism, xiv–xv, 9, 29, 57, 62–3, 67–8, 116, 120, 127; Border Region Years, 26, 37, 45–61, 84; Comintern, 58–9, 123–9; Epistemology, 6–15; Great Leap Forward, 34–41, 62–4; Gramsci, 93–113; Great Proletarian Cultural Revolution, 38, 43–4, 75–93; High Tide Years, 38–9, 61–75, 84; Long March, 45–6; New Democracy, 35–6, 56; Practice, 15–24; Production, 34–41, 62–4; Socialist Education Movement, 77–8, 83; Stalin, 58–9, 67, 127–9
on: writing, xiv; mistakes, 1, 79, 88, 117; dualism, 1, 79–80, 131–2; politics, 2, 70–4; 'wager on the people', 3, 5, 55–60; knowledge, 6–15; freedom and democracy, 13, 80–1, 89–90, 152n; consciousness, 20–1; cadres, 24–8, 52, 89–91; cultural relations, 30–3, 51; organisation, 36–7; General Line, 38–40, 86; methodology, 42–3, 58–9; armies, 46–8, 57, 87, 105–8; peasants, 48–53; co-operatives, 52–7 and *passim*; hegemony, 111–13; education, 117–18; socialist construction, 124, 129–34 and *passim*.
titles: 'Problems of strategy in China's revolutionary war' (1936), 48–9; 'On Practice' (1937), 7–8, 21–2, 143n; 'On Contradiction' (1937), 115; 'Problems of War and Strategy' (1938), 107–8; 'On New Democracy' (1940), 35–6; 'Get Organized' (1943), 36, 54–7; 'Some questions concerning methods of leadership' (1943), 24; 'Spread the campaigns . . .' (1943), 55, 56; 'We must learn to do economic work' (1945), 37; 'Methods of work of Party Committees' (1949), 25–6; 'On the question of agricultural co-operation' (1955), 38, 62; 'High

206 Index

Mao Tse-tung (contd)
   Tide of socialism . . .' (1955), 33,
   38, 64–74; 'On the Ten Great
   Relationships' (1956), 39, 63;
   'Speech at the CPC Conference on
   Propaganda Work' (1957), 22–3;
   'On the correct handling of contradictions' (1957), 40, 63, 67, 114;
   'Talks at Chengtu' (1958), 40;
   'Sixty points' (1958), 40, 61; 'On
   Democratic Socialism' (1962), 84,
   90–1; 'Where do correct ideas
   come from?' (1963), 6–7; 'Talk on
   questions of philosophy' (1964), 7,
   82, 84; 'Fifteen theses on socialist
   construction' (1964), 27, 31; 'Bombard the Headquarters' (1966),
   83, 153n; 'Sixteen articles on
   GPCR' (1966), 31, 34; 43, 87
   bibliography: 168–87
   sa Agrarian production, Learning,
   Mass-line, Party

'Maoism', xi, xiv, 29, 83
Market-relations, s Capitalism, Pro-
   duction
   world, 121–3, 138
Marx, K., 2, 8, 9, 12, 13–14, 15–16, 35,
   69, 76, and passim, 164–6 bib
   Capital: 1, 79–80, 98, 111, 130–1;
   Grundrisse: 7, 162n
Marxism, passim, sa Historical mat-
   erialism, Theory, marxist
Mass-line, 3, 23–33, 55, 66, 73, 86, 90–
   1, 128, 131, 133–4
Material incentives, 48, 84–6, 136, 153n
Materialism, s Historical materialism
Mauger, S., 4, 5
Metaphysics, s Idealism
Military affairs, s War
Mistakes, errors, 1, 23, 25, 76, 87–8
Modernisation, s Development/Mod-
   ernisation
Mongolia, 54
Mutual Aid Teams, 23, 54–6, 64, 70, 90

'New Democracy', 35, 36, 152n

Opportunism, 21–2, 28, 56, 106–7, 121,
   131

Pai Chi-hsien, 118
Paris Commune, 12–13, 89, 151n
Party, 11–12, 21, 23, 24–33, 43–4, 62,
   74, 114, 121, 130–2, 134
Peasantry, 23, 30, 36–7, 48–9, 61–75,
   102–4, 117–18, 133
Peng Chen, 82
People's Communes, 64, 119, 125, 128
People's Liberation Army (PLA), 46–
   61, 87, 106–8, 119–20, 147n
People's Republic of China (PRC),
   xvii, 112
Phenomenal forms, 48, 66, 79–80, 134
Philosophy, 1, 6–15, 16–17, 43, 80–1,
   142n
Piccone, P., 93–4
Planning, plans, 38, 40, 90–2, 119, 124
Politics, political relations, 2, 24–33, 61,
   70–5, 108–13
Practice, 6–7, 13–14, 15–24, 99–100
Production, 3, 5, 18, 20, 34–41, 121,
   123, 130–1
Production brigades, 119, 144n
Proletariat, s Working class, sa Class
Public Opinion, 108, 133

Red Army, Chinese, s People's Lib-
   eration Army
Red Flag Canal, 41, 145n
Redness, 2, 61, 155; sa Theory, marxist
Reformism, s Adventurism, Dog-
   matism, Opportunism, Revision-
   ism
Relations, s Culture, Epistemology,
   Politics, Production
Relative autonomy, s Base/Super-
   structure
Rent, s Fiscal policy
Revisionism, 26, 51, 77–8, 115, 133
Revolution, xv, 3–5, 20, 41, 49–50, 75–
   93, and passim; sa Socialist
   construction
Rossanda, R., 4–5
Ruling class, s Bourgeoisie, Landlords,
   State; sa Class

Sartre, J. P., xii
Schram, S. R., xiii, 14–15

Index

Second International, *s* Internationals, Second

Second World, 112

Selden, M., 50, 52

'Sinification thesis', xii, 58–9

'Sinology', 125–6

Smedley, A., 46, 48

Snow, E., 46, 48, 53, 88

Socialism, Parts II and III *passim*

Socialist construction, 3, 12–13, 18, 26, 38–9, 52–3, 66–7, 75, 84, 102–4, 114, 116–23, 129–34

Socialist Construction and Marxist Theory, ix, xv, 28–9, 62, 112, 116, 137, 140, 160*n*

Socialist Education Movement (SEM), xviii, 77–9

Soviet Union, *s* Union of Soviet Socialist Republics (USSR)

Speculation, *s* Idealism

Stalin, J., 35, 58, 66, 76, 79, 112, 116, 123, 127–9, 167–8*bib*

'Stalinism', xi, 5, 93, 123, 127–9

State/Stateforms, 2, 20, 75–91, 99, 105–13, 119–21, 130–4; *sa* Base/Superstructure

State Planning Commission (PRC), 137, 161*n*

Struggle, *s* Class, Experience, Practice

Subjectivisim, 11, 12, 22–3, 27, 54–6, 75–93; *sa* Dogmatism

Sun Yeh-feng, 84

Superpowers, *s* First World

Superstructure, *s* Base/Superstructure, State

Sweezy, P., 4, 6

Tachai, 142n, 161n

Taching, 119

Taxation, *s* Fiscal policy

Taylorism, 37, 125, 137

Teng Hsiao-ping, xv, 85–6, 135–40
   General Programme; Twenty Points; Outline Report, 137–9

Thatcher, M., 126, 135

Theory, *s* Epistemology, Experience, Intellectuals, Practice

Theory, marxist, 6–15, 41–4, 100, 143*n*;

sa Epistemology, Historical materialism

Theory of Productive Forces, 121, 125–6, 136–40, 161*n*

Third International, *s* Internationals, Third

Third World, 112, 135–6

Thompson, E. P., 29

Three Great Differences, 44, 117–18, 129, 136, 146*n*

Three Worlds Thesis, xv, 112, 135–6, 161*n*

Trade, *s* Foreign trade, Market

Transformation, *s* Exemplary transformations, Socialist construction

Transition, *s* Class, Production, Socialist construction

Trotsky, L., 69, 74, 105–6, 116, 167*bib*

Tsai Cheng, 119

Tse Ka-kui, ix

Tung-sheng Co-operative, 70

Ultra-Leftism, 83, 84, 87–90, 154*n*

'Underdevelopment', 125–6, 149*n*; *sa* Development

Union of Soviet Socialist Republics (USSR), xi, 39, 40, 49, 105, 109, 112, 115, 119, 124–9, 135

United States of America (USA), 126, 135

Vietnam, 50

Wang Che, 137

Wang Hung-wen 135

War, strategy and tactics, 46–61, 104–8, 144*n*

'Western marxism', xii–xiii

Williams, G., 95, 99

Williams, R., 10

Women: emancipation of, xv, 47, 117–19, 130–1, 134

Working class, 15, 31, 75–91, 102–3, 113, 114, 130–4; *sa* Peasantry

Yang Hsien-chen, 83–4

Yao Wen-yuan, 135

Yenan, *s* Border Region Years